THE FLOW

40 Days to Total Life Transformation

TARA MEYER-ROBSON

Outskirts Press, Inc.
Denver, Colorado

The Flow
40 Days to Total Life Transformation

Interior design by Lori Ewen
Cover design by Melanie Shellito
Author advisor: Laura Young

Outskirts Press, Inc.
http://www.outskirtspress.com

Library of Congress Card Number: 2007934844

Hardback ISBN: 978-1-4327-0913-6
Paperback ISBN: 978-1-59800-983-5

PRINTED IN THE UNITED STATES OF AMERICA

DEDICATION

This book is dedicated to my husband, John. You are my soul mate, my unconditional love, and my constant source of support. Thank you for sharing the beauty of your love with me, and for believing in me even on days when I did not believe in myself—this book would not exist without you. I love you with all that I am—today, tomorrow, and always...

ACKNOWLEDGEMENTS

There are so many people I want to thank for their part in this creation. First, to my beloved Gramma VA, Virginia Shanahan: You were one of my greatest cheerleaders in the process of writing this book. Thank you for believing in me—your support, love, and friendship still glow within my heart. I am so blessed to have had you as a grandmother. To my wonderful grandfather, William Henry Meyer III: Your kind and beautiful approach to life radiated a joy that I miss dearly. Thank you for always being there for everything that I did, and for watching over me in spirit now. To my mom, Patricia: You are my greatest writing and teaching influence, helping me to develop into the writer that I am today. Thank you for always being a guiding light in all ways throughout my life—I love you. To my dad, William: I am so grateful to have a father who has such a warm, kind heart. Thank you for opening yourself up to the possibilities of life, and for our many father-daughter walks over the years. I love you, "Great Thunder." To my sister, Maureen: I am fortunate beyond words to have been so blessed to have a sister like you. Our friendship is one of my greatest treasures—I love you. To my brother-in-law, Mike: I said it before, and I will say it again—you are the brother that I never had, and I could not have chosen one that I would love more. To my in-laws, David and Judy Robson: Thank you for bringing John into the world and for sharing yourselves and your lives with us— I love you both. To my sweet dog, Chester: Thank you for being my "assistant" and constant guardian during the long hours of writing. To the "kofe hous girls" (you know who you are) and Anne and Jay Fowler: Thank you for letting me be exactly who I am. Your friendship is a great joy in my life. To Andy Cohen: Thank you for believing in this from the start. Your interest gave me the confidence to believe that I had something to say—or, at least, something that someone else would actually like to hear! To Roz Kern and Steve Posner: You two were the spark that started me down this path. Thank you for your energy and friendship—and for believing in me from the first day we met! To Reji DiSalvatore and Sarah Thomas: You two are my "oldest" friends. Although we do not get to talk or see each other as much as I would like, I want to thank you both for all that you have both meant to me. To Todd and Stephanie Ramsier: Thank you for the discussions, picnics, and dreams shared. To all my friends throughout the years: You have all influenced me in some way. Thank you for sharing life with me in whatever capacity. To everyone at Outskirts, most especially Laura Young, Melanie Shellito, and Lori Ewen: Thank you for bringing this book into its most perfect creation. I could not have done it without your creative effort! To all those that I have worked with: You are lights in the world. I am privileged to have co-created moments with all of you! To all the visionaries who inspire me: I offer you my deepest gratitude. You are courageous in bringing your light and perspective to the world, and you make the world a better place with your energy.

CONTENTS

PRELUDE

It seemed like an average Saturday, but little did I know that **this** day was to be like no other day.

This day was to be the day when I realized with shock, dismay, and a touch of horror that if I lived to 80 years old—a ripe old age, mind you—I would have lived only 29,200 days. Something about this number felt wrong—so wrong, in fact, that I computed it several times, certain that I had not multiplied correctly. However, each time that I hit the "enter" button, the answer was the same: 29,200 days.

I stared at the number and realized that it seemed so **small**—or, at least, so much smaller than I had ever thought. Somehow, I had always imagined that we had somewhere nearer 100,000 days to live. And yet, the truth was that if I made it to 80—a bit past the average life span of an American woman—I would not have even cracked the 30,000 day mark.

Worse, I realized that as a 32 year old woman, I had already used 11,680 of these now incredibly precious days.

I was stunned. As I began to rifle back through the days of my life, I found myself wondering—how many days had been wasted to struggle, strife, illness, and difficulty? How many to feeling so stressed out that I could hardly move? How many more to worrying about what someone said about me, or how he or she felt about the decisions that I was making or even my life in general? How about the days used staying in a job or relationship that I did not enjoy? How many more had I spent feeling angry, dissatisfied, and afraid—or to just simply feeling that I didn't like myself?

Could it be 3,000 days? 6,000? Dare I even say 8,000?

Whatever the number, it was simply too many. I was absolutely not willing to waste any more.

At that moment I asked myself: What if I could live every day in the flow with the most positive aspects of life? What if I could feel joy, passion, wonder, success, health, and optimism in **all** aspects of my life **every**day—not just some of them, some of the time? What if I could create the life that I truly desired—**and** could live it every moment?

And—this was the really radical one—what if I could find a way to have all of this with ease?

I felt the answer in my soul: That would be a life fully lived. That would be a life that would truly delight me.

Better yet, what if I could help others to do the same?

Now, **that** would be a life I could be passionate about.

From that day on, that is just what I did.

PART 1
The Flow Principles

PRINCIPLE 1
You Deserve Everything You Desire

I want you, for a moment, to imagine everything that you really want: a new relationship, a job promotion, a cure from disease, a beautiful house and car, a child, or any other experience that you dream of. Close your eyes and see yourself having it all right now—this very instant. Try to make this as real as possible. Now say to yourself, "I deserve everything that I desire, right now, right as I am." As you say this, notice the reactions in your body and mind. What thoughts come to mind? Do you find that you have tightness in your body or a sense of uneasiness in your stomach?

It is likely that you do, and that is okay—all this indicates is that you hold a belief that you really **don't** deserve the experiences that you desire. In fact, were you to put your real feelings into words, it would probably go something like, "You know, I don't really think that I will ever have any of that. I don't feel that I am truly worthy of that kind of life."

How do I know that you are thinking this? Because most of us start with this belief—it is programmed into our brains from a very young age, and causes a lot of problems for everyone. It is time to get rid of it.

What's your balloon made of?

To understand how this belief became part of your system, I want you to consider this little story:

I want you to imagine that a man gives you two identical balloons. You look at them, and sure enough, they are **exactly** the same color and size, and appear to be made of the same material. The man then tells you that you may only have one of the balloons. As they are identical, you immediately take one and give the other back. The man stops you, and says that there are some things not immediately evident to the untrained eye that you should know before making your choice final. He informs you that one of the balloons is actually made of exclusive French plastic, and the air inside the balloon was bottled in the Alps in an area known for its clean, pure air. "See here," he says, "how this balloon seems more flexible and firmer to the touch than the other?" You touch them, and they feel exactly identical to you! The other balloon (the one that you were going to choose), he says, "was made of recycled toilet bowls, and the air inside was gathered from Los Angeles smog." He tells you to look at the balloons again, and asks, "Do you now notice the difference?" As you look at him doubtfully, he goes on, "Can you not see the subtle color variations of the balloon hand-dyed by Turkish artisans? There is such a contrast to the balloon colored with ordinary dye!" You look again. Yes, now you start to see it! There is a difference—a depth of color perhaps—in the hand-dyed balloon! Moreover, it is certainly much better to have the French plastic and Alps air over the recycled toilets and LA smog! You decide to choose the balloon that is clearly so very much better. You thank the man and leave, happy with your beautiful new balloon.

If this sounds like a con to you, it is—but it is exactly what has happened to you since you were a child. Whether you know it or not, you were trained to believe that certain objects were simply made of better material than others—making them much more desirable. In fact, you were even taught to believe that certain **people** were made of better stuff than others—making them more deserving of the better objects and a better life.

Think about this: How do you know that a $100 dollar bill is more valuable than a $1 dollar bill? Like the balloons, if you were presented with the two bills and you did not know the difference, you would see them both as simply pieces of paper, made of the exact same stuff. However, through learning that a $1 dollar bill does not buy you as much as a $100 bill, you now would easily assess that the $100 dollar bill is more valuable.

They are made of the same stuff, but you are taught how to **judge** one as more valuable than the other.

This does not just happen with currency; it happens with everything that you encounter in your day. Two purses look exactly the same, but one has a different label than the other, and so, is more valuable. Two houses are exactly alike, but one is in a better area of town, and so, you pay double for that one. Two people look alike, but one has been from a "better upbringing" than the other, and so, is judged to be a better husband who makes a better income.

On and on it goes. Every moment of every day, you are judging the worth of everything and assessing your **own** worth against every other person you meet. Like the balloons or the money, you have been convinced that some things and some people are made of a superior substance, and therefore, are more valuable.

I am here to tell you that **we have all been conned**. Everything is made of the exact same stuff, no matter what anyone tells you. In fact, no matter how you feel about yourself right now, there is absolutely nothing different about you than all the people and things that you admire. In a very real way, you are the exact same as everyone else—regardless of what you look like, think like, or act like.

A particle is still a particle by any other name

You are made of a whole lot of a little something called particles.

What are particles, you ask? They are infitismally small and are the building blocks of the universe, functioning a good deal like Legos—snapping together to form every single thing in your life, the galaxy, and beyond.

The really amazing thing is that all particles are completely identical. As a matter of fact, if you took a particle from a distant star, one from the car that you are driving, and another from your arm, there would be absolutely no way to tell the difference between them—they would be, in every sense, the exact same.

Congratulations! You have now seen past the deception: you now know that no matter how anything looks to you, underneath it all, it is all the same. In whatever form it is taking right now, a particle is **still** a particle by any other name.

How does this bit of knowledge impact your life? Let's get right to it.

You are equal to everyone else—even the most successful, happy people you know

Think of someone who you consider to be very successful, perhaps someone that you strive to be more like. Do you think that you are equal to them? Do you think that you deserve the same success that they do?

You should, but you probably don't. You likely assume that they must be made of something intrinsically better than you are, and this allows them to be more deserving of success and abundance.

Enter your new understanding of the world. Remember, at a particle level, the people you admire are made of the exact same building blocks that you are. Because of this, there is nothing different about a Bill Gates or an Oprah Winfrey than you. They do not have, on any physical level, any better particles than you do.

Truth be told, you could exchange yourself as humans, and it would literally not matter at all in the grand scheme of things.

The idea of the from-a-better-family woman or the better-bred man is totally ridiculous. No particle is preprogrammed with any information at all—there are no rich or poor particles, no brilliant or idiotic particles, there is nothing pretty or ugly about them. At the particle level there is no race, no religious affiliation, no blood line, no genetics, no predisposition to weight or disease or anything else; there is literally no distinction between them at all. They are all a blank slate, and are distributed to everyone equally.

Your particles have come together to form the person that you are, and the collection that is "you" has every ability to have an amazing life **just as you are**. You do not need to change anything about yourself to deserve that success; you just need to decide that you are good enough to have it!

Don't believe me? Really look around at the kinds of people that have a life that you envy. Do they all look alike? Are they all intelligent? I am willing to bet that some of them are the guys that you knew in college who would dare each other to run around the quad naked! Now, they own multi-million dollar companies and hold public office. If **anyone** was not able to achieve any level of success that they wanted, then these guys would be jobless and living in their parents' basements, not running huge corporations and making public policy!

So think about it this way: If **they** have the particles necessary to make it big in this world, then you certainly do!

The meaning of all of this? Your particles are as good as anyone else's; therefore, you are every bit as worthy and important and fascinating as anyone else is—and as completely deserving of a totally wonderful life.

You are equal to everything that you desire

In the same way, everything that you desire is made of the same particles. The clunker car is made of the same particles as the expensive sports car. The house you own is made of the same particles as the house you **wish** you owned. The generic brand medicine is made of the same stuff as the name brand medicine. The plain old farm horse is composed of the same bits as the award-winning race horse.

Since that is the case, then what **is** the difference between the really expensive, desirable item and the less-expensive, less-desirable item? It is, as always, how you **perceive** its value. If you perceive something as valuable, it is; if you do not, it is not—it really is that simple.

In school you may have learned about the law of supply and demand. The basic idea here is that if there is a high demand for a product and low supply, then the item's price goes higher. Of course, if there is little demand for the item with a surplus of items available, then they end up on the clearance table at your local shopping center.

Please notice—there is nothing different at all about the item when it was in high demand with high prices or when its price was reduced—it is **exactly** identical. The only thing that changed is how people perceived its value, and that changed the price that you had to pay for the item.

This point was really brought home for me when I caught *Antiques Roadshow* and was stunned to see a Frisch's Big Boy statue priced at $5000. Apparently, Big Boy is enjoying a resurgence in popularity, and these collector's items are hotter than ever. Amazingly, the owner of the statue bought it at a garage sale for $50. Quite a nice profit on that, I'd say!

The statue is made of the exact same material now as when it was just junk at a garage sale, but the **perception** of its value has increased due to public interest and the state of the antiques market, and this, in turn, led to a very exciting moment for one garage sale shopper.

Apply this same idea to your life. Realize that **you** are the antiques dealer of your life. You assign worth to every single thing in your life. Nothing is inherently better or worse than anything else. **No one** is inherently better or worse than you. You make the call. **You** decide whether you deserve to have it in your life or not.

If you perceive that an item that you desire is equal in value to you, you are sending out a signal to life that you are able to afford it. However, if you perceive that you do not deserve something that you desire—that it is more valuable than you, or too good for someone like you to have, then you will never be able to pay for it, energetically or otherwise.

When you decide that your particles are equal to everyone and everything, you can never be intimidated by anyone or anything ever again—you will realize that every person is just the same as you, however they appear. In situations where you would normally feel intimidated—maybe meeting a very successful, wealthy person, or looking at expensive cars, you can choose to not be intimidated by thinking to yourself, "There is nothing better about this person (or item) than me. I am equal in value to this and everything in life."

Here's the question, then: Do you want to make your own value equal to everyone and everything in the whole world? Are you able to allow that to happen? Are you **willing** to allow that to happen (it is going to take some change from you!)?

When you truly see yourself as equal to the things that you want, you will start to see them coming into your life, simply because you will truly value yourself as much as you value the things that you desire. Right now, you have all the particles necessary to have anything that you want, and better yet—**you deserve it all, just as you are**.

Choose—right now—to believe this, and make it true for you every day and in every way.

Exercises:

1. On some poster board, make a collage of all your goals and desires. Take a great picture of yourself and copy it several times. Put your picture next to a big equal sign which is pointing at your goal. For example, take a picture of a car that you want, and put a picture of you

next to it. In between the two, put an equal sign.

2. Each time that you see something you want, say to yourself, "I deserve everything that I desire, right here, right now, right as I am."

3. Get a blank notebook, and make it your **"Flow Journal"** (you will need this throughout the book for many exercises). Journal about the times when you have felt unworthy of something or someone. How did you feel? Why do you think that you felt that way?

4. How many people in your life have made you feel that you were a failure or not deserving of some aspect of life: for example, respect, love, money, or promotions? Write out each of these circumstances in as much detail as possible. Then, write each person's name down, and next to it, "I forgive you for everything. I release you from my life, and I move forward with confidence." How difficult is this for you? Do you find that it is very hard to even imagine forgiving this person? If so, come back to this exercise for several days, and see if it becomes easier for you.

Retuning statement: "I deserve the very best in life, right here, right now, right as I am." For the next few days, please repeat this statement to yourself (either aloud or silently) over the course of the day. In addition, you can write it out several times a day, or even say it into a tape recorder and listen to it.

PRINCIPLE 2

You Can Change Anything About Your Life

Perhaps you can remember a time when, as a child, you watched a magic show. Excitement turned to complete amazement as the magician pulled flowers and bunnies from thin air, made people and watches disappear (hopefully to bring them back again), and pulled money from behind ears and out of hats and sleeves. Your little eyes filled with wonder—how in the world was this possible? How could anyone have the power to make things appear and disappear at will?

And then you became an adult, and you learned the magic **behind** the magic—this magician was not endowed with special powers, rather, ANYONE has the ability to make things appear and disappear as long as they know how to do the trick. If you learn the steps involved, practice them for speed and accuracy, then you, too, could pull money from thin air and make objects and people disappear.

In essence, you realized that what appeared to be true was, in fact, an **illusion**.

Actually, this is exactly what you are discovering how to do with this book. Like learning a magic trick, you are learning the reality behind the illusion, and by doing so, becoming skilled at performing life-changing magic in your own life. While it seems impossible that you possess the power to make things appear and disappear in your life, I am here to tell you, **you've got the power**. You can make a tumor melt into thin air. You can have money appear to you as if out of thin air. You can make perfect relationships, fulfilling careers, beautiful houses, and whatever else you desire appear in your life.

But—in order to use this power, you must figure out the trick behind the trick, and by doing so, understand that the way that you are viewing things now is just an illusion—a diversion that is used to hide what's really going on. In order to perform magic in your own life, you must understand the reality of the situation, learn the steps involved, and use them every moment of every day.

By doing all of this, you will find out that you are capable of instant, magical change in your life (in fact, you are doing it now). As you learn and accept the reality behind the smoke screen, **you** become the magic in action.

The reality of reality (or letting the illusion go)

I got my first real lesson in what happens when one solid object runs into another when I was very young. I was a very active child, one of those that was always playing, jumping, and running. Unfortunately, I was also not able to consider the day a complete success unless I came home dirty, scratched, and bruised. Needless to say, I was always looking for new ways to entertain myself, and one day, upon noticing a large rock outside my apartment building, an idea instantly came to mind: "I know! I can jump on and off this rock over and over again!" (I didn't say that I came up with particularly **good** ways to entertain myself, now did I?) I proceeded to do this, not only entertaining myself, but also amusing my little friend who was not interested in jumping on the rock **herself**, but was more than happy to watch me as I did it. I suppose we could have spent a good afternoon in this pursuit of fun had I listened to my mother—just that once—when she told me, "Tie your shoe; you're going to trip on that loose shoelace!" Prophetic words indeed, as much of motherly wisdom often is. On my hop up one side of the rock, I caught my loose shoelace and tumbled head first into the brick wall directly in front of me. Needless to say, my head was hard, but the wall was harder—and I ended up with a pretty lovely gash on my forehead. A trip to the emergency room, several stitches, and a lollipop later I was all fixed up, but I realized that day that solid objects do not often move just because we would wish them to.

Because of these kinds of experiences (and who hasn't run into their fair share of walls?) it certainly seems that some things are quite solid, and, by that token, quite unchangeable. However, like a magic trick, there is a deeper reality that, once learned, can be applied to life.

That deeper reality?

Nothing in life is solid. It may look solid, it may even **feel** solid, but it is not. It is all energy, and energy can be moved, molded and changed at will.

It is true. Every particle that makes up life (the little building block from Principle 1) is actually a bunch of energy that has, for that time, become a solid particle. These solid things can be changed and broken down, and when they are, they then release this energy, which will go off and become some other solid thing. Best of all, this is happening all around us all the time.

To understand this better, think about a fire. To start a fire, you need a few logs, maybe some kindling, and a match (some outdoorsy types can start a fire without a match, but for the rest of us, a match is an essential fire-starting tool). You start the fire and watch it burn, maybe even making some s'mores and basking by the heat of the fire. Finally, the fire burns out, becoming just a pile of ashes.

What happened to the logs? Where did all that solid matter go?

If you have taken a physics class, you may be aware that the logs' mass did not just disappear, rather, as they burned the logs converted some of their mass back to energy (the same energy that you used as the heat to toast your marshmallows and keep you warm). So, solid matter **is** changeable—it can be changed to energy—which implies that the solid things and circumstances in our lives might just be changeable after all.

In fact, this is the discovery inherent in Einstein's famous equation $e = mc^2$. This equation means, literally, energy (e) equals mass (m) times the speed of light squared (c^2), which is a huge revelation in and of itself. This explains that energy can be neither created nor destroyed; it is simply converted into one or the other. All the energy that is ever going to be created has already been created, and it is just waiting around to become the matter that you have in your life. It forms temporarily into the solid things that you see in life—things like cars, bodies, and buildings—and then converts back into energy when it is done being solid. Matter is energy, energy is matter; energy creates matter, matter breaks back down into energy.

Observing, disturbing, and somewhat perturbing

This actually gets more interesting. When you think of energy, you probably think of a substance moving in waves—like light waves, microwaves, electricity, and sound waves, for instance. Actually, this is quite true—all energy does move in waves, and so, has its own frequency. In contrast, when you look at something like the table in front of you or the chair that you are sitting on, you do not think that it is moving in waves; as a matter of fact, it is very likely that you don't think that it is moving at all (reasonably enough).

However, to the shock of the entire scientific community, they actually discovered that every single particle in life—whether it appears to be energy or solid—is actually both moving in waves and being a bit of matter all at once. For example, the chair that you are sitting on is both hanging out as a solid **and** is energy that is moving in waves right now. You can no longer describe a particle as just a particle, and you cannot describe energy as just energy—everything in the entire world is **both at the same time**.

This may seem very strange, and perhaps even a little disconcerting (it is, actually), but when scientists were using particle detectors to attempt to identify whether a light particle (photon) was a solid or a wave, they noticed that when they looked for the light to act as a solid it did, but at the instant that they turned off their particle detectors, the light went back to being a wave. This meant that particles are either psychic, or the aspect that they decide to show has something to do with the person that is looking at them.

After a good bit of considering, scientists decided that particles are not psychic, per say. What they figured out is that the determination of whether you see something as solid or energy depends on two very important factors: one, whether you are looking at it or not, and two, **what you are expecting to see**.

Werner Heisenberg, a brilliant physicist, summed this entire issue up with his famous uncertainty principle: **"To observe is to disturb."** What this states is that by observing anything, you are actually changing the outcome of any experience. To put this more simply, this means that you are very active in creating what you are seeing and experiencing in your life—you are actually affecting the formation of reality all around you just by being alive. What's more, this indicates that your expectations are actually creating your experiences in a very real way. In terms of the experiment, when the scientists turned on the particle detector, they had the **expectation** of seeing particles, so that is what they saw. In the same way, you are active in creating your life through **your** expectations; each moment that you are awake, you have your own "detector" flipped on, and you are actively looking for the experiences that you expect to get, and by doing so, getting exactly what you expect.

This **also** means that by changing your expectations of any situation, you will change your observation. This will, of course, disturb the outcome, making the outcome not so perturbing.

While I am sure that all of this seems fascinating to you, you may be wondering what this has to do with your life, specifically.

Alright, here goes:

You get what you expect to get, nothing more, nothing less

Perhaps you have heard the old philosophy question, "If a tree falls in the woods and no one is there to hear it, does it make a sound?" I always supposed that it did, simply on the principle that whether I was there or not, sound happened. In my opinion, my involvement had very little to do with what happened naturally with the tree.

It turns out that I would be wrong.

The **correct** answer would be that not only would the tree not make a sound, the whole forest does not exist because I was not there to see it.

If particles are only showing themselves as solid when we are looking at them and are wave when we are not, it stands to reason that all of reality is actually in wave form until you **specifically** are there to experience it. It pops into form as you experience it and goes back to waves when you are not looking (or sensing) anymore.

This is a bit of a wild notion, to say the least. Your house exists when you are there and does not when you are away. Your spouse leaves for work in the morning, and he is not just at work, he is literally just a bunch of waves. You have lunch with your mom, and when you part ways, she just goes back to being a bunch of waves that are flowing at the frequency of "mom" until you see her again.

This means that every moment is a completely new act of creation based on your expectations at that moment in time. You are, in a very real way, **creating** every moment of your life. Life is not stagnant, rather, it is constantly flashing in and out of existence all the time, creating and re-creating experiences based on your observations.

Since you are now playing the role of the particle detector in the experiment, you can think of yourself as a **life** detector. You have certain expectations about how your life is going now and how it is going to be in the future. These expectations can be conscious thought, or they can be beliefs that you are not even aware that you hold. Regardless, the combination of these beliefs is acting as a particle detector—only it never turns off. Because of this, your expectations are always influencing the outcome of any experience. In short, you get the experiences in your life because that is what you expect to get.

When you change your expectations, you will change the outcome of any experience in your life.

If every moment is a completely new act of creation, then how do things keep presenting themselves to you in a certain way? For instance, when you come back to your house in the evening, I suppose that it looks pretty much the same as it did when you left. All that is happening here is that you have accepted the way that certain things look, and your mind is programmed with these expectations. It is banked in your mind as a memory of the characteristics that you expect, and that is what pops into being when you come home.

It is no different for anything else in your life. I'll go into this in much more detail in the next few Principles, but essentially, you are tuning into the experiences in your life by expecting the same things over and over. You have accepted that your life and your experiences are going to be a certain way, and you are actively looking for more experiences matching these expectations. In essence, your "life detector" has been set, and it just needs to be reset to tune into the life that you desire.

It is that simple: you get what you expect to get; nothing more, nothing less. Of course, there is an upside to this—you now know that by working on changing your expectations of the experiences in your life, **you *are* changing your life at a very real and physical level.**

However, in order to use this power, you must start at every moment to observe the thoughts that you have about anything. Each thought that you hold represents an expectation that you have about your life. Start to notice the way that you talk about money, illness, your body, your job, and your relationships. As you now know, whatever you say is a verbalization of your expectations, and that affects the life that you receive.

When you say, "I have cancer," you are telling the waves all around you, "I expect that I have cancer." They respond by continuing to present you with the experience of cancer. Likewise, when you say, "I am poor," you are telling the waves around you that you expect to be poor, and so you get the experiences of poverty: too little money, a run-down car, low-paying jobs, and so forth.

If you change the way that you look at and speak about your life, you can change your expectations. For instance, you may have cancer now, but every time that you speak of it, you can say, "I had cancer. I am being cured of it now." By doing so, you are verbally showing your expectation that you are being cured. By the same token, you can change anything in your life in this way. Change, "I am poor," to "I easily attract wealth to my life." Instead of, "I am so sick of dating abusive people," try, "I attract wonderful, kind people to myself." Rather than, "I really wish that I could afford that (house, designer dress, car, etc.)," speak the truth of, "I easily afford all that I desire. Money comes to me in many wonderful ways." Change, "I have a terrible time losing weight," to "I easily maintain my perfect weight."

Send the right signal out to the waves all around you, and they will bring to you everything that you desire. Make sure that your life detector is looking for the right things, and the right things will present themselves to you with ease.

You create magic each moment

As each moment passes, it just goes back into non-existence. You cannot observe a past moment anymore, so it is just a bunch of waves. This means that the past does not exist at any real level. You may have memories of past events, but they literally have nothing to do with the present moment that you are observing and creating. Your past has no hold on you but the hold that you allow it to have in your present mind.

Likewise, your future does not exist at all. There is no way to observe future moments, so they are just waves of potential. They have the potential to be created in any way that you choose, based on the expectations that you hold for that future moment. **You** are in control of choosing the expectations that you hold on to—and whether or not you allow negative thoughts about yourself created from negative past experiences to have any hold on the "you" that you are creating today.

This is important, because so many of us think that our future is determined by our past—that we are literally chained to our past selves and cannot be anything more than we were before. In addition, it often seems that we have no influence on the future— that it is out of our hands and left to fate, destiny, or luck.

This, too, is illusion.

You actually have great control over your future by controlling the expectations that you are using to create your present moment. Like setting a button on your radio to the frequency of a station that you really love and that makes you feel good, you can be assured that you will continue to tune into positive future experiences by always tuning into positive expectations right now, in the present moment. You see, if every present moment is in alignment with what you really want in life, then you can be assured that each future moment will be as well.

What do you expect to have in your future? You must expect that it is real right now, in your present. You can only create this moment; no other moment exists. The past does not exist. The future is just a bunch of waves waiting to become something else. If you tune your expectations into the very best that you can imagine right now and believe that it is so in this present moment, then **it will be so in your future**.

To take this one step further, you actually are a completely new you each morning. When you sleep, you are not there to observe yourself, your body, or your surroundings. It stands to follow that you are actually in wave form while you sleep—you are just a bunch of waves that flow at the general frequency of you. You, in the form that you are at this moment, do not exist in the night. In the morning when you wake, you are a completely new creation of you—you are totally recomposed upon waking. In a very real way, you can look at this like being **totally reborn** each and every day.

This re-creation of you is based on your expectations of how you are going to look and act in the morning, and what you expect the state of your life to be that day. That being the case, why not change your expectations at night by making sure that you are programming yourself with positive beliefs overnight? Try repeating a positive belief over and over as you go to sleep each night. You can even speak a set of beliefs into a tape recorder and listen to it as you drift off to non-existence. By doing so, you will be actively changing the expectations that you will have of yourself in the morning, which will change the way that your energy and particles come back together.

Use your magic overnight to create the "you" that you want to be in the morning. You will be amazed at the changes that you witness just from this simple practice.

You can release what you do not want, and attract what you do

If you can, please go to a mirror and look at yourself. If you cannot do this, look down at as much of your body as you can. What do you notice when you do this? First, some fairly nasty judgments about yourself and your appearance may come to mind, but just put these aside for the moment—you'll be dealing with those soon enough. What else do you notice? I will give you a hint: do you seem solid? I know that there is that jiggly part under the butt and around the middle that may not seem totally solid, but please disregard that for now.

I am guessing that based on your observations and expectations, you **appear** to be solid.

Let's see if you can observe yourself another way. I want you to imagine yourself as a staggering amount of energy. (Please take a moment and visualize this so that you really get the idea.) Imagine that you are just an image on a computer screen. In this state, you are **completely energy**—there is nothing solid about you at all. Imagine that someone types in a command that changes your hair color. See that color change instantly. Imagine that the person makes you a bit taller, changes what you are wearing, or decides that you would look better with a different eye color. Whatever it is, see it change instantly.

Imagine stepping out of the computer screen just as you are. Feel the energy that has created your body. See yourself as glowing with energy all over your body. If you can, imagine this energy shifting and moving—flowing within your body like gentle waves of electricity.

You have now seen beyond the illusion of you—you have seen the trick behind the trick. You really **are** flowing with energy all the time, and this energy is changing at every moment. You are literally being created and re-created each instant.

When you look in a mirror, is the image that you see actually you? No, it is simply a reflection of the solid that is you right now. Just like the image of yourself in the mirror, your body **itself** is an illusion. Yes, it appears solid and unchangeable, but it is actually a huge amount of energy that has decided to become the solid form of you at this moment. If you decide to change your observation about yourself, you can change what you see. And, like a log converting to heat energy, this should not be a struggle; it is simply the totally natural process of changing states of being, and it is going on in you and around you all the time.

While this may sound nice in theory, let me give you a practical example of how this energy conversion stuff can help you in your daily life. Let's say that you decide that you want to lose 10 pounds. You begin to diet a little, but you know that the real key to permanent weight loss is exercise. "You've got to burn that fat!" people tell you, or you go to an aerobics class and the instructor shouts, "Feel that burn!" with the kind of glee that only a woman causing an entire room of people to think that their thighs are **actually** on fire could ever muster up. What does this happy sadist mean by "burning"? When you get onto the treadmill and "burn" 400 calories, what you are really doing is releasing 400 units of energy from the mass that is your body. When you do work (exercise), you actually are converting mass (as in, that jiggly part under your buns) to energy—and you end up weighing (and jiggling) less!

The same thing happens when you eat food. The food is solid, and your body breaks it down, turning the solid into the energy that fuels your body. If you eat too much, your body turns that energy back into solid—fat cells—where it is stored until it is needed again to fuel you. At that point, it is broken down into energy once more.

Your body **is** $e = mc^2$ in action (and it does all this converting of solid to energy effortlessly, every moment of every day).

This applies to more than just fat, however. If you develop a tumor—a solid, scary mass in your body—your body has simply used energy to form into this as well. This tumor is merely excess energy that your body has formed into a bump that you do not want. If your body has the power to **make** the tumor, then your body also has the power to turn it back to energy and let it float away from you like smoke from a fire.

Whatever you do not want in your life is just waiting around to be turned back into energy and released from your life.

Better yet, all this released energy coming from everything around you is floating around waiting to become the things that you experience in life. Since that is the case, why not see that energy as becoming the things that you truly desire? It has to become some kind of matter at some time, so why not have it become the experiences and objects that you would really enjoy?

Start seeing everything in your life and all of your desires as what they really are: energy. For instance, the car that you want is just a bunch of energy. The money that you need to buy the car is simply energy that has become the paper you recognize as currency. The promotion that you need to get the money to buy the car is simply an energy experience—all the players involved are energy, as are you.

So, the next time that you see something you really want (like a nice purse or a beautiful home), just see it as energy. Say to yourself, "Well, that is just energy. It is the same energy that I am made of, and I accept it into my life." If you have a relationship that you do not want in your life, simply see it as energy—and say to yourself, "This relationship represents energy that I no longer need in my life. I release it and ask that the energy come back to me in the form of a positive, fulfilling relationship." This statement works for anything that you no longer want—cars, houses, clothes, jobs, or anything else. Just change the "relationship" part to the word for what you are working on, for example, "This **car** represents energy that I no longer need in my life. I release it and ask that the energy come back to me in the form of the car that I really want."

Try this each time that you are confronted with these experiences. Believe me; you will be surprised at the results!

Remember, if all matter is changeable, then everything material about us and our circumstances is changeable **at all times**. Use this reality to break through the illusion and change your life.

Energy is neither good nor bad—it's just energy

If you had a serious, life-threatening form of cancer, I would assume that you would view those cancer cells as very bad and could not imagine seeing them as anything other than a negative, scary experience. This perspective is both very human and totally understandable.

As you have just learned, you can change those cells back to energy and release them. These cells can go off and become ANYTHING else—even positive experiences for you or others. The former cancer-energy can become the car that you really want, or it can float off and provide food to a hungry child. It could become more money in your pocket, or even clothing for a person halfway around the world.

In terms of the universe, energy is just energy. It doesn't matter where it comes from or where it is going, it is all neutral. Rather, it is your perception (what you **expect** from the energy showing up in your life) that assigns the labels of "good" and "bad" to it.

You can think of this like a huge energy swap meet. In a

normal swap meet, you bring something that you do not need anymore to swap for something that you like and want. Further, the item that you take home is something that someone else did not want anymore, but will bring you happiness. For instance, perhaps you have an old lamp just sitting unused in the basement, and you swap it for a truly beautiful vase that you display prominently and that brings you joy each time that you look at it.

In the universe, the exchange of energy is exactly like this. You release energy from your body or life that you do not want to swap with energy that you **do** want. It is not a struggle, you are not losing anything important to you, and you always get back something more useful and better for your life.

Moreover, energy that you thought of as bad or useless to your life is swapped for something useful and helpful to your life or to someone else's. It is recycling at its very best!

Clean out your life with wild abandon! Get rid of the fat that you don't want, the objects that you don't want, and even the relationships that you don't want. Don't hold on to them with the fear that you will have nothing to replace them with. Rather, send anything that you no longer want (or perhaps never wanted) into the big swap meet of universe—and expect to get back something better and more useful for you. Do this, and you will get back your desires, and more.

Additionally, when you are faced with things and experiences that you do not want in your life, do not label them as bad or negative—they aren't. They are simply energy that is temporarily something that you do not want—swap that energy for something that you **do** want!

You are so much more than you think you are

What do you really want to do or be? Do you ever feel like you just do not have what it takes within you to really accomplish what you desire? Perhaps you have felt that you are only one person, and cannot possibly make the impact that you wish.

24

If so, it is time to banish that thinking forever. You are much more than you ever thought.

The energy swap meet I spoke about a moment ago applies to **everything**, even your body. The "you" of today is formed out of a bunch of bits of recycled energy.

You are actually composed of particles that were once Shakespeare, Ghandi, or Mother Theresa. Other particles came from former Presidents, rocket scientists, and millionaires. You even have particles that were, at one time, Jesus, Krishna, Buddha, Mohammed, and every other great spiritual figure. You see, you are **not** just one person. Rather, you are made of the energy of the people that have gone before you—all the people that you admire or want to emulate are actually part of you.

If you have always wanted to be a great playwright, at some level, you already are. Perhaps you have dreamed of being a real estate tycoon or a fashion designer; you've got a bit of that inside you as well. **Whatever** it is that you dream of being or doing, some of your particles have "been there, done that."

This is very important, since so many of our expectations about the kinds of experiences that we are allowed to have come from our physical and mental attributes: race, gender, sexual orientation, and religious affiliations. Because of this, you may expect that only certain experiences are appropriate for a person "like you," while others are not something that you can take part in. Because of your body and personal characteristics, you may believe certain things about how others perceive you or the kind of life that you can have, and if these beliefs are negative, they will create negative experiences that match those expectations. Further, you may judge others because of their traits and choices, seeing yourself as superior to them.

This, too, is illusion.

The truth is that you are made out of particles that have been every race, religion, color, or sexual preference under the sun. So, regardless of the religious, sexual, or racial group that you feel an allegiance to in this life, you are, at a particle level, totally, completely multicultural. You have many particles that were at one time female, and many others that were at one time male. You are

25

also made of particles that were, at one time, even homosexual or transgender. This is likely hard to fathom and maybe even a little uncomfortable to think about. In today's society, much comfort is taken in belonging to a certain group, and this group affiliation is involved with how you perceive your place in life. However, it is time that we realize the truth that we are more like mutts in a pound—made of a little of this, and a little of that—than we are purebred dog show winners (actually, purebreds are not really purebreds either!).

No matter how it appears on the surface, the reality beyond the illusion is that you are composed of every single culture on earth. Given that fact, it seems rather silly to have such hatred between different groups of people, doesn't it? From now on, when you catch yourself feeling hatred or judgment toward people because they seem different from you—remember, they are not so different after all. In a very real sense, you are actually made of some of them, and they are made of some of you.

Of course, that concept does not just cover people—it extends to include every single thing in life. You also have particles that were once part of **anything** that you can imagine. Some of your particles were once a beautiful house. Others were an expensive car or hundred dollar bills. In this way, you are truly a walking universe—because you have particles that were once planets, stars, trees, animals, and other people.

Whatever you can think of, whatever you could possibly want in life, you are made of particles that were once those exact things. You are, at a very basic level, everything that you could possibly dream of. Right at this very moment, you **are** the manifestation of your dreams.

Questions:

1. What changes would you like to make in your life? What do you feel are your limitations? What are your attributes? What would you do if you thought you could

not fail?

2. Imagine yourself connected to the reality that you desire—where all your goals come true. What would you feel like? What would you look like? Visualize this reality every day this week.

3. What are you afraid of losing? What are you really attached to? If you achieved everything that you desire, do you think that you might lose some of these things? Is this fear holding you back?

4. What have you always wanted to be or do? What has stopped you? Can you now see that you have no limitations on your dreams? How would you feel if you truly took on the new belief, "I have no limits on my life"?

Retuning statement: "I can change anything that I choose. I am unlimited." For the next few days, please repeat this statement to yourself throughout the day. In addition, you can write it out several times a day, or even repeat it into a tape recorder and listen to it.

PRINCIPLE 3

You are Connected to Your Wishes Right Now

I once had a dream that I was running through a huge obstacle course trying to win a golden trophy. A strange man told me that there were very specific rules I had to follow; breaking a rule meant that the obstacles would change, become more menacing, or actually transform into sinkholes in the earth that I had to try to cross. I remember at one point in the dream I broke a rule that I was not aware of, and suddenly, a huge sinkhole appeared in front of me. The golden trophy was on the other side of the chasm, and I had no way to get across.

On one level, this dream is just my nocturnal musing; on the other, it is indicative of how I felt life to be at that point, and how you may be experiencing life now. Each day you are faced with a series of tests with incomprehensible or unknown rules, leaving you far away from the prize that you were after in the first place. Maybe your golden trophy is to win the sales contest at work, but every appointment is a nightmare and you end up with no sales at all. Or, your trophy might be a promotion, but your boss keeps changing what he is looking for in a candidate, causing you to run around trying to hit a moving target. Perhaps you wake up each day **swearing** that you are going to stick to that diet, not have a cigarette, give an hour's time to a charity, or stop yelling at your kids, but one thing after another pops up, causing you to go back on your promise to yourself once again.

Just like my dream, the obstacles shift and the rules constantly change. What was necessary to achieve what you desired the day before is radically different today. After putting forth all that effort and **still** coming up empty, you head home beaten and weary. Is it any wonder why all you want to do at the end of the day is flop down in your easy chair and watch TV?

After all, getting what you want from the TV is easy. Once you learn how to use the remote control, the rules never change. You punch in numbers or hit the up and down buttons, easily surfing through endless options of programs, all of it accessible with no trouble at all. Whether it is love, anger, violence, or joy that you're after, you can experience it without even getting up—you are connected to a whole world of options just by sitting and choosing. Talk about struggle-free!

Wouldn't it be nice if getting what you wanted out of life was as easy as surfing through TV stations? If, instead of struggling to earn what you desire, you would be instantly connected with any option of your choosing?

Nice wouldn't even been the word for it—it would be **incredible**. Thankfully, I've got good news for you:

You are connected to all that you desire now

In the last Principle, you learned that your expectations are actually affecting the reality that you are living right now. This being true, it just stands to reason that when you change your expectations, you change your life.

It sounds easy enough, but there is a major problem with putting this into practice: that is, **you believe that you are**

disconnected from your desires. In fact, just as my expectations were in the dream, **your** expectations have been set to believe that you must struggle, suffer, or pass some mandatory spiritual or physical tests in order to have your wishes granted by sources outside yourself—"power brokers" like your boss, your spouse, your customers, or even whatever higher power you believe in. If you gain the approval of these powerful entities, you **might** get what you desire in return (and that is a mighty big "might").

It is as if your life is a big TV, with a different set of life experiences on each channel. But, instead of having free access to connect to any channel that you wish, various powerful people have blocked some of the experiences that you'd like to have. To tune into a blocked experience, you must prove to these power brokers that you are responsible enough, smart enough, or just deserving enough to be given the code to see that channel. In this scenario, you are powerless; you are like a child pleading with a parent to be able to watch a program that has been deemed off limits.

There is no doubt that this is a common belief, but it is still false. The truth is that you do not have to look anywhere but **inside yourself** to gain access to anything that you desire. There are no power brokers that have exclusive access to experiences; no one else holds the code for granting your wish. Right at this very moment you are connected in a physical way to every single thing that you could ever want in the entire universe. Just as changing the channel on your TV is easy for you now, when you learn to communicate with life in the correct way with the right expectations, you will easily tune into everything that you desire.

I can say this with such confidence because of the scientific concept called "non-locality." Non-locality is a term used to describe the completely amazing reality that every particle in the entire universe knows what every other particle in the entire universe is doing at any moment in time. Furthermore, every particle is communicating with and responding to every other particle instantly, whether the particles are 12 inches, 12 feet, or 12 billion light years apart. Whatever happens to one particle affects all particles at the **very moment** that it happens.

Put in day-to-day terms, the instant communication that particles display is like having telepathic ability so strongly that you could read another person's mind at the exact instant that they had a thought. It seems impossible, but it is precisely what is happening right now with the particles that make up your body and mind and the particles of everything in the entire universe. In fact, your particles are communicating instantly with the particles of a man in Japan, a redwood tree in California, and a star at the farthest reaches of the galaxy. Your particles are aware of and responding to anything that is happening to any friend or loved one in the entire world, and their particles are instantly connected to and communicating with you. Moreover, your particles are having an instant conversation with all the money, cars, and homes in the world, every wish you have, and brilliant idea you'd like to have. Even more importantly, all of these particles are instantly responding to and communicating with you at all times—your connection is never broken.

No matter how disconnected you seem from everything that you wish for, you are **never detached** from any of these things; rather, you are, at all times, physically connected to and communicating with the entire universe. Never believe that you must prove yourself to anyone in order to gain access to your dreams, because, whether you know it or not, you have an open line of communication with all of it. By changing your expectations, you will be able to bring your desires into being in your life as easily as you now change the channels on your television!

Faster than a speeding...particle?

A particle communicating at a speed faster than the speed of light is quite a dilemma. After all, **nothing** is supposed to travel faster than the speed of light!

The wave nature of reality provides the answer to this quandary. After thinking about how faster-than-the-speed-of-light communication is occurring, Physicist David Bohm put forth the theory that although each of us experience life as a set of individual particles composing solid things, perhaps the reality is that there is actually nothing but wave. Maybe underneath it all, reality is one fluid system—like a big ocean with no beginning and no end—no separation between anything. This fluid, waving system has an order that is imperceptible because of each person's limited perspective, but order is there—an order that gives birth to the particles and everything else in the universe. You cannot see this deeper wave reality because by the time that you are there to observe something, it has sprung into the solid forms of life. In essence, according to Bohm, your perception of reality is faulty, because it is impossible to look at anything without your perspective affecting it (but if you could, you'd just see waves).

There is not actually faster-than-the-speed-of-light communication, because everything is really a waving oneness. Two particles may **seem** to be breaking the speed of light by communicating, but in reality these particles are part of one whole, undivided system.

This also means that no matter what you are experiencing, the truth is that you and everything in the entire universe are one. The impression that you are separate from anything or anyone is, in actuality, just an illusion.

Bohm calls this deeper reality "quantum potential," and says that it is here that all the wave information to produce any experience of life resides. There is a unique order that, while complex and difficult to understand, organizes and gives birth to everything in the entire universe—turning wave frequency into reality as we know it. Quantum potential calls up the wave frequency of a seed and allows it to become a certain kind of tree in a certain place. You sprung forth into reality from quantum potential, and you go back to quantum potential when you sleep— back to this oneness, this place of wave.

Even when you seem solid and separate from others, you are part of this oneness. At this very moment, you are one with everything that you desire, everyone in the world, and any possible experience that you could dream of. You are one with that fantastic car that you want, the money that you need to start a new business (and indeed, with all the money in the whole world), the solution to every problem, the people that you love, and even those that you hate.

Your sense of separation is an illusion—oneness is the reality. Shift your perspective to expect that you are connected with all that you desire, because you are!

Quantum potential shaken, with a twist of Jung

While this notion of a waving oneness creating reality seems strange (it is, actually), quantum physics isn't the only place where scholars talk about having a deeper reality that is a source of common creation. In fact, Transpersonal Psychology was founded on this concept.

You may have heard of the term "collective unconscious" and of the psychologist Carl Jung, founder of Transpersonal Psychology. Jung theorized that the collective unconscious is a deeper reality that all humans are tuned into, connecting us at all times to a collective world of symbols. These symbols are unconsciously understood by every human, regardless of their cultural affiliation, gender, or race. He called these symbols "archetypes," and they run the entire gamut of emotions and situations—covering the best and the worst that humanity can dream up.

The idea of working with different archetypes is to go beyond your normal daily experience and connect directly with the deeper root reality. By understanding what archetypes you are pulling up, you can understand why you are creating your particular experiences. By changing the archetypes that are in your life now, your reality immediately shifts.

Choosing the archetypes that are in your life is a bit like changing the channel on your TV. Just as your TV tunes you into anything that you choose, **you** are consciously or subconsciously selecting the archetypes in your life, calling them up to be played out. Your selection causes you to live and act in ways that are consistent with that archetype, even when you might want to do otherwise. If, for instance, you have selected the "anger archetype" to tune into, you will have many experiences in your life where anger is a theme. If you become aware that you have selected an archetype that you did not really want, you can mentally choose another one. So, you can choose change the channel to tune into the "peaceful archetype," causing only peaceful and flowing experiences to play themselves out in your life.

By combining Bohm's and Jung's theories, a new understanding of how each of us creates our lives emerges. Each person's perceptions and expectations are pulling up matching waves of reality out of this larger oneness. Each experience in life is a flowing "wave-archetype"—a specific frequency matching your expectations. By identifying and understanding the wave-archetypes that you are working with now, you can choose to send them back into the deeper reality and start to select better wave-archetypes to experience. While you may not be able to see or experience the collective unconscious or quantum potential, the reality is that you are connected to, and part of, absolutely everything that the universe can create. You have direct access to these experiences through your mind, and if you change the archetypes (wave frequencies) that you are working with now, your life immediately changes. There is no limit to the life that you can live, nor the reality that can be created. There is only **potential.**

Alright, you may be thinking, "That's great and all, but how do I use this information?" Let's get to it!

You can choose any experience that you want

Since you are one with quantum potential, you are connected to the waves necessary to create any experience that you desire, and can choose to tune into these experiences by fine-tuning your expectations. Quantum potential itself is like a powerful TV signal—one that contains all the wave information necessary to see any experience of life at any moment. Moreover, **this** TV signal has a huge storage capacity, because it must be able to store all of this wave information for easy retrieval. After all, quantum potential needs to be able to create an infinite amount of experiences in the past, present, and future.

How is it keeping all this information? It would take an immense computer to be able to save even a small percentage of that data. And, if this information is there, why can't you see it? Why would you just see waves? More importantly, how are you interacting with these waves to choose the experiences of your life?

It turns out that quantum potential is a hologram containing everything in the entire universe, and by shining your personal light on it, you choose the experiences of your life. (I know that this sounds abstract—hang in there. It will all become clear soon!)

To understand how this could be, you need to understand a bit about holograms and holographic film, and also what makes them so different from normal camera film. You are, I am certain, familiar with normal camera film. When a picture is taken of you with normal camera film and that film is developed, you can look at the negative and see your image. If you print the picture, you'll have a nice, two dimensional photo of yourself. If you turn the negative into a slide that you put into a projector, you can shine the same two dimensional image of yourself up on a screen or wall.

Not so with holographic film. If you had a holographic picture taken of you, upon looking at the negative (film), you would see nothing but a bunch of concentric rings; you would not see your image. However, the energetic signature of you would be stored on that film; by interacting with the wave information correctly, you would be able to see what you were looking for: **your image!** If you shined a strong light through your piece of holographic film, you would suddenly see a complete 3-D image of yourself. It would be exactly like you in every way, down to the smallest mole and tiniest wrinkle. Moreover, just like the real you, you could walk completely around this holographic you. This image would simply be you as represented by waves—your "wave-archetype," as it were.

To put this in terms of TV, let's say that you had the ability to stick your head in your television and actually see the waves of information that produce TV shows. These waves would not look like a TV show to you because you did not have the correct tool to be able to actually decipher this information. However, tune your television to the right station, and these same waves would be translated onto your screen as a picture that you would easily recognize. If you imagine that your brain and body are the television, you cannot see the waves that compose the things that you are experiencing in your life (quantum potential), but your brain is the tool that is translating these waves into the life that you experience around you. Everything is still wave, but you experience it as solid due to your brain's perspective—you are the light shining through the hologram of life to produce that which you experience.

To take it a step further, what if you could take a holographic picture of quantum potential—with every possible experience in the entire universe—past, present, or future? On that film, you would have the wave information necessary to be able to produce any experience, person, or thing just by interacting correctly with the hologram. Of course, upon looking at the actual negative, you would not see anything that you would recognize as you, a planet, or a tree. However, it would all be there, captured as wave frequencies representing the energetic signature of every possible and potential experience that has ever been or ever will be. If you shined a light through the part of the hologram containing your image, you would be able to see you, in 3-D, standing there. You could choose any other experience and do the same.

Amazingly enough, this is exactly what scientists think is going on. Because everything is innately wave, each item in life has its own energetic signature—the unique frequency that produces just that object, person, star, or building out of the waves of quantum potential. This means that you are a holographic image; just waves of potential being formed and re-formed out of wave particles. You have a frequency that is just "you"—your "wave-archetype"—which is the combination of the waves of all the particles that make up you. Moreover, every single thing in life is also a holographic image, each with its own frequency. The people that you love are holographic images. The car that you desire is a hologram. Each and every experience that you encounter is a holographic bit of film being played out and produced from quantum potential—and it has its own wave frequency that matches your desires (conscious and subconscious) exactly.

You see, life truly **is** flowing.

Better yet…

There's more than enough for everyone

I remember the first time that I heard someone say that "life is infinitely abundant!" To be truthful, I thought that the person was full of it, especially since I was experiencing so much scarcity, limit, and difficulty. At that point in my life, it was difficult for me to believe that there was no limit to what I could create in my life, and further, that everyone else had the same opportunity, and there would **still** be more available.

Ironically, I am now going to tell you that life **is** infinitely abundant—and, just so you don't think that I am full of it, I am going to prove it to you.

Once again, it comes down to holographic film. If you took the holographic film containing the picture of you and cut it into two pieces, you would have two complete images of you—one on each side (not half on each side, as with normal camera film). You could shine a light through **either** side of the holographic film, and you could still see a 3-D image of you—as complete and whole as if you had the complete piece of film. As a matter of fact, you could cut this film into an infinite amount of pieces and **each piece would retain an entire image of you.**

What if you did the same with the piece of holographic film containing the picture of quantum potential? If you cut this film in half, you would have two complete quantum potentials. What if you cut this film in enough pieces to be able to give one to every single person on Earth? Now quantum potential would be cloned billions of times, allowing every person to have the wave information necessary to be able to pull up and experience any experience of life that they could possibly dream of. Each person would literally have the **potential of the entire universe**.

Better yet, every person could experience as much as they wanted of anything that they desired, and there would still be infinite amounts available to everyone else.

Sounds like a nice world, doesn't it? Frankly, it would not just be nice; it would be a **dream** world—one with limitless potential available to every person at every moment.

Well, this dream world is reality. In fact, whether you know it or not, this is exactly how the world truly works—you hold the quantum potential hologram within you, as does everyone else. Your piece of the quantum potential hologram resides (as much as it can "reside") within your mind. In your mind, you are not only connected to every possible experience of life, but you can access these experiences by choosing a mental state matching the frequency of that experience. It is exactly like shining the right frequency of light through a piece of holographic film in order to see the image captured there, because your thoughts are simply waves of electrons that have their own frequencies. As such, they are waves of potential that illuminate different parts of the quantum potential, resulting in matching experiences popping into being in your reality. When you match your mental waves of potential with the experiences that you desire, you suddenly have that experience flowing in your life.

To begin flowing with all that you desire, start to view everything in your life as it really is—simply waving holographic images that represent a certain energetic frequency. Your body is a flowing holographic image created by your mind and processed by your brain out of the frequencies of your expectations. Every object in your life is a holographic image flowing at a frequency matching your expectations of yourself and what you believe that you deserve right now. Everything that you desire is a holographic image that you are connected to now, but, in order to actually experience these desires manifesting in your life, you must adjust your beliefs and expectations to the proper frequency. Most importantly, every bit of this is being pulled up and generated by the quantum potential, based on the frequency of your expectations and the collective expectations of all of the minds in the entire world.

Expectations are a thinking person's remote control

I know that all this talk of flowing holographic images and your mental power to select your experiences may be a little confusing, so let's put it in TV terms to make it easier to understand.

In order to create a TV show, a camera films the show, translating physical reality into waves. This wave information flows through your cable or via your satellite into your TV, which decodes this information back into the images that you see on the screen. When you change channels, you are requesting that your TV tune into a different frequency—and thus, a different channel.

The quantum potential hologram can be thought of as the waves of information flowing to your TV. The TV itself is your brain—it acts as the tool that decodes the wave information in a way that you can comprehend. Your mind is the remote control—tuning you into and out of experiences as your thoughts and beliefs change. Each experience of life can be thought of as a different TV show, each with its individual frequency. You see, life **is** reality TV at its best.

Without knowing it, you have used this to your advantage to find this book. At some point you decided that you were ready to truly transform your life. You started surfing through all the frequencies of the quantum potential until you tuned into the energetic signature of this book. Of course, if you had asked for information on how to build houses, you would have looked for home-related programming and would have tuned into a book experience flowing with **that** request. Or, if you wanted information on how to have a healthy pregnancy or learn a language, you would have sought out very different stations with very different programming. As always, you get what you are looking for, no more, no less.

Since this is how life works, tuning into what you desire should be an easy experience, but more often than not, it isn't. This difficulty is due to something I call a "preset." Presets are exactly like programming your favorite channels into your remote control, only, in the case of your mind, your presets are programmed based on your long-standing expectations of life. Just like favorite channels, your presets keep tuning you into the same kinds of experiences over and over again. For instance, you may have had many frightening and difficult experiences growing up, so your mind expects that life is not safe. Because of this "favorite" frequency, your mind is preset to tune into the station playing violent, frightening programming—causing you to live this frequency of experience over and over. Or, maybe you learned to expect that relationships are difficult, so this "favorite" frequency tunes you into the same problematic relationships and issues time and time again.

More than just repeat experiences, presets can cause serious frustration when you are trying to change yourself and your life. While you may have consciously decided, once and for all, that you want to change, your subconscious mind is still tuned into a preset frequency that works against your best efforts. As an example, let's say that you decide you would like to lose weight. However, you subconsciously expect that you will fail at your efforts (an old preset that was set because of past problems losing weight). Without your conscious knowledge, this preset will continue to tune you into the experience of gaining weight, so, try as you might, the weight stays (or even increases) when dieting. In TV terms, it's like deciding that you are going to tune into FitTV, but still pushing your "favorites" button on your remote to tune into FoodTV instead. While it is obvious what the problem is when you accidentally tune into the wrong TV station, it is not so obvious when your results are due to old preset beliefs and expectations. Understandably, you'll feel like a terrible failure when you keep gaining weight despite your best efforts, likely yelling at yourself for being so "weak" or "unfocused."

41

The thing is, you don't beat yourself up for accidentally tuning into the wrong TV station, so it doesn't make sense for you to beat yourself up or feel like a failure for simply (and subconsciously) tuning into preset expectations, does it?

The truth is that you are not a failure, and there is no reason to beat yourself up. When you get results that are different from what you desire, simply imagine that you have pushed the wrong button on your mental TV. Do not judge or yell at yourself (this only reinforces the preset frequency expecting difficulty). Choose to empower yourself by seeing the experience for what it is—some preset programming that you were not consciously looking for, but accidentally or habitually tuned into.

The setting of a preset: memory-holograms and you

If your presets are automatically choosing your experiences, then it is important to understand how they became favorite frequencies in the first place. And further, if everything is holographic in nature, why are you experiencing life as so physically real—with all the scents, sounds, sights, and textures of solid objects?

I'll give you that **does** beg an explanation, and here it is:

Your brain is taking in all the wave information around you and decoding it into your experience of reality. In fact, every one of your senses is actually a construction of your brain, allowing you to experience life in physical form. When you experience this physical reality, each moment is registered in your brain in the form of a memory—or rather, a "memory-hologram"—with its own frequency. The frequencies of all your memory-holograms combine to create preset frequencies that seek similar experiences from the quantum-hologram.

This process begins with your experience of your senses. Of course, your ability to sense life is precisely what makes it so hard to believe that everything is actually a set of waving holographic images. After all, seeing is believing, right?

Wrong. As real as it all feels and looks, each of your senses is just wave information that is being interpreted by your brain. In fact, when you touch something, the sensations of texture or temperature that you "feel" are actually waves of electrons that your brain uses to say, "Ah! I am feeling this!" to the rest of your body. Your eyes are simply tools that take in and send wave information through your nerves into your brain, where it is constructed into your visual experience of that moment. Likewise, your nose takes in odor particles, and depending on their frequency, sends the wave information into your brain, where it is interpreted in such a way that you can experience that particular scent. Your sense of taste is just the same—the wave information of anything that you eat is processed and sent on to your brain, where it is decoded and translated into the taste of chocolate or strawberry or potato chips.

Even emotions are created and processed by your brain in much the same way. While no one seems to agree on exactly how emotions are formed, there is much scientific evidence that your individual emotional response to different experiences comes from a certain set of waves in your brain that, through your experience of life, have matched with a specific type of event to create the physical and emotional responses of a particular emotion. For instance, as you grow up, you learn that you should feel sadness upon being in certain situations. Once this preset is set, your brain not only translates the frequency that identifies a situation as "sad," it also sends out the wave information that causes you to respond to sadness physically in your own preprogrammed way—be it with tears, silence, or whatever learned response that you have. In fact, research has found that different emotions can actually be seen showing themselves as unique activation patterns in your brainwaves, thus showing emotions as waves as well.

Likewise, every thought that you have (conscious and subconscious) is a little wave criss-crossing through your brain, making new wave patterns, creating new neural pathways and contributing to new holograms. In fact, there are different frequencies of waves for different activities—for instance, slower waves for meditation and faster waves for active concentration—

and these frequencies tune your body into and out of memorized responses as necessary for the situation. In addition, each word or phrase that you think or speak is a unique wave pattern with **its** own specific frequency.

In a way, your experience of life is an illusion—no more real than a TV program. Your brain is simply taking the waves around you and making sense of it all in the same way that a TV takes in wave information and translates it into a TV show.

When you live an experience, all of the wave information associated with those moments—everything that you felt, thought, or sensed—makes its way into your brain and bounces around, bumping into each other and creating memory-holograms for that event, allowing you to remember any experience in full sensory detail. It is exactly like the process of making a photographic hologram—only, your brain is the camera and your mind is the film. This interaction allows a unique wave-archetype of just that experience to be written onto your mind, permitting access to the memory in full detail whenever you like, just by accessing that frequency.

To give you an example of how this works, I would like you to think of your happiest moment. As you pull up this memory, do you notice that you have the same bodily response that you had when you lived the original experience? Can you recall what things looked like, smelled like, or even sounded like? Your ability to remember this experience in such sensory and emotional detail is due to the fact that the frequency "happiest moment" matched the wave-archetype of that particular experience. Because of this, that experience and all its sensory information were called up for you by your mind, which allowed you to relive those sensations now. If you asked for your "saddest moment," then your mind would tune you into a much different experience indeed.

Let's take this to the next step: what if there was technology available that would allow someone to take a holographic picture of your mind? Captured on a piece of holographic film would be everything that you had ever experienced in your life—all of your memory-holograms would be represented. By shining the right frequencies at the right angle through this piece of film, you would find yourself physically reliving any experience of your past. Your brain would decode the waves in the same way as when you lived the experience initially, and you would be completely convinced of the reality around you.

Further, if you were able to play one of these memory-holograms for another person, he or she would be convinced that **they** were experiencing your memory as real for them right then—complete with sensory experiences such as tastes or emotional responses.

And, while it may seem strange to think of a taste-hologram or an emotion-hologram, it is really not so strange. Because all waves behave the same, any kind of wave can make a hologram. Of course, the most common example of this is a visual hologram (like the one on a credit card), which is created by technology that has been around for quite a while. However, there is technology available now that is recording sound-holograms of live concerts. The most amazing thing is that, just like cutting a piece of holographic film in half, this type of recording is not just recording the experience; rather, it is **cloning** it. It is in every way the same experience as the original experience. In fact, if you listened to a sound hologram of a concert that you had previously attended, your brain would be completely convinced that you were at the live concert, and in a way, you would be. You would hear everything **exactly** as you heard it live—your ears would sense sounds coming from the exact direction where they were originally produced, and musical notes and voices would appear all around you as if out of thin air.

If that technology were developed further, you could add the sense of touch, taste, sight, and smell to the experience, along with a recording of the emotions and thoughts that you had while at the concert. If this were replayed for you, your brain would re-create the exact experience of the concert in full detail. You would literally be transported back in time, but living it today. And, although your senses would be convinced that the experience was real, it would really be an illusion.

Actually, for that matter, reality itself **is** an illusion.

And **this** is how life can be composed of waving holographic images, yet you experience it as very solid and sensory. This is also how your presets become set—through the making of memory-holograms—tuning you automatically into a life that you have come to expect, but that you may or may not actually want.

What problems are your presets causing you? And more importantly, how can you reprogram your presets to easily seek fulfilling, joyous experiences? It's time to find out!

You get repeat experiences because that is what you recognize

Do you notice that you seem to have negative habits that you just cannot break, no matter what you do? Or that you react the same way to certain kinds of situations, even when you are trying to respond differently?

While you might become frustrated with yourself for not being "strong enough" to break the negative habit or pattern, this has to do with memory-holograms and preset frequencies as well.

The truth is that your expectations tune you into more than just similar experiences—you also recognize certain frequencies, and your mind tunes you into favorite **responses**. This is due to something that I call the Priniciple of Recognition, and it explains what habits really are, and why they are so hard to break.

To understand the foundation of the Principle of Recognition, I need to take you back to the example of taking a holographic picture. Let's say that you take a holographic picture of an orange, and on the same piece of film you then decide to take a picture of a teddy bear wearing an orange scarf. Wherever there is a similarity between the two objects, there would be a bright spot on the film—in this case, anywhere that the color orange overlapped, there would be a bright spot. However, if you photographed an orange and then a teddy bear **without** the scarf, there would be no similarities, and therefore, no bright spot on the film. The holographic film actually **recognizes** similarities between two objects—it knows when there are matching frequencies.

Let's apply this to your mind. Let's say that you have a memory-hologram from your childhood of your mom opening a box of perfume and spraying it in the air on Christmas morning. This memory-hologram was photographed onto your mind by the combination of the waves of sight, smell, sound, taste, touch, emotion, and thought that occurred during that experience—each with its own distinct frequency that combined to make the wave-archetype of that memory.

What would happen if you smelled that same perfume today? Your mind would **recognize** the similarity between the smell waves of that memory-hologram and the smell waves of today's hologram, and that memory would be triggered—in all its sensory glory. Just like the teddy bear and orange example above, you would have a bright spot illuminating the similarity between the two!

It is amazing, but the frequency of just **one** wave—the smell of the perfume—is a trigger that causes the **entire memory** to be re-experienced. Exactly like the teddy bear and the orange, one similarity between two experiences will light up a bright spot on your mental hologram, tuning you into the matching memory-hologram—even if the two experiences were decades apart.

You can test out your personal recognition response right now. If you have an old record or CD of music that you listened to in high school or college, go get it. Pick a song that was played during a memorable experience and play it now. If you are married, perhaps you might want to choose to play the song from your first dance. How do you feel when listening to this song? Are you transported back to that age and that experience? Can you remember what you were thinking, saying, or doing in sensory detail? Is your heart racing, or do you feel the same excitement and joy that you did when the original memory was made?

Actually, you can try this little experiment with any of your senses. Maybe the taste of salt-water taffy instantly transports you back to your favorite amusement park. Perhaps the smell of chlorine or the scent of a baseball field instantly makes you feel like a kid again. Or, maybe there are certain words or phrases that instantly trigger good or bad feelings and memories for you.

No matter what, your mind has learned to recognize different frequencies of experience and associate those frequencies with not only a memory, but a memorized response. When you encounter a recognized frequency it becomes a trigger, and your response is automatic. This is important to understand, especially when it comes to breaking a habit—and creating a new one.

How this plays out in life is that you will find yourself doing and saying things in response to a certain kind of experience, even when you do not want to be doing or saying those things. For instance, let's say that your boss drops a bunch of projects on you at the last minute. You feel infuriated, but you don't say anything—you bite your tongue and do the projects, all the while wondering why you didn't stand up for yourself. After all, you had just decided that you were going to refuse any more projects until he gave you a raise! How could you have let this happen?

Simple. Your mind recognized a certain frequency of experience, which triggered you to tune into a **memorized response**; in this case, it was to accept more work and not make trouble. In fact, had you been consciously aware of the frequency of the beliefs that were causing your habitual reaction, you would have realized that it stemmed from your parents' assertion that you needed to be the best at everything—that second best was never good enough. Along with that belief, you were also taught that you could not question your parents, even if they were being unreasonable. This combination of beliefs has caused you to put aside your needs in order to do the impossible in every area of life, thus always being the best—or at least, your parents' definition of what is the best. When your boss gave you extra work, your brain recognized this frequency and that triggered the habitual response, which caused you to react in the exact same way that you would have had it actually been your parents giving you the extra work. To your mind, "your boss" and "your parents" are identical frequencies; they are both authority figures that you must please and cannot question. Due to your preset response to this frequency, you will react this way with **anyone** that your mind considers an authority of the same caliber as your parents.

It is exactly the same for any and all experiences that you have taken on as "how life is"—whenever you encounter another matching frequency, you react out of recognition or habit. For instance, you may have mentally decided that you are going to say "no" the next time that someone asks something unreasonable of you, but when your dad asks in "that tone" of voice, you give in automatically, acting exactly as you did as a child. Or, you might be trying to quit smoking, but when the clock clicks 10 o'clock you are unable to stop yourself from taking your regularly scheduled smoke break. Maybe you decide that you are going to stick to your diet, but when your favorite TV show comes on you find yourself pulling the ice cream out of the refrigerator just like you always do.

In every instance, you'll beat yourself up for not acting differently, but without conscious reprogramming of the memory-hologram (or preset), nothing could have changed. Your mind simply tuned you into the response that it recognized for that frequency, and you found yourself reacting accordingly.

This also accounts for our individual responses to different kinds of stimulus, or why one situation can cause one person to react with a stress response, while another finds it no big deal. For instance, my husband has associated the idea of a plane ride with "go to sleep." He literally falls asleep the instant the plane starts to move. I, however, associate "plane ride" with the physical response of heightened awareness, motion sensitivity, and being wide awake. So, while turbulence rocks him to sleep, it causes me to be wide-eyed and alert. However, in other situations, I am calmer than he is; for instance, public speaking is a joy for me, but it causes him great consternation.

No experience is inherently stressful—it is how you have been programmed to recognize and respond to a certain kind of stimulus that determines whether or not it is stressful to **you**.

Think about the kinds of experiences that cause you stress. What are your physical reactions when you encounter that frequency of experience? Is it different than other people that you know? Do you find some things calming, while others respond with great distress to the same situation?

This just shows that you can reprogram your mind to associate new responses with old triggers, thus changing your habitual response into one that you would desire. To begin this process, take out your Flow Journal and write down different situations that trigger a memorized response in you—both positive and negative. What situations cause you great stress? What reactions do these experiences trigger? When you find yourself reacting in a habitual way that you do not desire, jot down what the pattern is, where it seems to come from, and when it started. Once you understand this, become conscious when you begin to tune into an undesirable memorized response, and actively say to yourself, "This is not the way that I react to this situation (or trigger) anymore. I now consciously choose a new response."

Reinforce these statements by deciding to take actions that retune your mind into a desirable pattern, thus completely breaking the old pattern and reprogramming your mind to associate old triggers with new responses. In this case, little changes do make a big difference. A simple change might be to walk away when your boss starts the same old stuff, or to speak up for yourself when you would normally remain silent. Whatever it is, you just need to make new choices to send a message to your brain that you are not only expecting different (better) experiences, but that you also want to react to similar experiences in a new way. This will reprogram your preset, allowing you to make a positive way of living and acting a habit for you.

By using the Principle of Recognition coupled with the Principle of Repetition (coming right up!), you can program your expectations to seek personally fulfilling experiences—and to be truly in the flow with all that you desire. By doing so, you will watch one similar fulfilling experience after another light up your mind—and your life.

Repeat yourself. It's good for you.

Or bad for you.

Well, it depends. I'll tell you what—let me just explain myself.

At some point in your life, you have undoubtedly witnessed a child begging his mom for some crazy thing that the mom does not want to buy. The child begins a chant of "please please please please please…" until the mother either drags the child out of the store in disgust, or gives in, unwilling to fight any more.

Retuning your mind to the frequency that you are looking for can be thought of much like this. You have a frequency that your mind is flowing at now. As you would like to adjust this frequency to tune into the things that you desire in your life, you begin to use matching-frequency retuning statements and take new actions when faced with old triggers. After a couple of days, you aren't noticing anything too different in your life, so you decide that it doesn't work and go back to your old ways of doing things.

What happened? Quite simply, you did not repeat yourself enough to retune the overall frequency of your mind. You can easily understand this if you think of playing notes on a piano. Let's say that you play one note and hold it. You then add another note. The resulting sound is the combination of those two notes— it is a frequency **in-between** the two. The introduction of the new note does not eliminate the old note; it combines to create a new tone.

In your mind, you have certain beliefs and expectations that are flowing at a certain note—like a piano, they are tuned to keep playing these frequencies to create the life that you are living. Every time that you introduce a new thought or empowering action to your mind, you are adding that frequency to the current waves. This causes the overall wave frequency to change a little, but not very much. Again, it does not eliminate the old note, it adds to it, raising or lowering its frequency. However, as you keep introducing this frequency to your mind, you gradually retune your mind to match the frequency of your desires—each addition of this new note increases or decreases the existing frequency by steps, and you eventually get to the point where your intended frequency **is** the default—or favorite—frequency.

I call this the Principle of Repetition. If you want to retune your mind (and presets) to the frequencies of that which you desire, you must continuously introduce the new frequency to your mind in the form of thoughts, words, and actions matching that frequency. There are ways to speed the process up considerably, such as by adding sensory exercises, emotions, and energy to your words and thoughts—you will be given all of these tools in the "4 for 40" section of the book. However, no matter what, repetition is the key to truly longstanding, successful change.

Of course, you can have just the opposite effect by using this in a negative way. Every single time that you think or speak, you are introducing that frequency to your mind and adjusting your overall flow. If you repetitively say nasty things about yourself or others, you are asking to tune your mind into those frequencies.

That being true, I would definitely suggest that you stop it!

Fine-tune your beliefs, retune your life

I know that I keep going on about how you need to match your beliefs with the frequencies of all that you desire. You may be wondering what exactly I mean by "the frequency of a belief" or "expectation" (and why shouldn't you? After all, you did buy the book). Okay, here it is: in terms of life-changing, the frequency of a belief can simply be described as the **feeling** or **emotion** that the belief or thought conveys.

While this may seem abstract, it is actually very common sense. For instance, what frequency would you say that love has? Would you say that it is a positive frequency? What sensations and thoughts does love evoke for you?

Now think about hate. Is there a difference in what you sense or feel? I would bet that there is a BIG difference in how you feel and think about each. If you held only loving and kind thoughts about yourself and all of life, would you expect to have different experiences of life than someone who embodied hate?

When looked at this way, it becomes clear how the different frequencies of emotions that are attached to an experience or thought can actually produce very different experiences of life.

Every single one of your expectations conveys a feeling or

emotion, and it is this frequency that is selecting experiences from the quantum potential and projecting the life that you are living. If, for instance, you truly believe that a person "like you" is not good enough to start a business, achieve success, or find a kind and decent person to love, then you will certainly tune into experiences that prove this out. In frequency terms, this belief is tuning into the frequencies of hatred toward self, fear of not being good enough, and belief in limitation.

In order to begin to change your expectations (and thus, your life), start to evaluate each of your thoughts and beliefs in terms of their frequency or feeling. If your thoughts and beliefs are contrary to that which you want to achieve in your life, you will not be able to achieve those goals, plain and simple.

In energetic terms, this is the phenomenon of constructive and destructive waves playing out. When waves encounter each other, they size each other up. If they are alike, they will add their frequencies and double their energy (constructive). However, if they are different, they will actually negate each other, flattening out and decreasing their energy (destructive).

Apply this to your beliefs and expectations. If you hold positive beliefs that flow with the frequencies of hope, success, prosperity, love, health, and joy, you will flow easily with matching experiences, doubling your energy (double positive). However, if you hold **negative** beliefs and encounter positive experiences, you will negate the positive energy, making you totally unable to flow with positive experiences, no matter how hard you try. For example, if you encounter a wonderful person who could be the love of your life, but immediately think, "too good to be true," or, "He'll probably end up to be a freak, since I'm a freak magnet," then you'll wipe out the positive energy of the situation (destructive), and that experience will just fade back into the quantum potential. Worse, while you turned this experience down (energetically, anyway), the next person that you attract will likely be a person who matches these beliefs exactly (and may I say, "**Yikes!**")!

Do **you** think that your beliefs and expectations flow with a frequency matching all that you desire? As a quick exercise, take out your Flow Journal and write down some of your beliefs and expectations. Look at each one. Does it flow with the frequency of love, faith, joy, pride, success, prosperity, and abundance? Or does it flow with a frequency of hate, disappointment, guilt, worry, fear, limitation, sadness, and pessimism? Your life will flow with experiences matching the frequencies that these beliefs embody, so be sure that your beliefs are tuning you into what you really want!

If reality is illusion, then illusion is reality

When I was first developing this system, I worked with my father as a benefits consultant for hospitals. At this point, I had read book after book talking about how it was possible to visualize the reality that you wanted and connect to that reality. These books claimed that by doing this, this exact reality would come to pass.

After reading many tales of people's real experience with visualization, I decided to give it a whirl. I knew that I had a very important meeting with a large hospital system coming up—one that would be very beneficial both to myself and to the business. About a week before this meeting, I began to lay in bed at night visualizing everything about the meeting. I imagined myself driving up to the hospital, and I imagined in great detail what the hospital would look like. I imagined where the front door would be, and where in the hospital my potential client's office would be located. I imagined exactly what he would look like—down to the color of his tie. I imagined exactly how the meeting would go, and how the meeting would end. I saw myself being successful in every regard.

The day of the meeting came, and my dad and I drove up to the hospital. To my utter amazement, the hospital looked exactly like I had imagined. Without thinking, I told my dad, "You need to go that way. The Human Resources department entrance is in the back." This was a huge complex, with no signs to tell us where to go, and yet I knew just where to go. My dad looked at me with amazement as we found a parking spot right by the entrance (which also looked just as I had visualized). We entered the hospital, and without stopping at the information desk, I told my dad to follow me down the hall. Sure enough, at the end of this long, winding hallway, there was the office, just as I had imagined. We walked in and were greeted by our potential client, and he looked just as I thought that he would—down to his bright red tie.

Long story short, the meeting went perfectly, and we came out of the appointment as successful as I had visualized that we would. My dad thought that I was developing psychic powers, but I was really developing **creative** powers—I had learned to connect to the reality that I wanted by pre-constructing that reality in my mind first.

After all, if your mind is constructing the reality that you experience, then everything that you experience—even in meditation and visualization—is as real as when you open your eyes and consider yourself "awake." You are literally building reality through the frequency of your expectations, so by building the reality that you desire in your mind first, you are simply assuring that what you want **will** come into being.

In essence, you are simply using your mind to construct sensory holograms that have the frequency of your desires. These holograms, when built correctly, must come to pass, since your mind is simply seeking out matching-frequency experiences from of the quantum potential.

Pre-constructing your reality is a skill that I call the "Art of Connecting." You know that you are already connected to that which you desire—you cannot exist and be separate from anything. You only perceive yourself to be disconnected from these desires due to your beliefs and expectations now. When you repetitively use visualization to pre-construct your reality, you radically change these expectations and shift your reality to focus on your connection to your desires. In essence, you reset your presets to tune into exactly what you desire.

The Art of Connecting is ridiculously easy, and the little effort that it takes is certainly worth the results. To do this, sit quietly and begin to visualize yourself in the exact reality that you desire. Imagine every color. What are you wearing? What are other people wearing? What does each person look like? Are there any smells? Are you holding anything, or shaking anyone's hand? What does that feel like? What will you say? What will you be thinking?

And most importantly, what emotions will you be feeling? Allow yourself to feel those emotions fully—become caught up in everything that you would be feeling. For instance, if you feel that you would be smiling, allow yourself to smile in reality now. If you want to actually act this reality out, do so. You can even use objects to "become" things that you would be holding—for instance, use a necklace to represent an award or medal, a piece of paper to represent a certificate, or a voided check to represent the check that you'd like to give to charity or use as a down payment on a house.

By doing this, you are creating a new hologram in your mind that brings that reality into **your** reality. You are simply connecting yourself to that which is already in existence at the quantum level and programming that frequency of experience as a "favorite," allowing you to tune into that experience with ease.

Practice the Art of Connecting each day, and you, too, will develop "psychic" powers—or should I say, very creative powers. You now have the ultimate control over your life by simply choosing to pre-construct your reality with your mind.

Your unlimited creative power also means that nothing is impossible for you to create, choose, or do. There are no limitations to what you can do with The Flow system—you can cure a disease, be successful beyond your wildest dreams, get solutions for the world's problems, or do what has never been done before. In fact, when you understand how this works, it is easy to see why some people can walk on fire, put 3000° F coins in their mouths without pain or injury, or cure themselves of an "incurable" disease by praying or meditating. It is this same truth that allows people to lift immense amounts of weight to free a trapped child, or to have a life that is, at every moment, exactly what they desire. If you truly believe that you can do any of these things and you repetitively train your mind to flow at the frequency of this expectation, you will experience these things, just as you expect. After all, there are countless studies about the fact that more optimistic people have better, healthier, and just generally easier lives—and I say, "Of course they do!" They are **expecting** the best, and, due to the laws of the universe, the best must flow to them.

The good news is that whether you tend to be optimistic or not, you can train yourself to think and believe in ways that actively seek all that you desire, and flow with all good things. And, when you see your desires coming into reality, you will be a very optimistic person, indeed!

Competition is seriously over-rated

And very unnecessary, actually.

I know that I talked earlier about the fact that life is infinitely abundant—meaning that you and everyone else can create any life that you desire and there would still be more for all of us.

However, I have found that the idea of being in competition with others is so ingrained in our minds that even knowing this, many people still feel that they need to compete to be the **first** to connect to their desires—less someone else tunes into it before they do.

Yes, that is common thought—but it is not true.

You never have to compete with anyone to get what you want out of life. You can have what you want, and even if someone else wanted the exact same thing, they could have it as well.

Remember, the quantum potential hologram that we each house in our minds contains the wave information to tune into **any** experience of life that we want. You could cut that piece into a thousand pieces, and you would have a thousand more exact clones of quantum potential.

To ease your competitive spirit, think of this like a video game. In a video game, you always start on Level 1, fighting your way to the top level where you are a "winner." In life, you also begin on Level 1, struggling to stay alive, hoping to just make it to the next level where you might do a little better for yourself—maybe getting a better job, finding a new love, or picking up a free pass for less back pain. All that you can see and experience right now is Level 1, but that doesn't mean that Level 32 doesn't exist. Of course, Level 32 **is** quantum potential—it has all the riches, health, happiness, life satisfaction, and love that you could possibly want. In essence, it is the ultimate "winner's circle."

So, you are playing the game, and suddenly, you discover a secret passageway to go straight to the "winner's circle" with absolutely no effort. Would you stick it out and keep fighting your way up the levels, or would you take the secret passageway? I am sure that you would stroll right up that passage to the winner's circle and claim all the goodies that you could possibly want, laying claim to a totally fulfilled life without any struggle at all.

The Flow system is giving you the secret passage to a fulfilled life. And, like a video game, just because you can't see the deeper reality yet doesn't mean that it doesn't exist, or that you do not have access to it. It **is** there—you just need to choose to take the secret passageway by consciously choosing to live life in the flow.

Moreover, you and a friend could be playing the same game on your own computers, and you could both win as many goodies as you could possibly want. After all, a videogame doesn't suddenly say to you, "Yeah, I know you won the game, but that other guy just did it, so you don't get anything. Sorry!"

Has this **ever** happened to you when playing a video game? I would imagine not—because this **doesn't** happen with a video game, and it doesn't happen in the game of life either. No matter who you are or how you did it, when you get to Level 32 you get access to the same stuff as anyone else who has gotten there before you.

Since each of us has a clone of the quantum potential hologram in our minds, there are **infinite possibilities for each of us**—there are an infinite number of fully stocked winner's circles available to every person. No one has more or less wave information; each piece of the hologram, no matter how many times it is cut into pieces, always contains all the wave information necessary for every person to have access to any experience, even if an infinite amount of people are "winners" as well.

Better yet, **your** Level 32 is perfectly stocked for what you desire, and your friend's will be perfectly stocked for him or her. After all, each of us has a different sense of what it means to be fulfilled in life—success and happiness for one person is not the same as success and happiness for another. By fine-tuning your beliefs to seek a fulfilling life for you, your winner's circle will present you with the life that meets **your** needs and desires exactly. It is life fulfillment personalized for you, your values, and your expectations.

It all comes down to a choice on how you want to live and how you decide to use your power. Each of us lives differently and learns lessons at different times, resulting in a totally unique experience of life. For instance, you might have learned about a secret passageway to your dreams a long time ago, and are living the life that you desire now. A friend of yours may have missed it or been programmed with more problem beliefs than you, and is still struggling with a difficult reality. A totally fulfilled life is there for him, but he is either unaware of it, or chooses not to move toward it in the same way that you did.

As you begin creating the life of your dreams, there will likely be times that you will feel the need to be in competition with someone else for a coveted prize. Stop yourself. Remember that although it appears as if there is only enough for one of you, there are infinite amounts of experiences matching your desired frequency available to you. If you do not get this particular experience, you will get another that exactly matches your desires.

Questions and exercises:

1. Each day this week, put the Art of Connecting to use by taking the time to visualize an experience that you desire. Create your reality by using the Principle of Repetition to retune your mind's expectation.
2. Begin to use the Art of Connecting to change your memorized response to a problem trigger. See and feel

yourself successfully changing a bad habit or response.

3. I'd like to expand on an analogy put forth by physicist David Bohm for how you could see certain experiences and not others. Take a piece of paper and write down one of your goals. Fold the paper up so that the words are on the inside. Looking at the folded paper, you only see blank paper—you can't see your goal. Of course, this doesn't mean that the paper doesn't have an inside, or that your words are no longer there. You must make a choice to open up the paper to see what you cannot see now. Now, apply this to the "real" world. Just because all you are seeing now is trouble and difficulty does not mean that your dreams are not there. You must make choices to align yourself with the frequency of those goals, and suddenly, the inside of the paper shows itself to you—showing you that your dream was there all along! Keep this piece of paper. When you doubt that you will ever see your dream in reality, remember, it is already there. Open that paper up and connect to that reality.

Retuning statement: "I am connected to all that I desire now. I choose to see all that I desire in reality." For the next few days, please repeat this statement over and over. In addition, you can write it several times a day, or even say it into a tape recorder and listen to it.

PRINCIPLE 4

You are a Life-Creator

While watching the *The Wizard of Oz* recently, I realized that not only is it a highly entertaining and fanciful film, but it is also quite a fitting metaphor for how life actually works. As the story goes, a young girl named Dorothy has a great adventure where she ends up in a strange land, and upon arrival, she is told by the Good Witch that the only way to get back home is to go on a long journey to the Emerald City, where she will find a Wizard that will grant her wish. So, she starts down the yellow brick road, meets some special friends, and encounters considerable obstacles and strife—finding her way through scary forests and past flying monkeys, all the while trying to keep the Wicked Witch at bay.

After all of this, she finally arrives at the Emerald City, only to find that all the effort that she had made was **not** a guarantee that she would get her desire. As a matter of fact, the Wizard refuses to help her, and to make matters worse, she finds out that he is not such a Wizard after all—he is just a scared little man without any real magical powers. In a final ironic twist, the Good Witch shows back up and tells her that the difficult journey (the very same one that she sent Dorothy on) was actually unnecessary, as the truth of the matter is that Dorothy had the power to grant her **own** wish at any time—she just needed to click her heels, and she would be instantly back home.

At this point in time the movie, I often wonder what I might have said to the Good Witch, had I been Dorothy. I think it might have been something like, "Are you **serious**? Could you have mentioned that at any point before I got picked up by a bunch of flying monkeys and had a Wicked Witch threaten my life? And why exactly did you tell me that I had to see the Wizard for anything? You call yourself a "good" witch. You should be ashamed of yourself." And then click, click—I would have been out of there.

Well, prepare yourself. By the end of this Principle, you may want to ask just these same sorts of questions to some "Good Witches" in your own life!

Be your own Good Witch

Like Dorothy, throughout your life, you've had "Good Witches" and "Wizards" teach you about your personal power to change your life, and what it takes to get what you want from a higher authority. In fact, it is very likely that your entire concept of a higher authority—and your understanding of your relationship with that higher authority—has been given to you entirely by the Good Witches and Wizards in your life.

Good Witches are people who have helpful intentions—they teach you what they believe that you need to know in order to live a good life and have a good relationship with "the divine Creator," whatever they called this higher power. What they teach you may not end up being helpful or even true, but it is not because they were intending to give you false information—they were just doing the best that they could at the time with the knowledge that they had. For instance, your mom or dad may have played the part of a good witch when they told you that you must go to church a certain number of times a week in order to be considered moral or worthy. Your priest, rabbi, preacher, or other spiritual teacher may have been acting as a good witch when he gave you specific instructions on how you could wipe away your sins or receive God's blessings on you. According to these good witches, if you accepted **this** teaching, did your prayers just **this** way, or you gave exactly **that** amount to money to the church, then God would look on you with favor.

You may have also encountered some unscrupulous Wizards on your personal journey. Just like the Wizard of Oz, real-life Wizards have no actual power, but they **pretend** that they do in order to get money, power or respect from others—usually resorting to fear and intimidation tactics to keep people under their spell. In order to trick their followers into giving them what they desire, Wizards convince people that they are wiser, holier, and have a more direct connection to a higher authority than anyone else. This creates the illusion that they are beyond question—strongly implying that you **must** accept their word as the Word of God. Worse, if you question a Wizard, you risk both their wrath and the wrath of other followers. Obviously, some evangelical preachers fit into this category, but so do some healers, psychics, and even CEOs of large corporations. Put simply, a Wizard is **any** leader who knowingly misuses their position of leadership by falsely representing themselves as holier than their followers.

While their intentions are very different, Witches and Wizards have one thing in common: they teach you that any higher authority is an all-powerful being who must be convinced that you deserve a good life in order for you to receive blessings. In this scenario, there is a Creator who does all the creating of life, and you are the created—always destined to live by the Creator's whims.

However, the holographic model of life provides a different understanding of a Creator. In the last Principle, you learned about quantum potential and the master hologram of life where the creative force is contained. This master hologram **is infinite potential**, organizing and creating all that is, will be, and ever has been.

If that is not the definition of the ultimate Creator, I don't know what is. Quantum potential is **the** Source of all life—it is **the** Creator, whatever name you call It by. In fact, in order to remove any preconceived notions about God, I am going to call the concept of a creative Divine force "the Source"—but please feel free to exchange "the Source" for whatever name you use to identify a higher authority, if you wish to. Whatever name you use, the concept is the same—it is the Creator; it is quantum potential; it is oneness.

Moreover, because you contain the flowing hologram of quantum potential within your mind, this means that **you have the Source—and all its creative power—*within you*.**

Further, if everything is one at the quantum level, then you cannot be separate from the Source and you cannot be Creator and created, rather, you are in a never-ending **partnership** with the Source to co-create your life.

The Source-power within you allows you to create new moments as your mind sends out fresh wave information in the form of thoughts, words, and actions. These waves work **with** the Source to create a life that is in alignment with your expectations. Think positive, unlimited thoughts and take actions in alignment with those thoughts, and you will have a positive, unlimited existence. Think negative, limited thoughts and you will have a negative, limited existence. This powerful partnership allows you to create your existence in the way that **you** choose.

I know that the idea that you are co-creating your existence can be daunting to grasp, especially if you have been raised to believe that you are powerless when it comes to the experiences of your life. However, the holographic model of life—and in particular, the idea of memory-holograms—can help you to understand how you can be part of and connected with the Source, and how the collective experience of life comes into being.

Memory-holograms, consciousness, and creation, oh my!

As you know, there is a master hologram—what I will now call the "Source-hologram"—that is quantum potential. The Source-hologram is creation itself, with endlessly abundant possibilities for every moment. At this level, everything is one—there is no you and me, there is no Creator and created—there is just oneness.

As part of the creative process birthed by the Source-hologram, **you** flow into existence. In fact, the wave-archetype of "you" is actually a memory-hologram of the Source—a "you-hologram"— that creates and re-creates you out of the oneness every day, and chooses experiences that match your personal frequencies. Of course, this you-hologram is not static—just as I talked about in the last Principle, every time that you think, speak, or simply exist, you are changing your personal memory-hologram in various ways. Each moment, you are not only co-creating with the Source, but you are also one with its infinite potential.

In between the "you-hologram" and the "Source-hologram," there is the collective consciousness—or, in hologram terms, the "collective-hologram." This is the memory-hologram created by the frequencies of all of the minds in the entire universe. Each person's personal creative power combines with everyone else's, and this collective frequency shines through the Source-hologram, causing universal or shared experiences to come into being in a way that our collective consciousness expects.

The world as we know it is a product of this collective-hologram. Every thought, word, and action that is created by each of us combines like multiple notes on a piano. It is as if every person in the entire world had their own piano, and all at once, each of us hit the key of our choosing. The combination of those notes would produce a specific frequency. Likewise, the combination of all the thoughts, words, and actions of every person on earth creates a unique frequency that produces matching-frequency experiences from the Source.

And yet, even when experiences and people spring into being from the quantum potential, none of it is ever separate from the Source. Like trying to pull a single wave from the ocean, you cannot exist and be separate from the Source.

Better yet, your own Source-power means that you don't need

any "Witches," "Wizards," or any other go-between for you to communicate with the Source, because you are every bit as connected to the Source as anyone else. You are one with the Source and are not only communicating directly with It now—but you *always have been*.

Save yourself the difficult journey with tests, tribulation, and even flying monkeys—there is no need to seek a Wizard's help to get what you desire. Instead, learn from Dorothy's experience: choose to believe in your co-creative power, click your heels together, and grant your **own** wishes now.

If everything is the Source, then nothing is not the Source

Every religion has its own way of identifying what the Source is.

One might say that God is an old man in heaven judging whether you are good or bad. Another might say that the Source is the ultimate Goddess. Yet another sees the Divine as a light or a Flowing Oneness. Another describes the Creator as the sun and moon, or even a multitude of different gods, each with a specific purpose.

Which concept of the divine Source is the correct one?

All of them.

If quantum potential is the Source, and quantum potential includes everything, then everything in life **is** the Source. The Source is every definition of God that has ever been or ever will be. The Source is both male and female, good and bad, judging and loving. It is every race, every sexual orientation, every religious inclination, and every person you meet. It is all the things that you find beautiful and desirable and everything that you find distasteful and ugly. It is this moment now, every moment in the past, **and** every future moment.

Understanding the Source in this way is absolutely in alignment with a belief shared by many religious traditions: that is, the Source is the Alpha and the Omega, or the beginning and the end. This statement is often taken at face value, thinking that it simply means that the Source created the world and will also end the world. However, if you view this statement in terms of what you now know of the Source, it takes on a more significant meaning: if the Source is the beginning and the end, then the Source must also be everything in the middle. Nothing exists that did not start with the Source, and nothing can end without being the Source. The Source **must** be all of it—every single bit of existence.

Take the Source-identifying statement, "I am who am" to heart. The Source is "who am"—whatever exists in thought, energy, or form. You are "who am" as well—you cannot exist and be non-Source.

When you say "I am," you are using your co-creative power to declare what your expression of the Source is for that moment. If you say, "I am poor," you are choosing to express the Source as poor. When you say, "I am sick," you are creating the experience of sickness. If you say, "I am powerful, I am good, I am love," you choose to express your Source-power in alignment with these qualities.

Actually, the concept that the Source is within every person is present in many religions, but is often misunderstood. As a child, I remember being taught to "see Jesus in everyone." In that context, I understood this to mean that you should be as kind to others as you would be to Jesus himself. However, I now see that there was a very different meaning—that **each of us** is the Source-made-flesh. Likewise, the Hindu greeting "namaste," often used in Yoga classes, means, "The God in me greets the God in you," although scores of yoga students do not likely believe that this is meant literally.

Well, it is! Become aware of the Source in yourself and in others. See everyone and everything as the Source presenting itself to you. Observe all life from a place of wonder and awe at the Source-creation that you are co-creating.

Most importantly, choose to see yourself as you really are: a life-Creator co-creating life with the Source, and who is filled with the light of the Source itself. Use this power with conscious responsibility—make this moment, and every moment, a creation

67

that is the very best for yourself and for all life. After all, isn't **that** what the Source would do?

Every moment is a prayer...

And **every** prayer is answered.

In the holographic model of life, every moment of your existence is a prayer that is instantly answered as creation forms around you in alignment with your expectations. Every thought ripples out over the waves of the Source-hologram, and increases or decreases the frequency of your life (and all life in the universe), in that instant. Every word or action does the same. The life that you live as a result of all of these "prayers" is the **exact** life that you asked for—in thought, word, and deed.

Change the way that you think and speak about your life to a way that is in alignment with a fulfilling life, and you will have those prayers answered by pulling matching life experiences from the Source-hologram.

This is very different from what most of us were taught about prayer. In my own life, I was taught to get on bended knee and pray to God for what I wanted. More often than not, the prayer would end up being a kind of barter with God, such as, "If you give me the money that I need to repair my car, I promise to give 10% of it to charity." In the case that I thought I had offended God, I learned to do certain numbers of prayers to cleanse my soul and earn God's forgiveness. If I did not get what I wanted out of life, then I must not have done something right—I needed to pray harder, search my soul for further indiscretions, or give more money to the church.

You may have been taught something similar—most people have been given some version of this approach to prayer. However, the holographic model of life provides a new understanding of what prayer is, and how it truly works. After all, since you are co-creating each moment of life, then you cannot barter with **anyone** to get what you want—you are actually just bartering with yourself, which seems a bit pointless. You will only get what you believe that you deserve—every moment ripples out over the oneness of the Source-hologram and brings experiences to you that are in alignment with the frequency of your beliefs. If you believe that you must barter with the Source to get what you desire, then that is the reality that will present itself to you—each time that you get what you desire, you'll find yourself in a position where you have to give something else up.

Moreover, the idea that you can offend the Source is impossible. After all, how can you offend a neutral creative force? The Source is simply pure creative potential—how you use that creative potential is up to you, and **only** you. If you decide that your higher authority is one that will be offended by certain creations, then it will be. If not, it will not. If you expect that the Source is a judging force, then you will get a life built around that reality. If you expect that the Source is unconditionally loving, then that will be true. Amazingly, *even in the very definition of what the Source is*, the Source-hologram can only bring into being what you ask for, no more, no less. **You** decide how you want the Source to show itself to you; the Source that you ask for is the one that you get.

This does not release you from the responsibility of using this power in the best possible ways—on the contrary, it puts the **complete responsibility** on your shoulders to create a kind and wonderful life. You have the power to create a life filled with distress and difficulty, or you can create a fantastic life for yourself and for others.

Become fully conscious that every moment is a prayer that is instantly answered. Choose to think, speak, and do in alignment with the highest good that you can imagine. Accept your life-creating power, and begin to live each moment with the focus on making life better for all life on Earth.

That is a prayer that everyone will be grateful to have answered.

You may have heard it before, but judging is really, really bad

This new understanding of the Source has profound implications on our comprehension of every religious text in existence. In fact, reading the religious text of your choice with the new knowledge that you are co-creating life with the Source is an enlightening experience. For instance, the biblical quote, "Judge not, and ye shall not be judged; condemn not, and ye shall not be condemned, forgive, and ye shall be forgiven," (*Luke* 6:37) takes on a whole new meaning—and a whole new level of truth.

What you give out in terms of frequency, you must get back—this is the way that the world is created. Give out judgment, condemnation, and hate, and you will see these flowing into your own life. Send out love, non-judgment, and forgiveness, and your own life will flow with these qualities instead.

To take this a step further, by judging others, you are literally **judging the Source itself**, since everything is created from and part of the Source. There is nothing in life that is not part of the deepest intelligent potential, meaning that every object, every action, and every person is an expression of the Source, whether or not you would judge it so.

This means that the murderer is as divine of a creation as you are. The homeless person or crack addict is as much an expression of the divine as the socialite or successful business owner. In fact, everything that you would judge as "dirty" or "bad" is as much a Source-creation as everything that you would judge as "pure" and "good." It all comes from the creative power of the Source, and our personal choice on how to create. **Nothing** can be non-Source.

The truth is that you may not like what someone is choosing, saying, or doing, but nonetheless, they are as much a creation of (and part of) the Source as you are. When you judge them, you are not only judging the Source, you are also judging yourself as part of the Source.

You are **also** bringing down the frequency of the collective-hologram, because when you think or vocalize these judgments, you are creating a wave vibration of judgment. By doing so, you are using your personal power to create that moment at the frequency of judgment, which not only adds itself to the collective-hologram, it also adds to your you-hologram, causing **your** mind to tune into experiences of judgment. So, while you may be joking about someone else, your subconscious hears, "**I** like judgment. Please search the Source-hologram for experiences that match that frequency." This frequency tells your mind that **you** expect judgment—and you know what happens with expectations! Suddenly, you have many experiences in your life where **you** are judged harshly or are put down by others. You may not be able to consciously make this connection, but you are getting exactly what you asked for. Just as the quote above said, by choosing the frequency of judgment, you **receive** judgment in your life. It can be no other way.

Practice total non-judgment. See other people as simply an expression of the whole. Realize the truth that they are using their Source-power to create their reality in the way that they choose to create it, and allow them to do so without any negative thoughts or words. When you are presented with experiences where you would normally jump on the bandwagon and gossip about or make fun of someone, decide not to do this. If it is difficult for you to stop yourself, choose to remove yourself from the conversation entirely.

When you meet someone that is of a different religion, race, sexual preference, or political philosophy than you, choose to put aside your "differences," and open yourself to getting to know this person as a co-creator of life—not as a bunch of preconceived notions. You will be surprised how lovely most people are, and you will be shocked at how quickly your preconceived notions fall by the wayside. People are people. They all want to be loved, accepted, and admired. They desire the same things that you do, so give your best to them. Love them unconditionally, and you will be loved unconditionally in return.

The next time that you are about to say or think something judgmental, hurtful or critical about someone, **stop**. Choose non-judgment. Think about something loving or happy, or distract your brain from this desire to judge. Simply say to yourself, "Judge not, and ye shall not be judged." In fact, if there is only one thing that you take from this book, make it to stop judging anyone or anything—including yourself. If you do **just that**, your life will be profoundly changed for the better.

What you give out, you get back—so choose to give out non-judgment and love!

Love your tools

No, I don't mean the ones in your tool box.

The tools that I am referring to are your brain and your body—the very ones that you are using right this minute to experience life. After all, if you did not have these particular tools, your mind would be a free-floating bit of consciousness that would only be able to experience existence as waves—the body-less existence commonly known as spirit. In spirit form, you would still be the flowing frequency of "you" as part of the oneness, but you would not have the ability to create in the physical world. However, because your spirit is **connected** to your brain and body, it can use these tools to sort out the frequencies of life into that which you experience in physical form, allowing you to see and sense life in a way that you could not in just a mental or spiritual state.

Since this is the case, you would think that we would be filled with wonder about our physical experience of life, but all too often we take our brains and bodies for granted, becoming disconnected from the awesome experience of life. If you watch a child as they touch and smell new things, you will quickly become aware of how much we lose our sense of awe by the time that we become adults. A child will use their entire body to experience life, and will react with every emotion under the sun to each new experience. Every blade of grass, every sunrise, every giggle or smile is a new and wonderful sensory experience for a child; the simple experience of life as cold, hot, loud, quiet, rough, smooth, sweet, sour, and a myriad of other feelings is amazing. A child lives in the present—each moment is new, different, and exciting.

As adults, we ignore the present moment, taking for granted the beauty and excitement of an ever-changing physical experience of life. After all, do you ever stop to just look around you and be amazed that this very moment is a co-creation of your existence and will never exist again? Do you ever take the time to just be amazed that your brain is creating the sensory experience of your life, and that your body is a tool that allows you to sense life in all its glory? I didn't think so. Convinced that the future is scary, you are likely too caught up in planning the future to ever stop and be amazed by the present moment—and your hand in creating it. Worse, instead of embracing life as it changes around you, you may now **fear** change. This disconnects you from your child-like wonder in the new sensory experiences available to you each moment, and shuts you off from a willingness to embrace natural change as a path to awareness and true fulfillment.

It is time to love and honor your physical being once again. Part of learning to co-create your life from a place of power is to reclaim the sense of wonder in life that you once had. This does not mean just enjoying that which is easy or normal for you, it also means finding the beauty and depth in difficult and challenging experiences—indeed, to be grateful for the fact that you can physically experience the varied beauty of all creation.

I have found that this is very hard for many people to understand, especially those who are on a spiritual quest. Many spiritual seekers feel that they should detach themselves from their bodies and brains in order to sense themselves as spiritual beings. However, this is not the point of our existence as humans—the body is just as important for our development, spiritual or otherwise.

To understand this important connection, think of it this way: the you-hologram is always connected to the Source-hologram and is composed of **all** of you—mind, body and spirit—and all parts work together to co-create your life. As a body-less connection to the Source, your spirit is not only the holder of the memory-hologram of you, but it is also your personal creative potential. This "spiritual you" is composed of both your conscious and subconscious mind. Your conscious mind is **active**; it is here that you consciously make decisions, reason out choices, create with awareness, and decide to use words and thoughts to co-create life. Your subconscious mind is **passive**; it simply records all that your conscious mind, body, and brain sense and feel, and holds all of it in memory-holograms that compose your ever-changing you-hologram. Of course, this you-hologram is what seeks experiences from the Source-hologram as your active choices change the frequencies that you are seeking. At this point, your body and brain work together to become your *experiencing and learning connection* to the Source, allowing you to experience the product of your mental creation—to sense and feel the results of your mental choices and thoughts in a physical way. Without your brain and body, your spirit could make choices and create, but you would only experience waves—not the beauty and depth that is life as you know it.

So, instead of detaching from your body, be grateful for it! After all, you could not hold your child or hug your spouse without your physical form. Your body allows you to run marathons, climb mountains, and play sports. It also allows you to create amazing buildings, write beautiful poetry, create moving music, and express yourself in millions of ways that honor your spiritual nature and raise humanity to a higher level. I, for one, am very grateful for my physical experience, since I could not write this book in physical form if I was just experiencing myself as spirit. For me, my body and brain have become unique tools that my spirit uses to bring forth this physical creation in a way that I would otherwise not be able to, and I can help many people because of it.

Looking at it this way, you can see that your body is necessary for your experience of life—and **essential** for your spiritual journey. Your spirit is being allowed to create life in a physical way, and you are learning how to work with the Source to bring experiences into being. Each moment that you create, you are learning more about who you are as a human being, and who the Source is in relation to you.

Further, you get to experience the reality that you are the Source-made-flesh. When you look at your body and brain as tools that allow you to experience your ability to co-create life, you can view **all** life as a gift that teaches you how to control your mind to create a life of fulfillment. By bringing your awareness to this important process, you can begin to notice the presets that you have in your life. Using this information, you can use your conscious mind to change any preset pattern in an instant, thus tuning yourself into a better experience of life. Best of all, when you understand this process, change becomes as exciting as it was for you as a child—after all, when you begin to set your expectations to tune into a life of fulfillment for you, you can await each new day with a sense of expectation and joy. Even so-called "bad" experiences will be seen as part of the overall creative and experiential process and can be lived with awareness and optimism.

Most importantly, when you choose to use your personal mental and physical power in a positive way, you align yourself with the best attributes of the Source. Truly, the moment that you choose to change a negative, limiting pattern, you have just become more divine. In that instant, **celebrate!** You have just chosen to honor your spirit and become the best that the Source has to offer.

Make the simple choice to be grateful for all aspects of yourself today. Become an observer of your life, choosing to be aware of your power of co-creation. No matter what happens today, decide to react from a place of joy at your ability to experience life. If life is not going as you would like, calmly use your mind to change the pattern to bring a new experience of life into being.

When you start to see the results of your new ways of thinking and being, celebrate the beauty of you. Be truly grateful that you have been able to co-create this moment with the Source. Celebrate your responsible creation of the best in life, and be proud and in awe of all aspects of your existence—mind, body, and spirit.

Potential is all there is and all there ever will be

Do you think that you are fated to live the same life or have the same diseases as your parents? Do you think that there is a destiny that you must live out, one that you cannot do anything about? Are you reading about your personal creative potential and thinking, "Well, yeah, but this disease runs in my family," or "You can't change who you are"?

This may be what you have been taught, but it is not true.

Let me first state that it is perfectly normal for you to believe that you are given a certain lot in life, and there is little that you can do about it. It is also understandable that you believe that you are a ticking genetic time bomb waiting to go off with some dread hereditary disease. After all, if you turn on the TV or open a newspaper, you are bombarded with this perspective, convincing you that this is the way that life really is.

The problem is that quantum physics does not prove this theory out. If every single moment is a completely new act of creation from a flowing reality of waves, then how is **anything** predetermined? If your individual perspective creates the reality that you experience, then how can a doctor predict what you will or won't have in terms of disease or anything else? If even the most brilliant scientists can only make an educated guess where a particle is going to show up, then how can anyone say that anything is predetermined or fated?

Ask any doctor worth their salt, and they will tell you that there are a number of "factors" involved in predicting disease—they will start to mumble something about stress levels, eating habits, addictions, and so forth. Ask any psychic if what they are predicting is the absolute future, and they will tell you that it is not; it is only a possible future based on the current frequencies within your personal energy field (mental state).

Release the belief that you are fated to live a certain kind of life. You aren't. You have the ultimate control over your body and mind, and because of this, you have the ultimate control over the state of everything in your life. By making choices that communicate the right frequencies to all of life, you will tune into the best experiences from the Source-hologram.

You can make a difference in the world right this instant!

Have you ever wanted to change an injustice, but thought to yourself, "What can I do? I am only one person!"

If you are like me, you have. But, while your perception might be that you cannot make that much of a difference, it isn't true. Every single time that you think, speak, or act in ways that flow with the best aspects of the Source, you are making a **big** difference in the world.

Remember, while you may see yourself as separate from others, you are not. The reality is that we are all one, just part of a flowing ocean of energy that is creating and recreating itself based on the frequency of each different perspective. The collective-hologram is constantly changing as new thoughts and actions are created. Like individual notes in a song, each of us puts our individual frequency toward the whole, changing the overall frequency with the notes that we choose to play.

It is essentially the Principle of Repetition taken to a global level. Each thought or action that is of a positive frequency adds to the overall frequency of the collective consciousness, raising the frequency and changing our collective experience by seeking new experiences from the Source-hologram. When this frequency is repeated by many minds, this shift tunes into a better way of life for all of us—in that moment, **life has evolved.**

Each time that you choose to co-create a moment in alignment with the very best attributes of life, you are adding a note to the overall frequency of life that tunes all life into a better existence. By continuing to do this in each and every moment, you become a powerful signal that shifts the universal energy to a better way of life.

I call this "**conscious evolution.**" While much evolution happens at a subconscious level (such as the development of opposable thumbs), you can use your conscious mind to create evolution by making positive choices in your daily life—and this changes the wave-archetype of humanity for the better. By staying consciously aware of your individual impact on the frequency of the collective-hologram, you can choose to improve all life on Earth by always choosing to tune your mind into the highest frequencies.

Furthermore, the choice to consciously evolve and stay connected to the Source will provide you with solutions to problems that can have an impact on not only your life, but on the lives of a multitude of others. Author Neale Donald Walsch is the perfect example of this, as his trilogy, *Conversations with God,* was written entirely from his positive connection with the Source. I have used this same connection to write this book, as has every other author whose intention is to better the lives of others. Beyond just the written word, this same conscious connection can provide you with the cure for diseases, the concept for new technologies to make the world better, the idea for a business that can provide a needed service, and anything else that you can dream of (and more than that!). By opening yourself up to the highest frequencies of life, you will be provided with everything that you need to make the world a better place in a way that is in alignment with who you are.

Again, **every** creation ("good" or "bad") is a Source-creation, but you can consciously choose to evolve in such a way that you connect with the highest attributes of the Source, and thus, create your life in ways that make a real difference to the world.

Make **this very moment** one that flows with the best frequencies. In that instant, you will have made a real difference in the world. Keep it up, and you will be a powerful force for positive change!

The Art of Connecting, part 2: connecting to the Source...

And creating your own "conscious evolution."

In the last Principle, you learned how to use the Art of Connecting to pre-construct your reality and connect to your desires. Using the same concept, I would like for you to experience your connection to the Source in a very real way, and also to use this skill set to consciously evolve in the ways of your choosing. To help you to visualize all of this, you may want to read the rest of this section into a tape recorder to listen to as a meditation.

First, sitting in a comfortable and quiet location, imagine that you are standing in the ocean. Allow yourself to sense how the waves feel as they lap around your body; imagine the smells and sounds of the seaside. Once you feel fully relaxed, imagine that your body slowly turns into water and flows out into the ocean, becoming one with the water all around you. Imagine that every other person on Earth has turned into water also, and each of you is represented as a wave. Repeat the word *"love"* to yourself, and watch as this thought ripples out over all the other waves, changing their frequency as well. Choose other words or thoughts, and see your instant impact on your own wave and all the waves around you.

Now, imagine that a "wave" far away from you has a thought of hate. Feel the instant impact of that individual's creation on you, affecting the height or strength of your own wave. Imagine that you send out loving thoughts to that waving consciousness, and visualize that wave affected positively with your creation.

See the waves around you begin to come together to reform into your body. In this physical state, you are still connected to the waving ocean of potential, but you are able to experience yourself as an individual. Imagine that everyone and everything else in the world pops into being from the ocean of consciousness as well— watch as people, animals, trees, and mountains form around you from the waves. Repeat the word *"peace"* to yourself, and watch that wave ripple out and affect the entire world with its frequency. Try the word *"compassion."* Now, try the word *"acceptance."* Watch as each of these words creates a rippling frequency that instantly affects the entire world.

Let's use the Art of Connecting to pre-construct solutions to the world's problems. Maintain your sense of flowing connectedness with the rest of the world, but now, imagine that you are able to create world peace, end world hunger, or create a sustainable world. What would this look like and feel like? How would you feel if you were able to create this kind of solution for the world? What would others be saying to you? What would life taste like, sound like, or smell like? Make the experience as real as possible—truly see and feel yourself creating this reality as if it were happening right now.

How would you feel about yourself if you were able to bring this reality into being? Each morning from now on, choose to focus on and connect with that feeling, and then stay connected to it as you go through each day. Create the day in alignment with the reality that you **are** a person that makes a real difference in the world. Imagine that your positive thoughts are having an instant impact on the entire Earth. See them flowing all around the globe and creating food for a hungry child, providing trees and food for endangered animals, or freeing a political prisoner from jail.

Stay connected to this reality today and everyday. Your positive thoughts are combining with the thoughts of the whole universe and bringing new solutions into being from the Source-hologram. Each time that you choose to stay connected with the most positive attributes of life, you **instantly** impact the whole world in a wonderful way.

Exercises:

1. To have a physical experience of the above visualization, get in an actual body of water—such as a bathtub or a pool. Try to move just one part of the water without affecting all the water. Can you do this? Watch as that small motion ripples out over the entire body of water. Imagine that you are sending out the thought of love each time that you move your finger or hand. Watch as this positive thought affects the oneness of the water.

2. Try this non-judgment exercise: This week, strike up a conversation with someone who you would not normally talk to—maybe the Harley rider, hippie, or gay couple standing next to you in line, or perhaps you

decide to choose the guy in the next cubicle who you avoid because he seems "strange." Try smiling and saying "hello," give them a compliment, or ask what they are drinking. It does not have to be a big drawn-out conversation on the wonders of the universe; just a simple greeting counts. Afterward, write down what you learned through this practice. Were you surprised by the experience? Would you be willing to make this experience a habit?

3. Choose a day this week to be "Non-judgment Day," where you will make an effort to not judge anything at all—not yourself, not others—**nothing.** For the entire day, commit to observing life from a place of understanding and connection with the Source. See everything in the day as an aspect of the Source that is showing itself to you. Become aware of whether the people that you normally associate with are judgmental as a habit. If you notice that someone is judging another person, say something nice about that person instead. I will warn you that this will likely frustrate the heck out of the person that you are with, but it doesn't matter. Just do it. See what happens. Notice how judgmental you tend to be about yourself. If you become aware that you have started to judge yourself, simply stop yourself and end the sentence with something positive or nice instead. At the end of the day, journal about your experience. How hard was this for you? How different did you feel? What did you learn? Would you be able to try this for two days? A week? A lifetime?

4. Pick up your favorite religious text. Open it anywhere, and reread it from the new perspective that you are part of the Source—a life-creator. How does this change the meaning? Is it different from what you have been trained to believe? Does the text make more sense from this perspective?

Retuning statement: "I am co-creating my life with the Source. I choose to create in ways that flow with love, respect, and harmony." For the next few days, please repeat this statement over and over. In addition, you can write it out several times a day, or even say it into a tape recorder and listen to it.

PRINCIPLE 5

No One is an Authority on Your Life but You

Your alarm goes off in the morning, and you slam it off with a curse. Following your morning ritual you turn on the TV, and the news starts blaring at you about a murder halfway around the globe or the latest terror threat. You get dressed, and as you do so, you hear a commercial talking about how you will turn everyone away in horror if your teeth aren't their "whitest and brightest" or your skin is not flawless and wrinkle-free. You look in the mirror and sigh, thinking that you just aren't cutting it.

You get to work and notice that there is a note on your desk telling you that your boss has decided to reject the brilliant idea you came up with on the grounds that she "just doesn't think that it fits the company vision." Then, your co-worker comes in and, upon noticing the color that you are wearing, says that it really isn't very flattering on you—you should try a brighter tone. Irritated to the core of your being, you decide that you need something to eat, so you go to the break room and grab a donut. As you start to gorge yourself on its chocolate-y goodness, another co-worker sees you and says, "Oh, I **never** eat donuts. Do you have any idea how many calories are in one of those?"

Sigh. You head back to your desk, only to receive a call from your mother. Upon telling her that you are having a bad day, she says, "Well, sometimes you need to put up with things that are difficult to get ahead. You won't get anywhere if you decide to quit your job now. Just stick it out." You get off the phone with her, manage to get a few hours of work done, and then go out to lunch with a friend. At lunch, you tell him about the day that you are having and how unfair your boss is, and he says, "What is wrong with you? If I were you I would quit this instant—what are you doing still working there anyway?"

Does it ever stop? Does everyone have to have an opinion on every aspect of your life?

Sadly, yes they do. However, you can train yourself to block out the opinions that you do not want, allowing in only opinions that match the frequency of the life that you really desire. To do this, **you must decide that the only opinion of you and your life that matters is yours**. Read that last sentence again, please. It is that important—because once you have mastered this level of detachment from others' thoughts about you, every single day will be filled with moments that fulfill **your** dreams, instead of trying to live up to other people's unrealistic standards.

It may seem impossible to do, but it can be done. In order to begin this process, you need to recognize a new truth:

UFOs are real

Well, **U**nidentified **F**oreign **O**pinions are at any rate, and they have been taking you up into their ship and reprogramming your mind all your life.

UFOs are any beliefs or truths that are not your own. They are unidentified, because they have not been processed by you. They are foreign, because they came from an outside source—some other person. And finally, they are opinions, because every single thing that anyone tells you about absolutely anything is NOT a truth—it is simply his or her **opinion**. *You* get to decide whether or not to believe it and therefore take it on as a truth, which becomes an expectation that you build your life around.

Please be warned: UFOs are coming at you from everywhere. **Everyone** has an opinion on positively everything, and they disguise these opinions as "facts," "absolute truths," or "just the way things are." From what you are supposed wear and how you are supposed to look, to what a person "like you" or "at your age" should or should not be doing, these opinions are inundating you constantly. Just turning on your TV exposes you to **millions** of them, as you are subjected to others' opinions on what you need to buy, the zillion ways that the world is getting worse, or why you cannot be healthy and happy without pills or plastic surgery. UFOs are sneaky because the people sending them out are experts in making it sound like you **must** believe what they are saying—often quoting statistics, religious passages, or experiential examples to prove that their opinion is true for all people everywhere. The implication of this deluge of "facts" is that you are wrong, a bad person, or simply stubborn and argumentative if you do not believe this particular fountain of knowledge.

Yep, they are a stealthy lot. Without even knowing it, these UFOs try to take over your mindpower—converting **their** beliefs to **your** beliefs and causing you to start to choose experiences that are in alignment with the vibration of their way of thinking. If all of these UFOs made it into your personal hologram your mind would be totally fried—you would be a mess of wavelengths that did not know which way to go, and who had no idea of who you really are. You would be a zombie, doing anyone's bidding any time (actually, you may feel a bit like a zombie right now!).

Thankfully, you have a way of protecting yourself from unwanted opinions—much like a shield on your personal spaceship. Better yet, by fine-tuning what your shield allows in and what it blocks, you can easily create the exact life that you desire.

Who is in your Captain's chair?

If you have ever watched any episodes of Star Trek (yes, I am a closet Trekkie), then you have inevitably noticed that the Captain's orders are always followed. In fact, it doesn't matter if the Captain is asking the seemingly impossible out of his (or her) ship and crew; somehow, they always manage to pull it off. So, when the Captain asks for more power, the engine room is able to produce it, even when the ship has been damaged by an attack and two of its engines are down.

No matter what, everyone must do what the Captain says, no questions asked. Of course, the Captain has earned this respect by years of training, analyzing and learning about many, many different circumstances, and having the kind of foresight expected of a leader. It is he or she who has to use this experience and knowledge to analyze threats, decide to bring someone aboard (or not), and make sure the decisions made are the best decisions for the ship and all aboard.

You can think of your body and mind as your own personal ship—one that you are very much in control of. Like any Captain on the Starship Enterprise, you use your conscious mind to instantly check each UFO as it approaches you, analyzing it for content, truth, and its security level. If it finds the opinion true (or just qualified to be let past your "shields"), it then sends it off to your subconscious mind. Your subconscious sees this conscious qualification as an order—and translates this into a frequency that becomes what flows into your life.

Like the crew on the Starship Enterprise, your subconscious mind cannot question any orders given to it—it just adds the new frequency to the you-hologram, and brings into being whatever your conscious mind has decided is truth for you. When you have taken on a new UFO as a personal truth (expectation), your subconscious accepts that frequency and then searches through the collective potential to find answers to problems, look for experiences that match the frequencies of what you believe and expect out of life, and pull up the best possible matches. It's a lot like when the Enterprise's Captain Pickard issued an order and then directed, "Make it so"; at the moment that your conscious mind accepts a thought as truth, you have issued a precise order that must bring into being the exact matching-frequency experiences.

When you think about it, it's really a great system so long as you are aware of your personal power and use your conscious mind properly, only issuing well-thought out orders and blocking negative UFOs from taking over your mind and turning your life into a confused mess. Sadly, the system fails more often than not because you were not taught the importance of the conscious mind, so you take on beliefs from everyone and everything around you like a drunk, spineless, drugged out Captain, recklessly beaming aboard anyone and anything that crosses the ship's path. This results in a life that is full of struggle, illness, and stress, because your expectations are being (unknowingly) set by others, but your spirit wants you to live a life that is truly authentic to you. When you take on UFOs that work against your spirit's inherent desire to live a perfect, balanced, and thriving life, you flow with a life filled with difficulty. However, when you work **with** this inherent desire, you have a life that is wonderful beyond your wildest dreams.

It is time to take back your rightful place as Captain-Extraordinaire-Final-Authority of your life, and realign yourself with the Source's best intention that you thrive and are fulfilled in every way. After all, your subconscious mind has the ability to allow all the systems of your body and your mind to work at their optimal levels, but it cannot stop your conscious mind from issuing an order that is not for your best, puts you in danger, or could kill you. Even if you are taking on beliefs and thoughts that are going to tune you into difficulty and sickness, your subconscious mind cannot stop you from messing with its inherent mission.

It is easy to understand how this works when you consider all the life-giving systems of your body. Right now, your subconscious is easily running all these systems without your conscious thought. Your lungs are breathing, your heart is pumping, and your stomach is processing food (and this is just the tip of the iceberg). As a matter of fact, your subconscious is running your body functions in such a complex way that even the most sophisticated computers could not match its efficiency. You have been hard-wired to **live**, and your subconscious makes sure that everything is going along well in order to make that happen.

However, you can use your conscious mind to mess with all of this if you choose. Right now, I would like you to hold your breath. Keep holding it. You will begin to notice a sensation that indicates, quite clearly, that your body **wants** to breathe. If you did this long enough, the need to breathe would become so uncomfortable that you would either gasp for breath, or you would pass out (but please don't go that far!). In fact, you can choose to change your regular breathing patterns any way that you want, from panting quickly like a dog, to extremely slow breathing, causing your heart rate to drop. You see, your subconscious **wants** you to breathe at a good and regular rate for you, but you can consciously mess with this intention and your subconscious must allow it, whether or not your request is for your best.

Clearly, what you consciously choose to do, think, or say sends an automatic, infallible, executive order to your subconscious mind to take this on as truth and to begin to seek matching-frequency experiences. This is good news, because, as the Captain of your own ship, you can choose to beam aboard only viewpoints that match your desires precisely.

Please understand, while this is a good system, it is not fail-safe. In your life-training, you have been taught to always beam aboard the UFOs from certain trusted sources—allowing these people and entities direct access to your mind. Unfortunately, if these UFOs are negative, they really mess with your systems—tuning you into a life that is in alignment with others' beliefs, causing you to becoming an unknowing victim of UFO brain-washing.

They look friendly, but...

There you are, sitting and reading e-mail, when you see that your best friend sent you a note. You open up the note and notice that there is an attachment. You click to open the attachment, and a pop-up from your computer asks, "Is this from a trusted source?" Sure, it's your best friend! You download this innocent-looking attachment only to have a file-melting, hard-drive destroying virus hitchhike into your computer.

Suddenly, you are staring a blank screen, watching all your precious files turned to mush by this predator. Worse, you realize that there is nothing that you can do about it.

As this example shows, any kind of virus protection is only as good as the operator. When you, as the operator, decide to always allow access to a "trusted" source, viruses can piggyback right in, taking over your system with malicious intent.

It is absolutely no different in life. As a child, **everyone** was an authority over you. Because of this, you took in and trusted any information that came from these sources, especially if it was from your parents, teacher, friends, doctors, or religious leaders. You watched and listened as the adults in your life told you what to believe, what you needed to do, what life was like, and whose authority was absolute. You had no analytical power of your own—no shield to speak of—you just soaked in everything around you. You had no power to question, and, more than likely, you saw your own parents unwilling to question certain authorities in their life, even when they had serious reservations about what these authorities indicated was truth.

As you got older, you may have begun to ponder some of the things that these authorities had taught you to believe and likely were told to "take it on faith," "that's just the way it is," or "well, there are just some things that you don't question" ("Wizards" particularly like to use these kind of statements). At that very moment, your personal authority was compromised—and your shields were set to always trust UFOs from certain sources, allowing you to unconsciously take in beliefs that may or may not be for your best. Because of this, even as an adult, you likely trust everything that comes from your parents, no questions asked. When you watch the news, you assume that they are telling the truth and you believe their viewpoint on the world, no questions asked. You go to a religious function and you assume that the leader has done the homework to speak words of truth, so you believe whatever he says, no questions asked. You go to your doctor and you refuse to question her, even though she suggests a course of action that does not make sense to you. Of course, your own "trusted source" list is likely much longer than this—from friends and relatives to your boss and co-workers. Throughout your life, you have learned who you must listen to and trust, and what ability you have to question these sources or to protect yourself from personal attacks.

Again and again, you were taught not to trust yourself or your own feelings and instincts—but rather, to always believe outside authority figures. After all, they were wiser, had a better degree, had more life experience, were holier, or just simply should always be listened to, and so, you learned to always listen to them like a good little girl or boy.

And this, my friend, is where the system has failed you. You have been trained to give away your authority to other people, causing your guard to be down. By treating certain sources as "trusted," you unconsciously take in everything that they say, along with anything that you are feeling, smelling, touching, tasting, or hearing at the time, and these waves combine to create a new hologram of expectation in your brain. I'd call it a hostile takeover of your mind, only it's not hostile—you are **allowing** it to occur because you believe (consciously or subconsciously) that you have no choice. Because these people are "trusted sources," you download their UFOs automatically, and consequently, manage to get quite a few mental viruses this way.

It is because of this that you have been unknowingly creating a life based on other people's truths instead of your own. For example, if you have been taught that you must always believe everything that your father says about life, you will still hold all the old beliefs that you learned from him as you grew up. This will cause you to now have a life that seems to mirror his, with very similar experiences and illnesses. Or, if you always believe everything your doctor says (even when you are uneasy about it), then you will unconsciously manifest exactly what he or she has told you would happen (which is **particularly** not good if you are told that you have a terminal illness).

Let me just state—the big problem with this is that you take on these beliefs unconsciously. Without your knowledge, you have been programmed to tune into their truths and resonate with **their** view on you and your life, which causes you to flow with experiences in your life that match these authorities' viewpoints, not yours. It is much like the TV example from Principle 3, as these UFOs are acting as an unknown parental control on your ability to tune into certain experiences, and that is limiting your life. Of course, you would be spitting mad if someone did this to your television, and you should be just as indignant that these "authority figures" have been doing this to your **life**.

No matter what any "authority" has ever told you, **you** are the final authority on your life. You are the Source-made-form, and therefore, full of potential—you can do anything that you dream of, any way that you choose. Never let anyone tell you any different.

To take back the reigns of your life and get totally in the flow with your true desires, take a look at all of the people and sources that you consider authorities. Ask yourself whether their beliefs and viewpoints are of the same frequency as what you desire to have in your life. Then, take a good, hard look at why you feel that you must always believe what they say—and whether you want to give them that kind of power.

At every moment, you must use your personal logic and reason to decide whether you are letting a UFO on board or not. Become the observer. Most people that have authority over you have motivations for telling you one thing or another. When you hear one of their opinions (and all statements should be looked at as **opinions**), see if you can notice why they might want you to believe as they do. Is it from a place of wanting to keep you close? Do they want to get your money and support? Is it because they are tapping into their own unconscious fears and worries? Are you threatening their sense of self in some way? Could it be that they need to convince you that their truth is right in order to help them feel that **they** are right?

There are endless possibilities as to a person's motivations, and as you begin to be aware of this, you will be amazed at how much of a slant that most statements of "truth" have, and how much fear motivates people to refuse to see a different perspective. For instance, when I was 28 years old, I was having very irregular, very painful menstrual cycles. Since I was not usually a person to be unhealthy in any way, this was very distressing to me. For nine months, I kept a journal of each symptom, as well as what was going on at the time, and what I thought might have contributed to this. As I was in a very stressful business with many demands put upon me, I felt that surely there was a connection. I also researched a great deal and found that there were natural hormones, that, taken properly, would be of benefit to me, and help me to balance back out. I went to the doctor armed with this knowledge, and to my amazement, she was totally unwilling to talk about the natural alternatives that would surely cure my situation. Further, she looked at my journal and simply said, "Boy, you did write a lot," and cast the journal and all my information aside. She then told me that she would just put me back on the pill to "make me regular again." When I mentioned that this would not give my body a chance to balance itself out, and would likely result in my needing fertility treatments in order to become pregnant, she simply said, "Probably." This woman was, at the time, the **president** of our local medical association.

Needless to say, I did not do what she told me. I challenged her authority, and used my own tools to cure myself. When I developed The Flow system, I realized that what had been going on was a belief that I could not create what I really wanted to in my life at that time, coupled with low self-esteem. These two low-frequency beliefs eventually manifested in the problems that I was experiencing. I am now completely cured and healthy with no need for any kind of drugs. And, while my experience with this doctor was certainly less than positive, it also spurred me on to take back control of my own life. Standing back now, I realize that this doctor was reacting out of a need to be right and a fear of learning anything new. She had an over-busy practice, and to have someone challenge her view of how things should work surely caused her stress. She was used to being the authority and did not want to share that with anyone—therefore, she had to convince me that **I** was wrong in order for her to be able to keep her personal feelings of power and identity.

I tell this story so you can see that you can always question "authority," and you should. Every one of us is simply human, and we all come from places of preconceived notions and personal fears. Recognize this. Take back over consciously checking and rechecking the information coming from any source. Choose to take back "always trusted" status from anyone that currently has that honor. You can still decide to believe what people tell you, but run a scan on the information first—make sure that this is an opinion that you want creating part of your life. If the UFO does not match the frequency of that which you desire, or if it limits you and your creative potential in any way, do not beam it aboard!

Remember, you are the Captain of your ship. You are the co-creator of your life. You are responsible for who and what you take on board, and for the effect that these opinions have on both your life and the lives of others.

No truth is always true for everyone all the time

The thing is, **nothing** is true for all people, so no truth can ever be the absolute truth.

This may seem shocking (it is, actually). You have been told a very different story all of your life, but it has all been false. Everything is simply an opinion. You are responsible for deciding what you want to believe, and whatever you decide to be true **IS** true for you. You can hold a truth that is completely different from everyone else's truth, and you would still be right—and actually, so would they.

I know that this is hard to understand, but it is reality. Since you are creating your reality out of your expectations, then the only thing that **is** true is what you **believe** to be true. Everyone else's perspectives are true for them, but no matter how much they tell you that you must believe them, you don't have to. You get to decide what to believe and what is rubbish.

Actually, you don't have to just take my word for it; you can also listen to Albert Einstein. The basic idea of his theory of relativity is that everything in life is completely relative to your point of view, so you can only say that the way that you see things is true for you, but it may not be true for anyone else. Moreover, totally opposing truths can both be true at the same time.

This sounds unlikely, but it is a fact (at least according to myself and Einstein!). There is absolutely nothing that is true for all people all the time. Nothing. Take the concept of time, for instance. It would seem that this is a constant for all people; something that is always true all the time. However, one hour can seem like a minute or it can seem like a day, depending on what you are doing. After all, if you are stuck in a company meeting about financials, your perception of the hour will be a good deal longer than if you are at a sporting event where your team is winning. The passage of time, rather than being constant, is actually a matter of perspective.

It is the same for motion. Let's say that you are sitting in a car and drive past a person standing at a bus stop. That person would watch you go by and would think that you were moving past them. However, from your perspective, you are sitting still, and they are actually moving past you. In fact, if you threw a ball in the air in your car, it would come right back down in your hand, just as it would if you were sitting in your chair at home. Because of this, you could easily say that the world is moving past you, and you are sitting still. Neither viewpoint would be wrong, as whether or not you are moving is actually a matter of perspective as well. It is all relative.

When someone tells you that you "have to believe" what they are saying, or they are "absolutely right," "know better than you do," or are "the final authority" on something, you now know that none of that is true. What they are telling you is simply a UFO, and you can use your mental power to decide whether you want to believe them or not. You are the final authority on your life, and no one knows better than you do what your truth is and what kind of life you want to create for yourself.

Stop obsessing over other people's opinions

What? You obsess? Can't be.

Trust me, you do it. Your friend tells you that you look like you have gained some weight. Your mom or dad says something in "that tone" that really means that they highly disapprove of whatever it is that you are doing or saying. Your spouse or mate tells you that they don't think you will ever make the business that you dream of a success. While you try your best to act like you are totally unaffected by these comments, internally you are a **mess**. You play and replay these words over and over again in your mind. You wonder if they are right—that you are a bad person, don't have what it takes, will be letting them down, or will be going against your religious upbringing if you choose to do or believe in a way that is different from theirs, no matter how much you know in your heart that you disagree with their thinking.

Believe me, I know this is hard—but being authentic to yourself and your own sense of right and wrong is paramount to becoming all that you truly want to be. **True authenticity is freedom**—at the highest imaginable level. For instance, you may have started to change what you think about life just from reading this book. There are likely parts of you that feel conflicted about this information and this new viewpoint on the Source and your part in co-creating your life. You may be worried about bringing this information into your life, simply because it is so different than the way that everyone that you know thinks and behaves. What will they think of you? How will you ever be accepted?

It is totally normal to feel this way. As I put the pieces together for this book, I became both elated and shaken. On one hand, this was a momentous discovery—it shows the amazing power that each of us have in creating that which we experience. On the other hand, I worried about what people would think of me, and how much reproach or criticism I would receive from the scientific community or religious groups. I feared that because I was not a trained scientist, my viewpoint would be rejected on that basis alone. I worried that I would offend people or turn away those that I love.

However, at the end of the day, I realized that this was too important to worry or fear how it would be taken. The potential to truly help people—to even save lives—was more important than anything anyone might say to me. And finally, I realized that I was being totally, completely authentic to myself in bringing this discovery to light. What other people thought of it was not my concern.

I knew that some of these authority figures would rebel against this approach—it is radical and perspective-changing. However, I also knew that the simple act of only caring that I was doing what felt right to me and that matched the frequencies of love and faith would bring people into my life that would love and support this book.

I can tell you, it has—a hundred times over. You know, Eleanor Roosevelt once said, "**You must feel the fear and do it anyway**," and this assertion could not be more accurate. By challenging the structures that are tuning you into a limited life with compassion and self-confidence, you will turn fear into the frequency of faith. You will turn hate into the frequency of love. And perhaps most importantly, you will take back the reigns of your life in a powerful and amazing way—allowing the best, most life-affirming experiences to come to you.

By releasing others' opinions of you and your life, you will create a life of wonder and success. Do not let others' fears or preconceptions or authoritative "truths" keep you from creating each moment with the passion that is uniquely you. Release them, bless them, and let them go back into the Source-hologram, where they belong.

And remember, as Wayne Dyer says, "Other people's opinions of me are none of my business." Frankly, that could not be said better. Let 'em think what they want to. Go forward with all things good, and you will bring all things good into your life.

Your subconscious mind does not take a joke

You may consciously have a very silly sense of humor (I know that I do), and enjoy joking around and watching ridiculous shows. Of course, that's highly recommended behavior—humor is a great tool for stress relief and basic enjoyment of life.

However, there is another kind of joking that is not recommended—the kind where you make self-deprecating comments about yourself in an effort to be funny. Maybe you joke about how fat you are, how you are "no spring chicken," or how you are just a "dumb blonde." You may do this to deflect how you are really feeling about yourself (after all, if you make fun of yourself, no one can beat you to it), or you may do it just out of habit—something that you learned from parents or friends.

Well, stop it. Your subconscious mind does not think it is funny. It does not have the ability to distinguish between your jokingly saying, "That's a hell of a spare tire I have there," and muttering to yourself in desperation, "Oh god, I am so fat." All your mind understands is **frequency**. It understands the words that you are saying and thinking and adds the frequency of those words to the overall flow of your mind. So, when you joke about how you have a spare tire, your mind recognizes that as a **request** to have a spare tire. If you want a little extra fat around the middle, that's fine—but if you don't, you are unknowingly telling your mind that you do.

The next time that you are about to joke about what a loser you are, or how you never seem to have enough money, or how you are too old to try this or that, remember—you are actually asking that this be true for you. Stop yourself, and change that thought to a positive one, right that instant! Believe me, you will thank yourself in the long run for cultivating this little practice—it will keep you from having a lot of troublesome experiences and make you feel better about yourself to boot.

Stop the madness

One of my friends had a pet iguana that was rather remarkable. When it felt threatened, it would not fight; rather, it would just shut its eyes and wait for the threat to be gone. It seemed to be operating on the principle that if it couldn't see the threat, there **was** no threat. I honestly believe that Ghandi, were he still with us, would have been extremely impressed with this iguana's level of passive resistance.

You and I can channel the iguana as well. Now, I am not suggesting that you just shut your eyes when you feel threatened by someone, but you can certainly decide not to fight and just let them have their opinions. What happens all too often is that you get into a discussion with a person who feels very differently than you, and suddenly the situation escalates. You end up arguing with each other, and you both leave the situation angry and frustrated.

Why choose this frequency? The next time that you are confronted with someone that thinks very differently than you, just remember that they can hold their opinion and it can be true for them, and your opinion can be true for you. There is no need to fight or to try to convince anyone that your opinion is right—you are both, in your own ways and from each of your perspectives, perfectly correct.

I'd like to give you an example of how this works, so that you have a clear image:

Let's say that you are taking a painting class with your best friend and her five year old daughter. You are all told to paint a still-life of a bowl of fruit. You pick bright, abstract colors, and paint in the cubist style of Picasso. Your friend picks muted watercolors, and paints in a realistic, picturesque way. The little girl picks up some finger paints, and makes big, colorful circles and squares.

Upon looking at the three pictures, could you describe any of them as wrong? No, they would all depict the bowl of fruit, just from different perspectives.

Moreover, if you were trying to describe a bowl of fruit to a person who had never seen one, you would give the person a more complete picture of what a bowl of fruit is by showing him or her all three pictures. Each one would give the person a new perspective on a bowl of fruit, and each would complement the other, creating a more rounded view.

Is it possible that people with opinions very different than yours are simply seeing things as differently as three artists might see a bowl of fruit? And moreover, could these opposing "truths" actually complement each other, giving a more full and rounded view of life?

Yes and yes. Since you can never see life through another's exact perspective, you can never truly see another's truth. You can be sure of that which you hold as true, and the other person can be just as sure that they are right, and you both can be right from your own perspective, in your own way of looking at things.

If you maintain an open nature and recognize that opinions opposing your own are learning experiences that help you to define who you are, you can gain a more complete perspective of life. This does not mean that you need to take on someone else's beliefs or even agree with someone who sees life very differently than you. Rather, it simply means that you can approach all people and all discussions from a place of respect both for the other person **and** for yourself.

Better yet, this means that you never need to convince anyone that your opinions or beliefs are right. You can see things from a completely different perspective from everyone around you, and you can know that **you are right for you.**

The next time that you are faced with a person who thinks very differently than you, just remember—their truth is true for them; your truth is true for you. You never need to feel threatened by another person's beliefs. They can create their life based on their truth and it has no affect on you, because you choose your life experiences based on yours.

Just shut your eyes, little iguana, and let them be.

You can get to where you want to go any way that you want to

Have you ever been going along, personal life plan in place, goals in mind, when someone tells you, "That's not the way to do it! You should do it this way!"?

I should think that you have, as I am certain that it is not possible to be human and to escape this experience. In my case, I cannot tell you how many times this has happened in my life, but somehow, here I am, book written, living the life that I wanted to live, exactly the way that I wanted to do it.

As you set forth your goals and go about following your action plan to get them, you will have tons of UFOs about how to do everything. Each person that you encounter will be the expert, telling you "from experience" that you **must** do it this way, or that they have "tried everything" and this was the "only thing that worked" for them, or simply that "you can't possibly do what you have set out to do. It just can't be done."

The next time that you are given this type of UFO, remember that this kind of thinking would have left us in the stone ages hunting and gathering for our food and wearing fur (or less). Please believe me: there are **countless** ways to do **anything**. Things that have never been done before are just begging to be brought into being from the Source. I mean, can you imagine how many people told the Wright brothers that flying was impossible? Now, it is an everyday occurrence, moving millions of people around the world at every moment. I imagine that Bill Gates had people who thought that he was crazy when he started Microsoft. Now he is one of the most powerful and successful men on Earth. I cannot fathom how many people Oprah Winfrey must have encountered that told her that she would never be able to be what she is today. Ghandi, Mother Theresa, Nelson Mandela, Gloria Steinam, and Martin Luther King changed the world because they believed that it could be done. They knew that they could do something that had never been done before, they ignored the naysayers, and **they did it**.

The next time that someone tells you that you can't do

whatever it is that you are aiming to do, tell them that they are full of rubbish (in the kindest possible way, please). Go home, turn on the Biography Channel, and watch a few biographies on some famous people. If that is not possible, pick up some autobiographies from the local bookstore. Suddenly, you will see that bringing the seemingly impossible into being in a way that is authentic to you is the **only** sure path to take. For every person who is a successful actor, there are as many different paths that led them to that goal. For every successful entrepreneur, there are as many different ways to find success. For every person who has become President of the United States—not one of them took an identical path to the White House. The ways to get to your dreams and goals are as varied as the number of people on the planet. Your life is not identical to anyone else's; no one else has lived life in the same way, made the same decisions, or taken exactly the same steps as you have. There is no one else in the world exactly like you—and there is never one true path that you must follow to lead you to the life of your dreams.

Believe in yourself and your connection to the Source. Make choices that radiate the power inherent within you. Take all actions based on the frequencies matching what you desire to bring into being. Finally, believe that what you dream of is already in reality, because it is. Stay steadfast in your personal belief and let this flow into being in your life, however it chooses to do so.

You are responsible for seeking the truth

No matter how you look at it, the truth of the matter that is you have been given a lot of power by the Source to co-create life, and you cannot take this responsibility lightly.

Since you are creating your world (and changing the entire universe) with the frequency of your beliefs, you must be certain that every belief that you hold is one that you **want** to hold. You can never take anyone else's opinions on anything at face value; rather, you must choose to research everything. Question every perspective that you encounter. Read contrasting viewpoints on the issues of the day, and question statistics and experimental results. After all, if the scientists in the particle experiments were getting the results that they expected to get—don't you think that the people taking polls and doing experiments on new drugs are affecting the outcomes with their expectations? These kinds of statistics and experimental results must also be seen as opinions, not truths. You can find a well-documented counter-argument for every single viewpoint imaginable—so it is up to you to decide the viewpoint that you want to believe.

Question the common opinion on matters of the day. These opinions are formed by the collective consciousness of all of us, and are affected by the media, the fashion industry, and propaganda. If you need more proof that the media has an effect on the collective reality, you need to look no further than the fads and trends of yesteryear. How many times have you seen a picture of your mom or dad dressed in the fashions of the time and thought, "How in the world did they think that looked good?" Yes, it may seem silly to you now, but from the collective perspective at that time, this fashion trend was pounded into their impressionable heads, and they really thought that it looked absolutely great on them. It is the same with the standards of beauty, from the pleasantly plump beauties of Ancient Rome to the stick thin models of today. I am sure, given the conditioning that you have received on the standards of beauty, you have wondered how these ancient women were seen as the great beauties of their time. However, an Ancient Roman man, were he able to time-travel to this day and age, would find it hard to see our current supermodels as beautiful, due to his preprogrammed conditioning.

It is the Principle of Repetition rearing its head again. When you first see a new fashion trend, you likely think that it looks a little silly. Then, you see it in magazines, commercials, websites, and other media sources. You see some people walking around in these new fashions. After repeated exposure to the concept that this trend is attractive you are convinced of it, and end up buying a piece of clothing that you laughed at just a few short weeks before.

It is because of the power of the collective thought and trends of the day that you must be very vigilant on what you choose to believe. You can decide to buck trends, and choose whatever standards you want for your life, no matter how different they are from common thought. You must never be a follower, going along with other people out of a fear that you will not fit in or due to a lack of self-esteem. Whatever you believe, you create—take it upon yourself to make sure that everything that you believe is perfectly matched to the frequencies of love, faith, and abundance, whether or not that is in fashion with the people that you know or even society at large.

Better yet, even though your beliefs might seem strange right now, as more and more people choose these positive beliefs, you are tuning the collective-hologram to a higher level. Suddenly, the beliefs that others laughed at just weeks before are taken on as "normal" or "right." Every visionary who set out to change the world was ridiculed at first, but after more and more people saw the world through his or her eyes, the world was transformed.

Whether you are trying to change the world or simply trying to live an authentic life, it is important that you evaluate each new belief with these questions: Will believing this limit my experience in any way? Will I be unable to achieve my dreams because I believe this? Is this belief judgmental of myself or others? Does this belief foster a feeling of cooperation and love of all people, or does it create boundaries and encourage hate?

Whatever the frequency of the truths that you take on, you will bring the same into your life. If you want a limitless, abundant, loving life, make sure that all that you believe is limitless, abundant, compassionate, and loving. Anything else is a waste of time and energy, and will tune you into experiences that you will truly not enjoy.

On this point, I will just leave you with this quote:

"Believe nothing, no matter where you have read it or who has said it, not even if I have said it, unless it agrees with your own reason and your own common sense."—Buddha.

Questions:

1. Who have you been taught to believe are authorities in your life? Do you believe everything that they tell you? Have you ever followed their advice or teaching and found them to be wrong? Do these people tend to put you down? Do they tend to disagree with you, either actively or passively (through tone or under-handed behavior)? The next time that you are with one of these "authorities," notice what they are really saying to you when they give you their opinion on some aspect of your life. Write these opinions and your observations about them down, and consciously decide whether you choose to believe this perspective or not.

2. How do you usually handle conflict? Can you tell where you developed this habitual behavior? Think back to how you handled conflict and difficulty as a child. How did you get your way? How did others in your life get their way (parents or friends that were arguing, for instance)? Can you see a connection between how you deal with conflict now and your past history and influences?

3. Imagine yourself in a situation with a person that normally causes you distress—perhaps one that disagrees with you on you or your life, berates you, or refuses to listen to your point of view. I would like you to fully imagine a recent time when you were in a conflict or argument with them. Please note the smells, sounds, words used, and what you were wearing—anything and everything that was part of the situation. How are you feeling in your body right now? Does your mood seem to have improved or declined? Please note any observations in your journal. Now, take a deep breath. See yourself in the situation again, but imagine that you have totally detached from this person and their opinions. Imagine that you are perfectly okay with

their feelings and perspective, but refuse to let yourself feel a connection to their contrary position. Try to see this person and their words and actions as just another creation of the Source. What words might you use if you truly approved of their perspective, but felt no need to take it on as your personal truth? How does your body feel right now?

Retuning statement: "I fully accept my personal authority over my mind, my body and my life. I choose to be responsible for all my thoughts, actions, and deeds, and I choose to block out all perspectives that are not for my best life. My truth is perfect for me, and I trust myself to believe what is right and good." For the next few days, please repeat this statement throughout the day. In addition, you can write it out several times a day, or even say it into a tape recorder and listen to it.

PRINCIPLE 6

Living the Life of Your Dreams is Your Choice Every Moment

Have you ever wondered why some areas of your life are easy, while others are wrought with difficulty? Or why one person gets a certain kind of disease, while another is healthy?

I think we all have. It is especially frustrating when you see yourself having the same kinds of problems and patterns show up time and time again, **despite** your best efforts to break the pattern or cure yourself of chronic pain or disease. For instance, perhaps you are very successful in business, but continuously find yourself in "failed" relationships, no matter how many times you try to make things work. Or, maybe you have tons of creative and potentially lucrative business ideas, but you cannot find funding for your business, despite the fact that you have an amazing business plan. Maybe you are the one that manages to manifest the genetic disease, while everyone else in your family is in perfect health.

You may have also noticed that there seems to be a link between the issues going on in your life and the kinds of health issues you manifest. For instance, you end up suffering a heart attack the day after you have a severe argument with your son. Or, you develop ovarian cysts a few weeks after you lose your job.

It just doesn't seem like a coincidence, does it?

It's not. In fact, all of these patterns and problems are a result of the fact that you hold negative beliefs in one area of life, and positive beliefs in another.

And that is where The Flow Stations come in.

The Flow Stations

What are the Flow Stations?

They represent a completely new understanding of the connection between your mind, your body, and the experiences of your life.

Remember the TV analogy that I used in Principle 3 to explain how you choose some experiences and not others?

To refresh your memory, quantum potential (or the Source) can be thought of as the waves of information flowing to your TV, or brain—which acts as the tool that decodes the wave information in a way that you can comprehend and experience. Of course, your mind is the remote control—tuning you into and out of experiences as your thoughts, expectations, and beliefs change. Each experience of life can be thought of as a different TV show, each having its own individual frequency, or "wave-archetype," that represents just that experience and no other. In the same way, every part of your body is its own TV show, with its own "wave-archetype."

Just as the TV does, all the wave information of every experience in life is sorted out into separate frequency ranges, or as I call them, Stations. Each Station is responsible for creating your experience of a specific area of your life and corresponding parts of your body—showing you the critical link between your thoughts and feelings, your experiences, and your body. If you have negative beliefs and expectations in a certain Station, you will not only have negative experiences in that area of life, you will also have pain, illness, and disease in the corresponding areas of the body. If you have positive beliefs and expectations in a Station, you will have ease, prosperity, and health in that area.

Just as white light is actually made up of seven different frequency ranges of visible light (or visible colors), the Stations show the seven different frequency ranges of **life** that you are tuning into at every moment to compose your experience of life. Much like a rainbow, they range from low to high frequencies—from the lower frequency survival and group issues found in Station 1, to the higher frequency spiritual issues found in Station 7. But be careful—while you might be tempted to judge lower frequencies to be of less value than higher, that is not the case—to live a truly flowing life, you need to set your presets to seek the best frequencies in **every** Station.

THE FLOW STATIONS

	Parts of the body	Area of life
Station 1: The Commanding Influence of Groups	Immune system Legs Feet and toes Knees Ankles Rectum Bones Base of spine Tailbone	Group and physical survival issues
Station 2: The Energy of Individual Dynamics and Creative Power	Lower vertebrae Pelvis Sexual organs Bladder Large intestine Hips Buttocks	Individual relationships and physical creation

Station 3: The Force of Positive Self-Image	Liver Pancreas Stomach Upper intestines Kidneys Adrenals Spleen Lumbar spine Gallbladder The core of the body Addictive disease	Self esteem and the ability to be authentic

Station 4:
The Emotional
Connection to Life
	Heart
	Circulatory
	  system
	Ribcage
	Lungs
	Respiratory
	  system
	Breasts
	Shoulders
	Collarbones
	Arms
	Wrists
	Hands and
	  Fingers
	Thymus Gland
	Thoracic Spine
		Forgiveness and the
		ability to feel and
		positively express all
		the emotions of life

Station 5: The Strength of Positive Communication	Vertebrae of the neck Throat Trachea Thyroid Mouth	Ability to say and do what you say that you will

	(Station 5, ctd.) Jaw Teeth and gums Esophagus Vocal cords Skin of the throat and jaw Neck muscles	

Station 6:
The Power of
Mental Creativity
and Intuition
	Eyes
	Ears
	Nose
	Brain
	Sinuses
	Head
	Pituitary gland
	Skin of the nose,
	  cheeks,
	  forehead, and
	  ears
		Ability to make
		positive decisions and
		to create what you
		desire

Station 7: The Energy of a Higher Purpose	Muscular system Nervous system Skin of the entire body Scalp Hair Top of the head	Your personal connection to the Source and to the oneness of life

With The Flow Stations and The Flow system, you now have everything that you need to understand not only why you are tuning into negative experiences, but how to fix these issues in a way that is right for you as an individual. Looking at life with this awareness is empowering, enlightening, and liberating—because you **know** that you can change the outcome of any experience by simply identifying the underlying problem preset. For instance, if you find that you keep tuning into the experience of having an abusive boss, you will understand that this is a Station 2 (individual relationships) issue, and you'll be able to design a specific plan to change the problem frequency. Or, if you develop pain in your shoulders, you will be able to identify that as a Station 4 (emotional) issue, and you will understand that this pain is manifesting because you are feeling burdened by life and are blocking yourself from feeling joy. No matter what, every issue in your life is its own frequency—and when you identify the problem Station and negative preset, you can easily change the preset and **radically** change your life!

Understanding your mental connection to any disease or pain that you develop can actually **prevent** illness as well as cure it. In fact, when you train yourself to become aware of the first signs of tuning into negative experiences, you can actually fix the problem frequency before it manifests as an illness. Always remember— starting to have negative experiences in a certain Station is the **warning** that something is amiss. If you do not catch the problem frequency at that level, you will eventually tune that Station into disease due to the Principle of Repetition—every negative experience will add to the frequency of that Station and lower it by steps until disease develops. Not surprisingly, the disease that manifests will exactly match the negative experiences and issues that you have going on in your life.

For instance, let's say that you are tuning into some negative group experiences, which you realize is a Station 1 issue. One of the major issues that you are tuning into is that you cannot say "no" when your co-workers ask you to take some of their work to "help out the team." The truth is that you already do more than everyone else, but because you are preset with a negative belief about your ability and right to say "no," then whenever one of the team asks you to do more, a habitual reaction is triggered and you say "yes." Each time that you do this, you feel worse and worse, and, due to the Principle of Repetition, you tune your Station 1 into an even more negative frequency. If you catch it at this level, you can do exercises (such as the "4 for 40," which you'll be learning about soon!) and reset your preset to change the pattern. If you do **not** catch it at the "negative experience" level, you will develop pain or illness in a corresponding area of the body. In this case, you might notice that you are getting a rash all over your legs, and you know that legs are a Station 1 body part. By viewing the rash in terms of the underlying issue, you see that you are irritated by your co-workers and your own inability to say "no" in a group setting. Your preset frequency here is flowing with this irritation, and your mind begins to choose the wave-archetype of "irritated rash on the legs."

Instead of the development of disease being a mystery, you now have the power to understand **why** disease happens—and what you can do to heal yourself and others. Always view the disease as just a symptom of the real underlying problem—the negative beliefs and expectations preset in a certain Station. Because of these presets, your mind is simply pulling up exactly what you are telling it to—in mind, body, and spirit. If your presets match an unhealthy, blocked frequency, you get matching negativity and disease. If your presets match a healthy, flowing frequency, you get matching positive experiences and excellent health.

Of course, the new understanding of life and disease that The Flow Stations represent has a profound impact on your understanding of supposedly "genetic" diseases. The truth is that genetic diseases are not a predetermined reality. In fact, recent studies have definitively shown that the gene for a genetic disease or trait can actually be turned on or off depending on the affection and care of the mother. I am certain that future studies will show that it is not just the mother, but the entire environment around the child and even the personality and beliefs of the child himself that has this impact. From "The Flow" understanding, this finding makes perfect sense; if you are creating your life and body with the frequency of your beliefs, all diseases can be turned on or off based on fine-tuning that frequency. As I have said so many times before, nothing—not even your very genetic code—is unchangeable. You are in charge of your life and your body, and by bringing your awareness to the beliefs and expectations that you have in all seven Stations, you can and will flow with a great life and perfect health!

The Flow Stations also explain why you may have tried meditation, affirmations, or other techniques to fix your life or heal yourself and not seen results—or why diet, time-management, self-help, behavioral change, or success programs may not have worked for you, even when other people were successful with the exact same program. The truth is that it doesn't matter how hard you try or how perfectly you do a program, you cannot and will not change **anything** without changing the underlying problem beliefs that are tuning your "you-hologram" into the undesired pattern. Once you change your problem beliefs, you **will** succeed in breaking the habit (or resetting the preset, as it were).

Armed with this knowledge, you can change your life for good.

Custom-designing your life: putting The Flow system to work for you!

Are you ready to custom-design the life of your dreams and watch it flow to you with ease?

Good. Let's get to it.

In the next section, you will take a test to identify which Flow Stations are preset to create difficulty and disease in your life. You will then be directed to a workbook section that is designed to help you identify exactly which problem beliefs are causing you such difficulty—and how you can reset your preset with ease. To do this, each workbook section is filled with "retuning statements" that are designed to precisely change the frequency of that Station to tune into the exact experiences that you are seeking.

Once you choose the retuning statements that are specific to your issues, you will be directed to a second test. This is the "Reality Type Test," and it identifies your personal strengths, allowing you to design a perfect action plan to reset your presets in the way that works for you as an individual. Finally, you will use the "4 for 40" system—you will choose 4 exercises that work with your personal strengths to do for 40 days. By using this revolutionary program, you will be a completely transformed person in 40 days!

Now, how exciting is **that**?

It should **very** exciting to you—after all, you are only 40 days away from being in the flow with the life that you truly want to live! It doesn't get much better than that!

Whatever life you choose to create, make sure that it is in alignment with how **you** define success, peace, love, health, and prosperity—not how your family, friends, or even society views what is necessary to live a successful, fulfilling life. Success to you might be simply to have enough money to be a stay-at-home mom. For another person, it would be to finally make the decision to join the Peace Corps. For yet another, it might be to become the CEO of a major company or the top salesperson at their corporation. No matter what anyone might tell you, the truth of the matter is that a truly successful person is one who is creating a **personally** fulfilling life, feels unconditional love for the self and for others, and who radiates a true sense of inner and outer joy. A flowing life is not about how much wealth and riches you get (although, should you want that, it is an option for you) but rather, the **quality of the life that you lead**.

So, be proud of your desires, and confident in your ability to achieve them!

Better yet, you can choose to live the life that you envision right this moment. If you were living the life of your dreams right now, what would you be feeling? How would you feel about yourself? Would you feel joyous? Proud? Excited? Hopeful?

Every moment is a new act of creation, so by connecting with these "life of your dreams" feelings in this moment, you have just **become** the life of your dreams in reality. You have created a moment that is in perfect alignment with your desires. By choosing to stay connected to these feelings every moment of every day, then every moment **is** the life of your dreams.

Choose to unite the "life of your dreams" vision and feelings with who you are right now. From this moment forward, hold this vision of yourself at all times. Let these positive feelings flow into and determine your thoughts, words, and actions. Make every decision in alignment with this reality, and the reality around you instantly becomes all that you desire, and more. Each person that you meet and every interaction that you have starts to flow with the energy of your best life. Every moment of your day becomes exciting and satisfying—it all takes on a new glow of beauty and wonder. Each moment that you create while flowing with these positive feelings will be in perfect alignment with the life of your dreams, because it can be no other way.

Finally, **always trust the process**. You truly can move mountains by simply believing in your co-creative power. Do not wonder **how** you will achieve your goals or **how** you will become healthy—let the Source and your co-creative power do that. Just have simple faith that it is real for you now, connect with the best thoughts and feelings, do your "4 for 40," and let the reality that you desire flow to you.

You see, the choice to live the life of your dreams really **is** your choice, every moment. Live that reality now.

PART 2
The Flow Factor Test

FINDING YOUR
FLOW FACTOR

Y ou may know your I.Q. and maybe even your E.Q. If you
have ever done any career counseling, you might even
know your Meyers-Briggs personality type.

But do you know your Flow Factor? It turns out that it just
might be the most important number that you will ever know.

By finding out your Flow Factor, you can pinpoint the exact
problem beliefs that are tuning you into difficulty, disease, and
dissatisfaction in a particular Station. By doing the corresponding
workbook exercises and using the "4 for 40" system, you will be
able to reset that preset for good.

Best of all, there is no wasted time. There is no one-size-fits-all
approach that leaves you feeling like a failure. By taking the
revolutionary Flow Factor Test, you will get a custom-designed
plan for your success that works with your personal needs, desires,
and strengths. It's easy. It's fun. And **it works**.

In fact, it will work for the rest of your life. Anytime that you
start to notice negative experiences, pain, or illness show up in
your life, you can come back to the test once again and find out
which Stations have been tuned into the issues that you are
experiencing at that moment. For instance, right now you might be

119

dealing with issues of difficulty in your relationships as well as your ability to stand up for yourself. By taking the test, you will find that you will be directed to the workbook sections that are going to help you the most with those issues of immediate concern. However, as you know, you can take on new beliefs at any time, and, if they are negative, you will start to see conflict, struggle and disease in a corresponding area of your life. So, by doing the system, you fixed the Stations that are off right now, and everything is going great: you are standing up for yourself with ease, and you have wonderful relationships in your life. But, a few months down the road, you suddenly become very apprehensive about speaking in public, and your throat begins to hurt all the time. Right then and there you know that you have Stations that are flowing with negative, limiting beliefs. Immediately come back, take the test again, and get your new Flow Factor. Once again, it will direct you right to the workbook sections that you need the most at that moment to change what is going on in your life at that time.

If this is your first time taking the test, I would like you to evaluate the statements as they would apply **for your entire life**. For instance, let's say that you are taking the test, and you get to the statement: "I have had many difficult relationships." Ask yourself how true that statement has been for your for your entire life. Have you had a long-term pattern of difficult experiences? If so, you will want to say, "Agree completely," because you have had many difficult relationships throughout your life.

If you are retaking the test to identify new issues that have shown up in your life recently, please evaluate the statements for how often you have felt that way or had that experience in the **last few months to year only**. By doing this, you will receive a Flow Factor that is specific to your life and issues right now.

Ready? Go get your Flow Factor!

THE FLOW FACTOR TEST

Part 1:

Allow yourself 30 to 60 minutes to complete the test. Rate yourself on how strongly you agree with each statement or how true the statement is for you: 3 = Agree completely, 2 = Agree somewhat, 0 = Do not agree.

Station 1	Agree Completely	Agree Somewhat	Do not agree
1. I go along with whatever the group* wants to do, even when I do not agree; I prefer not to "make waves."	3	2	0
2. I do not feel comfortable in groups of people.	3	2	0
3. My family struggled to make ends meet, or to be able to take care of our needs for clothes, food, and shelter.	3	2	0

4. Fighting was normal in my family. I either yelled at my parents and others, or I was not allowed to speak up and question, even if they yelled at me.	3	2	0
5. I am afraid that if I make more money than my family, I will be making others feel less successful.	3	2	0
6. I don't feel like I fit in anywhere.	3	2	0
7. I make decisions based on what my family or other groups will think of me.	3	2	0
8. My own dreams for my life are in conflict with what my family or society expects me to do.	3	2	0
9. I feel a great deal of pressure to be the same religion as my family.	3	2	0
10. I have sacrificed my own desires in order to meet the needs of my family or other group.	3	2	0
11. I find myself afraid to stand up for myself when I am with my family or other group.	3	2	0
12. I am afraid that if I lived my life as I really want to live it, I will no longer be accepted by my family or other group.	3	2	0
13. I feel that I must live by the rules set forth by my family or other groups.	3	2	0

14. It is very important to me that my family is proud of my work.	3	2	0
15. I often feel judged by the groups that I am part of.	3	2	0
16. My family or religion taught me that people of a different religion, race, or group were bad or untrustworthy.	3	2	0
17. I find myself having to leave groups because they will not go along with my way of thinking.	3	2	0
18. As a child, I heard my parents talking about how difficult life was.	3	2	0
19. If I am not leading the group, I don't want to be part of it.	3	2	0
20. I believe that my family, religion, or other groups must always come first.	3	2	0
21. My family identity was very much defined by our religious affiliation, race, or financial status.	3	2	0
22. I have been labeled the "rebel" or the "black sheep" of the family.	3	2	0
23. When I am in a group, I often find myself doing more work than everyone else.	3	2	0
24. I believe that I am fated to live the same kind of life that my parents did.	3	2	0

25. For women: I feel worse about myself when I see images of women in magazines and on TV. For men: I feel pressure to live up to society's image of what a man should be.	3	2	0
26. I have had situations where a group turned against me or ostracized me.	3	2	0
27. I watch the news or read the newspaper often, and when I do, I feel that the world is becoming worse everyday.	3	2	0
28. I feel that it is very likely that I will get the same diseases that my parents or others in my family have because I am genetically predisposed.	3	2	0
29. I feel out of place in the world. I don't feel accepted anywhere.	3	2	0
30. It is important to me that I dress like the others that I am with; I would feel very uncomfortable if I looked different than everyone around me.	3	2	0

Subtotals: ____ ____ ____

Station 1 Total: Add all three subtotals together, and place the total here. _____

* The word "group" is used generically to describe any group: family, friends, neighborhood, church, co-workers, associations, or any other group that you are part of. Please assess the statement as it applies for **all** of these groups.

Station 2	Agree completely	Agree somewhat	Do not agree
1. I have many difficult relationships in my life.	3	2	0
2. I often feel taken advantage of in relationships.	3	2	0
3. I seem to attract people to my life that treat me badly.	3	2	0
4. I never seem to meet people that I really enjoy being with.	3	2	0
5. I never feel that I have enough money, and I don't think that I have the ability to create opportunities to make more money than I do now.	3	2	0
6. I am not proud of the work that I do.	3	2	0
7. I do not feel powerful in my relationships.	3	2	0
8. I notice that there are certain people in my life whose demands that I give in to, even when I do not want to, or when I have other priorities that are important to me.	3	2	0
9. I have a difficult relationship with my mother, father, sister, brother, or other individuals in my family.	3	2	0
10. I feel like I need to control other people—if I don't, they may leave me.	3	2	0
11. I play games in my relationships with others—using manipulation to keep them with me.	3	2	0

12. I believe everything that my doctor tells me, even when it doesn't seem right. I just don't think that I have a right to question him or her.	3	2	0
13. I feel that I am in competition with others to get what I want.	3	2	0
14. I find myself fighting with others a good deal of the time.	3	2	0
15. I am very afraid of not having enough of anything—money, food, work, or anything else that makes me feel safe.	3	2	0
16. I do not accept anyone questioning me or my control of a situation. I believe that my opinion is the most important.	3	2	0
17. I feel that I have to overpower others, or I am often overpowered.	3	2	0
18. I feel controlled by my need for success, money, or to have material things. I worry about losing these things.	3	2	0
19. I have seen many relationships in my life where people were unhappy, fought a great deal, or got divorced.	3	2	0
20. I think that other people should always be available to take care of me and my needs. I don't know if I can take care of myself.	3	2	0
21. I find it difficult to enjoy sex.	3	2	0

22. I do not feel that I deserve pleasure in any area of life. In fact, I often feel guilty when I am really enjoying something.	3	2	0
23. I have many creative ideas, but I either don't see them through, or others take my ideas as their own, taking credit for my creativity and hard work.	3	2	0
24. I have a difficult time at work—I never seem to get ahead, and I just miss out on promotions and prizes.	3	2	0
25. I am afraid that my sexual feelings or needs are bad, weird, or sinful.	3	2	0
26. I have relationships where I feel like that person's opinion of me and my life is more important and powerful than my own opinion about what I want or enjoy.	3	2	0
27. My relationship with my spouse or mate is very similar to my parents' relationship with each other.	3	2	0
28. I put up with situations at work that I don't like and/or feel good about in order to keep my job. Worse yet, the job just pays the bills—it is not my dream job.	3	2	0
29. When I do have money or other nice things, I feel guilty. I worry that I should give more away to charity.	3	2	0

30. I believe that it is normal to have difficulty in relationships.	3	2	0

Subtotals: _____ _____ _____

Station 2 Total: Add all three subtotals together, and place the total here. _____

Station 3	Agree completely	Agree Somewhat	Do not agree
1. I worry that I am unattractive.	3	2	0
2. I get very upset when others do not agree with me. I feel like I need to convince them that I am right.	3	2	0
3. When I look in the mirror, I don't like what I see. Actually, I really wish I could have a total make-over.	3	2	0
4. I worry about what others think of me.	3	2	0
5. I know that I do not have good self-esteem.	3	2	0
6. I am obsessed with my appearance—I constantly worry about how I look.	3	2	0
7. I wish that I was more like the people that I admire. I don't like I am as good as they are.	3	2	0
8. I don't feel like I am worth much if I gain weight, or if I am overly thin.	3	2	0
9. I judge my self-worth by how I look.	3	2	0
10. I only feel good about myself when others give me compliments.	3	2	0

11. I find myself obsessing over others' criticisms of me.	3	2	0
12. I have an addictive personality (for example, with smoking, drinking, gambling, food, or obsessive shopping).	3	2	0
13. I do not like myself much, and don't really feel like I am worth much at all.	3	2	0
14. I am afraid of others' opinions of me if I make the changes that I want.	3	2	0
15. I was made fun of a great deal as a child.	3	2	0
16. I worry that I do not have what it takes to be successful.	3	2	0
17. I feel like a failure because I have tried many diet, exercise, or success programs and have not had results.	3	2	0
18. I have difficulty accepting compliments.	3	2	0
19. I have had many experiences where I felt put down by others.	3	2	0
20. I do not feel worthy of prosperity.	3	2	0
21. When I have money, I give gifts to others—but rarely buy things for myself.	3	2	0
22. I feel like I have to earn the love of others.	3	2	0
23. If no one else feels the way that I do, I feel that I am wrong.	3	2	0

24. I am very self-critical. In fact, I tend to be a perfectionist about everything that I do.	3	2	0
25. I am very afraid of speaking in front of groups, or have other phobias that limit me.	3	2	0
26. When I have difficulty in my life, I feel that I have done something to deserve it.	3	2	0
27. I have a difficult time deciding what I want to do without consulting others.	3	2	0
28. I feel that I must do more and more to prove my worth.	3	2	0
29. I am very afraid of rejection, and it affects my ability to do what I desire or to live my life fully.	3	2	0
30. I find myself avoiding some experiences in life, because I believe that I do not have the ability to succeed.	3	2	0
Subtotals:	____	____	____

Station 3 Total: Add all three subtotals together, and place the total here. _____

Station 4	Agree completely	Agree somewhat	Do not agree
1. I have a hard time expressing emotions and how I really feel about something or someone.	3	2	0

2. I worry that I am too emotional or not emotional enough.	3	2	0
3. I believe that real men don't cry, and women are overly emotional.	3	2	0
4. I feel angry, frustrated, or put off a good deal of the time.	3	2	0
5. When someone hurts me, I have a hard time dealing with this emotionally—it bothers me a great deal.	3	2	0
6. I hold grudges for a long time after I am hurt.	3	2	0
7. I empathize deeply with others, feeling their pain acutely.	3	2	0
8. I find myself becoming very jealous of other people's happiness.	3	2	0
9. I am afraid to deal with issues from my past, because I do not want to feel the pain again.	3	2	0
10. I have a very hard time letting go of anything.	3	2	0
11. I am very afraid of getting hurt. I have been hurt before, and I do not want to repeat the experience.	3	2	0
12. I have had many experiences where others have not forgiven me for mistakes that I have made, or have held them over me for years.	3	2	0

13. I do not forgive easily, and there are some people who I am completely unable to forgive.	3	2	0
14. If I am not getting my way, I bring up other's mistakes or how they have hurt me to make them give into my wishes. After all, they owe me.	3	2	0
15. I use my own emotional pain or turmoil to manipulate others into doing what I want.	3	2	0
16. I am still very upset over some negative experiences that happened many years ago.	3	2	0
17. I have been in many relationships with people who did not respect my emotional needs.	3	2	0
18. When I love someone, I focus only on their needs—to the exclusion of mine.	3	2	0
19. I am very emotionally attached to things in my life (for example, feeling sadness over changing offices or selling a house).	3	2	0
20. I don't know if I have ever truly been in love or ever felt truly loved.	3	2	0
21. I tend to be very moody, and can fly off the handle easily when I do not get my way.	3	2	0
22. I have been told that I am either overly needy or too logical.	3	2	0

23. I either feel sadness more deeply than other people, or I feel totally detached from my emotions.	3	2	0
24. I find myself feeling guilty over mistakes or personal failures, even years after the incident itself.	3	2	0
25. I have been so hurt that I became emotionally numb—I no longer felt anything for anyone.	3	2	0
26. I either do not think emotions are as useful to me as logic and reason, or I only make decisions with my emotions.	3	2	0
27. I feel like I have emotional wounds that have not healed, or I am still grieving the loss of someone important to me.	3	2	0
28. My parents did not show love, or did not show the kind of love that I desired.	3	2	0
29. I have difficulty figuring out how I really feel about something or someone.	3	2	0
30. I am emotionally attached to my work—if I lost my job, I would be heart-broken.	3	2	0

Subtotals: ____ ____ ____

Station 4 Total: Add all three subtotals together, and place the total here. _____

Station 5	Agree completely	Agree Somewhat	Do not Agree
1. I find myself gossiping at work or with friends.	3	2	0
2. I know what I want in my life, but I am afraid of telling others about my dreams and plans.	3	2	0
3. I mentally make decisions, but I find it hard to actually carry through.	3	2	0
4. I find myself in conversations that I am not comfortable with, but I have a hard time removing myself.	3	2	0
5. I know what my goals are, but I find myself making choices that are contrary to my goals. I feel like I undermine my efforts to improve myself.	3	2	0
6. I have been told that I speak either too loud or too soft.	3	2	0
7. I find it very difficult to put what I mean into words, especially in certain situations.	3	2	0
8. My voice gets shaky, soft, or strained in some situations.	3	2	0
9. I never feel like I am able to stand up for myself.	3	2	0
10. I have relationships where I have a hard time getting a word in.	3	2	0
11. I yell a lot and frequently start arguments.	3	2	0
12. I am worried about hurting others with the things that I say.	3	2	0
13. I do not feel like others truly hear me.	3	2	0

14. I make up my mind to confront someone, but I always find myself backing down or being convinced that I am wrong.	3	2	0
15. I find myself in many situations where I am yelling or talking over people to get my point across.	3	2	0
16. I do not feel comfortable with the way that I move.	3	2	0
17. I have been made fun of for my voice, my spelling and grammar, or the way that I walk or dance.	3	2	0
18. I notice that I think very negative thoughts about myself and others.	3	2	0
19. When I try to do something creative, I am so critical of myself that I cannot complete my project.	3	2	0
20. When I do get ill, I get a sore throat.	3	2	0
21. When I try to write something, I find myself starting over again and again.	3	2	0
22. I do not feel confident about the way that I express my thoughts and feelings.	3	2	0
23. I have difficulty speaking about aspects of myself that I am proud of, always downplaying my accomplishments instead.	3	2	0

	Agree completely	Agree somewhat	Do not agree
24. My parents talked in an overbearing way, or did not allow me to express my thoughts.	3	2	0
25. I avoid confrontation.	3	2	0
26. I know that I would like to change my life, but I don't think that I have any willpower.	3	2	0
27. After being with certain people, my jaw aches, or I feel tension in my neck and shoulders.	3	2	0
28. I have had many relationships where I did not speak my mind for fear of being hurt, or of hurting others.	3	2	0
29. I find myself in circumstances with others who frequently talk over me.	3	2	0
30. Even when I do stand up for myself, I am often ignored— nothing seems to change.	3	2	0

Subtotals: _____ _____ _____

Station 5 Total: Add all three subtotals together, and place the total here. _____

Station 6	Agree completely	Agree somewhat	Do not agree
1. I feel out of control of my life.	3	2	0
2. I am afraid of change.	3	2	0
3. I have some beliefs that I think are always true.	3	2	0
4. I am very attached to the things in my life, and am very afraid of losing any of it.	3	2	0

5. I feel like I struggle and struggle to make what I desire happen, but see little improvement.	3	2	0
6. I am afraid of finding out that some of my beliefs are wrong.	3	2	0
7. I feel like a victim. I expect bad things to happen to me.	3	2	0
8. I get frustrated when I don't get exactly what I want.	3	2	0
9. I have a hard time letting go of anyone or anything in my life.	3	2	0
10. I don't trust anyone else to help me.	3	2	0
11. I have had many experiences where I felt like I lost everything at once.	3	2	0
12. I frequently ponder memories of things and people that I miss, and wish that I had them back.	3	2	0
13. I look back on decisions that I have made, and wonder if I did the right thing.	3	2	0
14. I have never felt like I really took responsibility for my life.	3	2	0
15. I often blame others for my difficulties, or feel that others are out to get me.	3	2	0
16. I do not feel like a lucky person.	3	2	0
17. I have a very difficult time making decisions—I dither back and forth.	3	2	0
18. I have many experiences where I try to help someone who will not help themselves.	3	2	0
19. I have many headaches.	3	2	0
20. My parents had/have a victim mentality.	3	2	0

	Agree completely	Agree somewhat	Do not agree
21. I feel like I have tried to improve my life before, and failed at it. I am afraid that I will fail this time as well.	3	2	0
22. I do not feel in control of my destiny.	3	2	0
23. I relate to the underdog. In fact, I feel like an underdog.	3	2	0
24. I feel like others have control of many factors in my life.	3	2	0
25. I feel that hard work and sacrifice are the only ways to guarantee that you get what you want out of life.	3	2	0
26. I do not know anyone that seems in control of their life.	3	2	0
27. I have trouble focusing on anything for long.	3	2	0
28. I have difficulty seeing the good in bad or difficult experiences.	3	2	0
29. I am not smart enough to be truly successful.	3	2	0
30. I have a difficult time looking at problems in my life objectively.	3	2	0

Subtotals: ____ ____ ____

Station 6 Total: Add all three subtotals together, and place the total here. _____

Station 7	Agree completely	Agree somewhat	Do not agree
1. I am not sure that I deserve love from the Source*.	3	2	0

2. I often barter with the Source in order to get something that I want.	3	2	0
3. My notion of the Source includes an all-powerful being watching my every move.	3	2	0
4. I feel like I would be more successful if I were a better person.	3	2	0
5. I feel that I should have to suffer to earn the love of the Source. In fact, suffering makes me more worthy.	3	2	0
6. I want to know my higher purpose in life.	3	2	0
7. I do not enjoy things that I used to enjoy.	3	2	0
8. I feel like I do not fit in anymore with the groups that I used to have much in common with.	3	2	0
9. I have a hard time trusting that I will be given what I need in life.	3	2	0
10. I feel like I am searching for something, but I am not sure what it is.	3	2	0
11. I think that I have done something to deserve the bad things that have happened in my life.	3	2	0
12. I feel afraid of eternal judgment if I go against the teachings of my religious upbringing.	3	2	0

13. I tend to act in ways that I think will earn the assistance of the Source (for example, praying that I will give money to charity if I get something that I desire).	3	2	0
14. I believe that we all have sin or karma when we are born, and must live out experiences or make choices that remedy this karmic debt or original sin.	3	2	0
15. I believe that to be truly spiritual, you must give up all your worldly possessions and choose to be poor.	3	2	0
16. I don't think that my choices have any impact on the rest of the world.	3	2	0
17. I believe that the Source views me as a bad person.	3	2	0
18. I want to do something meaningful in my life, but I don't know what it is.	3	2	0
19. I have been feeling totally disconnected from everyone and everything in my life.	3	2	0
20. I am tired all the time and cannot find a solution for this.	3	2	0
21. I want to find work that contributes something important to the world.	3	2	0
22. I don't know what to think about the Source or any notion of a higher power.	3	2	0

23. I turned my back on religion, because I see the amount of hate that it can cause in the world.	3	2	0
24. I don't believe that I can do anything to make the world a better place. One person doesn't have that much impact.	3	2	0
25. I am afraid of the wrath of the Source.	3	2	0
26. I am afraid of what is going to happen next in my life.	3	2	0
27. I don't know what my purpose in life is. In fact, I am not sure that I have any purpose at all.	3	2	0
28. I am amazed to see others who have absolute faith in the Source.	3	2	0
29. I don't feel like I am ever doing enough for the world.	3	2	0
30. I have blind faith in whatever my church tells me about the Source, or about the proper way to live life.	3	2	0

Subtotals: _____ _____ _____

Station 7 Total: Add all three subtotals together, and place the total here. _____

*Please feel free to replace "the Source" with any name that you use to describe a higher power.

Part 2: The Body

For each Station, evaluate each body part for whether you have pain, disease, rashes, itching, deterioration, malfunction, extra weight, or any kind of difficulty at all in each area. Rate how severe the issue is from 1 to 10, with 10 being the highest. For instance, if you have arthritis in your knees, and it is a chronic issue that is very painful, circle "10." If you carry some weight in your stomach that you are having difficulty losing, you might want to give that a "6." When you are done with each section, add up the numbers, and write that number down as the "Body Total." In the "Station Test Total" for each Station, put the number from the corresponding Station test above. Add the two together to come up with the "Station Grand Total."

Station 1 Body:	
Legs	1 2 3 4 5 6 7 8 9 10
Knees	1 2 3 4 5 6 7 8 9 10
Feet and toes	1 2 3 4 5 6 7 8 9 10
Base of spine and tailbone	1 2 3 4 5 6 7 8 9 10
Rectum	1 2 3 4 5 6 7 8 9 10
Immune system	1 2 3 4 5 6 7 8 9 10
Ankles	1 2 3 4 5 6 7 8 9 10

Body Total: ._____

Total from Station 1 Test: _____

Station 1 Grand Total: Add these two numbers together, and place the grand total here: _____

Station 2 Body:	
Sexual organs	1 2 3 4 5 6 7 8 9 10
Lower vertebrae	1 2 3 4 5 6 7 8 9 10
Hips	1 2 3 4 5 6 7 8 9 10
Bladder	1 2 3 4 5 6 7 8 9 10

Large intestine	1 2 3 4 5 6 7 8 9 10
Buttocks	1 2 3 4 5 6 7 8 9 10

Body Total: ._____

Total from Station 2 Test: _____

Station 2 Grand Total: Add these two numbers together, and place the grand total here: _____

Station 3 Body:

Stomach	1 2 3 4 5 6 7 8 9 10
Liver	1 2 3 4 5 6 7 8 9 10
Spleen	1 2 3 4 5 6 7 8 9 10
Lumbar spine	1 2 3 4 5 6 7 8 9 10
Lower ribs and core of the body	1 2 3 4 5 6 7 8 9 10
Addictive disease (ex: alcoholism, eating disorders)	1 2 3 4 5 6 7 8 9 10
Kidneys and adrenals	1 2 3 4 5 6 7 8 9 10
Pancreas (insulin-related disorders)	1 2 3 4 5 6 7 8 9 10

Body Total: ._____

Total from Station 3 Test: _____

Station 3 Grand Total: Add these two numbers together, and place the grand total here: _____

Station 4 Body:

Heart	1 2 3 4 5 6 7 8 9 10
Circulatory system	1 2 3 4 5 6 7 8 9 10
Lungs and respiratory system	1 2 3 4 5 6 7 8 9 10
Rib cage/ middle and upper spine	1 2 3 4 5 6 7 8 9 10

Breasts/ chest	1 2 3 4 5 6 7 8 9 10
Shoulders and collarbones	1 2 3 4 5 6 7 8 9 10
Arms, wrists, hands, and fingers	1 2 3 4 5 6 7 8 9 10

Body Total: ._____

Total from Station 4 Test: _____

Station 4 Grand Total: Add these two numbers together, and place the grand total here: _____

Station 5 Body:

Neck vertebrae	1 2 3 4 5 6 7 8 9 10
Throat	1 2 3 4 5 6 7 8 9 10
Mouth	1 2 3 4 5 6 7 8 9 10
Teeth	1 2 3 4 5 6 7 8 9 10
Esophagus	1 2 3 4 5 6 7 8 9 10
Trachea	1 2 3 4 5 6 7 8 9 10
Thyroid	1 2 3 4 5 6 7 8 9 10
Gums	1 2 3 4 5 6 7 8 9 10
Neck muscles	1 2 3 4 5 6 7 8 9 10
Jaw	1 2 3 4 5 6 7 8 9 10

Body Total: ._____

Total from Station 5 Test: _____

Station 5 Grand Total: Add these two numbers together, and place the grand total here: _____

Station 6 Body:

Eyes, forehead, temples	1 2 3 4 5 6 7 8 9 10
Ears	1 2 3 4 5 6 7 8 9 10
Nose	1 2 3 4 5 6 7 8 9 10
Brain	1 2 3 4 5 6 7 8 9 10
Sinuses	1 2 3 4 5 6 7 8 9 10

| Pituitary gland | 1 2 3 4 5 6 7 8 9 10 |

Body Total: ._____

Total from Station 6 Test: _____

Station 6 Grand Total: Add these two numbers together, and place the grand total here: _____

Station 7 Body:

Muscular system	1 2 3 4 5 6 7 8 9 10
Top of the head	1 2 3 4 5 6 7 8 9 10
Scalp	1 2 3 4 5 6 7 8 9 10
Hair	1 2 3 4 5 6 7 8 9 10
Nervous system	1 2 3 4 5 6 7 8 9 10

Body Total: ._____

Total from Station 7 above: _____

Station 7 Grand Total: Add these two numbers together, and place the grand total here: _____

So what's *your* Flow Factor?

Review the "Grand Total" for each Station. Under "Your Flow Factor" below, put the highest grand total in the first box, the second highest in the second box, and the third highest in the third box. You now know the top 3 Stations that are preset to tune you into the most difficulty!

Your Flow Factor		

Customizing your action plan, Flow-style

To customize the perfect plan for you, first look at your Flow Factor. The number in the first box is the Station that is tuning you into the most negativity, and is therefore causing you the most problems. Please proceed to that Station—for example, if your highest number is 3, proceed to Station 3 and begin the workbook. When you are done with the first section of the workbook, go to the "4 for 40" section of the book. Take the Reality Type Test, and follow the instructions to pick your 4 for 40. When you are done with the first Station, proceed on to the second and third Stations, and do the same.

Go at your own pace with this process. Try to answer the workbook questions as completely as possible. As you answer the questions, just let your mind flow. Write whatever comes to you, even if it seems unrelated to the issue. By doing this, you will uncover old memories, thought patterns, and long-buried experiences that are actually related to the question (and the solution). By using this technique, you can become aware of the whole issue at hand, and realize the perfect solutions for you.

If you ever cannot remember what to do, come back to this page and review the steps to your success below. In fact, you might want to bookmark or dog-ear this page right now so you can easily refer back to it.

Now, go tune into life of your dreams!

Steps to your total life transformation:

1. Go to the Station section indicated as your highest total.
2. Work through the first section (or a few sections) of this Station's workbook.
3. Choose 2 or 3 retuning statements.
4. Proceed to the "4 for 40" section of the book.
5. Take the Reality Type Test.
6. Look through the suggested exercises for your Reality Type.

7. Choose 4 exercises that most appeal to you, and commit to doing these every day for 40 days.
8. Repeat this for the next two highest Stations, as indicated by your Flow Factor.
9. Watch your totally transformed life flow right to you! Enjoy!

PART 3
The Flow Stations

STATION 1

The Commanding Influence of Groups

Station Motto: I worry about the group's expectation of me.

Location of Station: Tailbone

Problem Playlist: If you are preset with negative Station 1 beliefs, you will find that you have some of these behavior patterns and difficulties:

- Having experiences where you do not stand up for yourself within the group.
- Believing that the group's opinions and needs are more important than your own—causing you to sacrifice everything in order to meet their needs.
- Having incessant worries about fitting in with the groups in your life.
- Having experiences where your efforts at changing or improving yourself are put down or made fun of by many people around you—causing you to stop making

a self-improvement effort and fall back in line with the group.

- Taking on more work than everyone else in every group, or constantly being volunteered (or volunteering!) for more work.
- Having a nagging feeling that you have never really fit in with any group, and an overwhelming desire to have somewhere that you feel accepted and understood.
- Issues where you have had groups turn against you.
- Being associated with a failing business, church, or community that cannot make enough money to survive.
- Having financial struggles with your current family, or your childhood family may have had to struggle to make ends meet.
- Dealing with issues of prejudice over your race, sexual orientation, gender, religious affiliation, or any other common group identity.

Station 1 Body Issues: If you are tuning into negativity here, you will find that you have disease, pain, or extra weight in these areas:

- Immune system
- Legs
- Feet and toes
- Knees
- Ankles
- Rectum
- Bones
- Base of spine
- Tailbone

It's a family thing

You are born into an enormous amount of groups, from your primary family group, to your religious affiliation, race, gender, and even nationality. As a baby, the only one of these that you were even aware of was your family; your experience with this primary group set the foundation for your entire viewpoint on life—and whether you expect life to be safe, accepting, and supportive, or dysfunctional, scary, and difficult.

As you grow up, you begin to seek other groups who can be thought of as "families-of-choice." If you have positive beliefs about yourself and a strong foundation for choosing wisely, you will select groups that flow with positive energy, becoming part of supportive, empowering groups—such as a great group of friends, a winning athletic team, or a human rights group doing good for the world. If not, you will choose membership in groups that are creating a negative collective experience, such as gangs, cults, or hate groups. At best, these kinds of negative groups will cause you to act in ways that are harmful to yourself and others; at worst, membership in these kinds of groups can actually endanger your life. From drive-by shootings to terrorist acts and the horrors of genocide, negative groups led by negative leaders can be one of the strongest forces for destructive, harmful creations.

Whether you are actually part of a negative group or just encountering one in your daily life, standing up against these types of groups takes great courage—but the reward is that you can change the course of many people's lives when you choose to do so. When you truly believe that you can make a difference—and you take loving action in alignment with your desire to transform a dysfunctional, damaging group experience, you absolutely transform the world at both a micro **and** a macro level. Each powerful choice that you make to align yourself with positive, loving groups and speak up for justice and human rights is one that tunes the frequency of the collective-hologram up a step or two. The more people taking loving action, the better the collective frequency, and as a result, the collectively created experience is seriously enhanced.

A sense of belonging...

Do you long to belong?

At some level, I think we all do. Being truly accepted by a group of people is a good feeling—it gives you a sense of having a place in the world where you are not only wanted, but **safe**. Needing this group acceptance is a primal instinct frequency that is programmed into your "you-hologram" from a time when a tribal allegiance would have been essential to your very survival. In modern times, this programming becomes the belief that the groups that you are part of should support, protect, and stand up for you no matter what—a basic need and desire echoed in the common phrase: "We always stick up for our own."

When this sense of safety is violated by a group that turns against you or abandons you in your time of need, your survival instinct will kick in, and the fear that you feel may develop into a belief that life will not be able to support and protect you at **any** level. Further, such abandonment creates a serious loss of self-worth. Although you may have done nothing wrong to have a group treat you so badly, you will likely take on the belief that you deserved this treatment, or that there is something unlovable and unacceptable about you. It isn't true, but the negative feelings created by such an experience can cause long-term issues with this Station.

Whatever your personal experience with the groups in your life, become aware that you have a relationship dynamic playing out with each group that is based on whether or not you feel powerful in the situation. By understanding this power dynamic, you can become conscious of any negative patterns that you have with groups, and learn to flow with the most positive group dynamic that you possibly can.

Group Dynamic #1: The group controls you.

This dynamic comes from a desire to be part of a group so

desperately that you will do whatever it takes to fit in. If this is a dynamic that you tune into, you will have many experiences where you go against your personal needs and sense of ethics to seek the approval and acceptance of the group.

Pleasing the group at all costs may be a lesson that you learned early in life, as you watched your parents sacrifice their individual needs and desires for those of their families, their work, or even the church that you attended. You may have been trained to believe that you must always put "family first" or "others first," triggering you to drop **everything** and **anything** whenever your family (or other families-of-choice) needs anything, even if their demands are unreasonable or conflict with your own needs and beliefs.

Group dynamic # 2: You control the group (or at least desire to).

If you are naturally a "leader personality," this is not necessarily a bad thing, but you must be aware that (as discussed in the former section) you can use your skills to lead a group either for a positive purpose or a negative one. If you consciously choose to lead groups in a way that creates a positive experience for all involved, you can create the very best group experience, and (as I have said so many times before) that changes the world. However, you can also create a negative group experience, especially if you are fueled by a desire to control people for your own gain or personal agenda, or for the simple rush that can come from having absolute power. Obviously, this is a negative use of your leadership skills, and will never tune you into the life of your dreams in any group relationship.

Ironically, the desire to control groups can actually come from a deep sense of being an outcast. After all, by being the leader of the group, you assure that you belong there—and having followers may make you feel that you are accepted and admired in a way that you never received from your family or other early groups. Unfortunately, this plan will likely backfire on you, because you are still choosing the experience of leadership based on a set of negative beliefs. At this point, you will tune into many experiences where the group becomes sick of your particular brand of leadership and votes you out. Of course, this means that you will now be back at square one: you will feel that same sense of abandonment and betrayal that you have so many times in the past.

Group dynamic # 3: You refuse to be part of any groups.

While an independent streak is not a bad thing, this dynamic is built on the beliefs created by the negative group experiences that you may have had in your childhood. To protect yourself from ever feeling unsafe, hurt, or abandoned by anyone again, you decide to be "the rebel," refusing to go along with any group. Believing that you don't need or desire to fit in anywhere, you will manifest experiences and behavior patterns that self-ostracize yourself from groups. For instance, you may continuously pick clothes that are opposite from the "norm," or direct anger and violence toward authority figures.

The desire to be a rebel can be increased if you have witnessed the harmful effects of others giving over their entire mind, body, and spirit to a particular group, allowing that group to totally control them. A fear of having this happen to you can keep you from being able to become part of **any** group, even those that would help you emotionally or creatively.

Group dynamic # 4: You are unconditionally loved and accepted.

This is the ultimate group experience. Every individual is totally loved for who they are, without condition or restriction; it is the manifestation of the best possible group energy. In this dynamic, the group forms to puts its collective energy toward a purpose, but still allows each member be and create however they see fit. By definition, you are **always** safe and **always** protected in this kind of a group, and there is never any question that you belong. It is the group experience that we all instinctively seek.

Whether you know it or not, you are already part of such a group, also known as "the Source," "quantum potential," or "the life-creators." As part of the flowing oneness that composes the Source, you **automatically fit in simply by existing**. And, as with any other group that you are part of, you have a necessary role to play as part of the Source: your role (and every person's role) is to be a life-creator, and you fulfill this role by making the choices that create life around you. In this perfect group, unconditional love is always shown to you just as you are, providing all that you need to create your desired life.

Isn't it time that all groups in your life were this unconditionally loving? I **definitely** think so. Let's get to it.

Questions:

1. List all the groups that you are part of. Make sure that you list groups like your race, nationality, religious affiliation, gender, sexual orientation, profession, and any other group that you can think of. Then, identify the group dynamic that is playing out with each group: #1, #2, #3, or #4.

2. Which groups totally control you (Group dynamic #1)? How does this feel? Why do you feel that you must go along with the group no matter what? Is this a pattern in your life?

Retuning statement: "I am powerful. I choose my own destiny."

3. Do you desire to control all groups (Group dynamic #2)? Are you naturally a leader personality? Do you desire the power, recognition, and acceptance that comes from the total control of a group of people? Is

this a negative pattern in your life? Have you ever been voted out of your position of leadership?

Retuning statement: "I choose to lead in flowing, positive ways. I am respectful of all people."

4. Do you play the rebel with any (or all) groups (Group dynamic #3)? Where does this desire come from? Are you afraid of giving away your power? Have you tuned into this pattern as a response to being made to feel like an outsider in life? Is your rebellion keeping you from creating what you want in life?

Retuning statement: "I can be part of unconditionally loving groups, where I am accepted for who I am. I now choose that group experience."

5. Do you have any groups where you are totally accepted for who you are, without condition? What is this experience like? How can you create this experience in the rest of your life?
6. Was your primary family supportive and loving (Group dynamic #4)? If so, what positive beliefs did you take from this experience? If not, what negative beliefs did you learn? How do you play out this same dynamic in other groups? Does your lack of power in your family group translate to a desire to control the other groups that you are part of?

What's your mission?

Every group forms for a reason or it would not exist—and this reason becomes its collective vision, or mission.

What is a mission? It is simply the goal that is to be achieved by combining the collective thought and action of the members of the group. When all individuals in the group put their energy toward that purpose, the collective frequency will tune the group into their exact desires.

In this case, the sum of the parts is more powerful than any individual could be on their own. For instance, perhaps your mission is to have a family. To achieve this goal, you need to find at least one other person to create this reality with you. Or, you might start a business with the goal of creating a global enterprise. Without others to help you with the aspects of the business that you are not skilled at, you will not be able to achieve this mission. Maybe you would like to have the experience of being on a winning team. Obviously, that can't be a reality without teammates.

To flow with the best group experiences, you must understand clearly what the mission is for each group that you are part of, and then consciously decide if that is a goal worth your time and energy. If it is not a goal in alignment with what you desire for yourself and your life, there is no point in continuing to put your efforts into it. Rather than draining your energy on groups that do not work for you, you must reset your preset to allow the groups that match your highest desires to flow to you.

It is important to understand that every group has a leader; the quality of the vision and charisma of that leader will dictate both the group's feelings about itself and the collective frequency it tunes into. Because of this, a leader absolutely has the ability to radically change the way that an entire group of people views themselves and their mission in life, for better or for worse. If the leader flows with negative intent and a desire for power for power's sake, it can create group experiences that are extremely negative for all involved. For instance, an abusive father or an alcoholic mother creates a very negative experience for everyone in the family, tuning the children into limiting, frightening beliefs. Or, a negative church leader can create hate toward other religions with his words or actions.

In contrast, when the leader brings the intention of leading the group to be greater than the sum of its parts, amazing and powerful change can happen. It might be the great coach that causes a losing team to envision themselves as winners. It could be the new CEO that turns a failing business into a global enterprise. It may be the visionary that changes the way a group of people sees their personal power in the world: Martin Luther King, Gloria Steinam, and Nelson Mandela are perfect examples of the power of such a leader. In any of these cases, the leader is able to radically change the collective hologram of the particular group with the power of their personal conviction. The strength of the leader's vision is so strong that it retunes the frequency for the whole group, tuning all members into a completely new reality.

You can choose to be the best kind of leader in your own life, however and wherever you lead. You may not think that you are a leader, but believe me, **you are**. You lead as the mother, father, or even the oldest sibling of a family. You lead as the manager or department head in your business. You lead when you are the captain of a team or the head of a church. Take this responsibility seriously; others **are** following your lead, so ensure that what you do and say is in alignment with the very best in life. When you bring your awareness to your leadership power, your words and actions can empower your group to be a force for good in your community, your nation, and the world.

Become aware of the mission of all of the groups in your life. Choose to only be a member of those that are doing good for the world—and are good for **you**.

Questions:

1. Assign a name to each of your groups. For example, your family group might be "the Smiths," or "the Loony Jones Clan" and your group of friends might be "the Girls," or "the Boys." Your race might simply be "Black" or "White," or more specifically, "African-American" or "Irish-American." Be creative, and have fun with this—pick a name that really speaks to you for each group. What does this name say about your group

intent and identity? Say each name aloud. Do any of the names cause you to feel uneasy or sick? If so, ask yourself what about that group makes you uncomfortable.

Retuning statement: "Every group in my life is loving and fits me perfectly."

2. Develop a mission statement for each of your groups. For instance, if your family is insane and dysfunctional, the mission statement might be, "We come together to create dysfunction, unhappiness, and difficulty." If you are part of a charity, it might be, "Our goal is to better the lives of others." If you are part of a corporation or healthcare organization, find your organization's vision or mission statement. Review each mission statement. What does the statement say about who you are and what you stand for as a group? Is this a goal that you want to be part of?

Retuning statement: "I choose to put my focus and energy into the groups that match who I am and choose to be. I release all others."

3. Do you have to wear a uniform in any of your groups? When wearing the uniform, do you feel different? What does this say about your individual power within the group? Do you feel pressure to dress a certain way in order to fit in? Would you still be accepted by the group if you decided to dress very differently from them?

4. Were you made fun of as a child? How did this make you feel? Did you try to fit in by dressing a certain way, or going against your own integrity to make yourself seem "cool"? How did you feel after doing this? Do you still feel pain over this now? Do you still operate from a desperate need to fit in—to have people like and accept you? Can you see that you are (and always were) a

beautiful, perfectly acceptable soul exactly as you are?

Retuning statement: "I am good enough in every way. I love and accept myself, and I flow with groups who love and accept me for me."

What are the membership requirements?

No matter what groups that you are part of, there are membership requirements that you must meet to first become part of the group, and then to remain in the group. For some groups, you are a member at birth, simply because of the color of your skin or your gender. For others, you **become** a member because of your financial status or chosen career. Yet others allow membership based on the simple payment of a membership fee.

While you end up choosing many of the groups in your life unconsciously, it is important to evaluate each group in terms of the required beliefs for membership. Looking at each group, ask yourself: What are the membership rules? How are you required to speak? Are there limits on how and why you can speak up or ask questions? How do you need to act to fit in? What are you required to believe in to be a part of this group? Do you even believe this group's set of beliefs?

And further, what is your reason for wanting to become a member in the first place? Are you looking for acceptance? Learning? Personal improvement? Become aware of your personal motivations for associating with the groups of your life. If any of your reasons for membership are based in limitation, fear, and low self-esteem, you are tuning into a group experience for the wrong reasons. You will limit your ability to create the best life for you by continuing to give your personal power to this kind of group.

This is especially true if membership is earned by going through some sort of hazing process or by accepting certain required core beliefs. If the process and beliefs are in alignment with what you want to create for your life, by all means, choose that path. However, if you are being humiliated, robbed of your individuality, and forced into a certain belief system that does not match your inherent desires for life, you are tuning into the belief, "My own needs are not as important as being accepted by others." Because of this, you will continue to tune into more and more experiences that negatively impact your sense of self and your ability to create your best life for you.

At the end of the day, realize that being accepted into any group is no different than being hired for a certain job (I know this sounds odd—just stick with me). In order to be hired into a certain job, the company must first decide that it has a need for your particular skills. You are then interviewed, found to match the present need, and hired.

The process is the same for membership in any of your groups. First, the group decides (consciously or unconsciously) that there is an opening that you just might be able to fill. For instance, maybe a group of friends needs a "cheerleader" personality or a "listener." Because you are able to fill that need, you are immediately accepted into this group of friends in that role.

What role do you fill for each of your groups? For instance, in your group of friends you might take on the role of "the funny one," or "the fat one." In your family, you might be "the black sheep," or "the peacemaker." For your church, you might fill their need for new members. In your work group, you might be "the leader," "the gossip," or "the tech god." Whatever it is, the role that you play is essential for the current group dynamic to continue; if you remove your personal frequency from the group, the collective frequency is retuned into a different group experience.

It is important to realize that while some of these roles are taken on by choice, many are taken on because of early programming by your family. For instance, if your parents were abusive when you were a child, you may have become "the protector" of your siblings, taking all the beatings yourself. Or, because your mom was constantly depressed, you were given the role of "caretaker" for everyone and everything. Because of that which you encountered as a child, you were simply programmed to

163

become what your family needed of you, and you are likely still operating in that role to this day.

It is time to become conscious of the roles that you play, and to resign from any that limit you. However, should you decide to leave any of your current groups or refuse to continue to play your current role, be aware that you will likely be greeted with much resistance and a good helping of group pressure designed to cause you to acquiesce to their needs. The group, feeling the loss of your energy, may try to push you back into your old role—either by outright begging (believe me, it happens), by making fun of you, or by making you feel guilty for the loss that they feel. If this is an issue for you, please go to Station 2 and work through the beginning sections on relationships, and also work through all of Station 3. These two workbooks will assist you in being authentic to yourself even in the face of serious peer pressure.

If you start to feel frightened or alone, always remember that you **always** fit in with the oneness of the Source (there is no better group). Further, as a member of the "life-creator" group that **is** the Source, you already have a very important role that you play. Believe in your unlimited potential, and create your life in alignment with unconditional love for yourself and others. Now, that's a role that you will **love** to fulfill!

Questions:

1. What role do you play in each of your groups? If this were a job, what title would you have? What are you required to do as part of this job—your "job duties"? Why is this role important to the mission of the group? What needs do you fulfill? Are you comfortable with this role, or would you like to "resign"? What role would you **like** to play? What can you do now to get this new job?

Retuning statement: "I am _____." In the space, insert your new job title, and end with "and I have the power to create that now."

2. Do you feel peer pressure to do or be a certain role in your groups? Do you feel powerless to change?

Retuning statement: "I have the right to create my life in a way that works for me. I create my own reality."

3. What are the beliefs of your group? Are these beliefs empowering and loving, or are they flowing with negativity, judgment, and fear? Do you disagree with any of the group beliefs? Do any of the group beliefs go against your innate sense of reason? Do you feel that you can question the leaders of your group (or the group as a whole) about the things that you disagree with? If not, why not? Would you be shunned from the group until you acquiesced?

Retuning statement: "I am able to think and speak for myself within a group setting. I have the power and right to stand up against the things that I do not believe."

4. Do you believe in an "us-versus-them" mentality? Do you have prejudices about any group of people? This week, research one or two of the groups for whom you feel fear, hate, or prejudice. What do you find out about this group of people? Do you find that the generalities that you believed in are actually false? Can you release your prejudice, and replace it with a new understanding of the oneness of all people? What would happen if you told others of your new understanding? Do you think that you could enlighten the groups that you are part of with this new way of thinking? If not, why not?

Retuning statement: "I choose to be loving to all groups of people. We are all one."

5. How accepting of new people (outsiders) is your family or other group? If they do not readily accept new members, what does this say about their group beliefs? What fears might they be operating on? Do you find yourself acting in the same ways with new people?

Retuning statement: "I am open to and accepting of all people. I choose to view life with love."

6. Are there any groups which you wish to leave? What fears do you have about leaving? How will your life change if you do leave?
7. Do you get any benefits by totally believing whatever the group says? Do you feel absolved of your personal responsibility for how you create by believing totally in the group's way of thinking? How are you rewarded for this behavior? Are you greeted with open arms when you agree to accept their way of thinking?

Retuning statement: "I know that I am responsible for creating my own life. I love and accept myself."

8. What must you do in order to prove your loyalty to the group? Have you ever done something against your personal ethics in order to fit in? How do you feel about that now?
9. What do the laws of your society say about your group values? Are different groups of people held up to different laws? Do the punishments really fit the crimes? If not, how not? How can you get involved in the process of changing what you see as unfair or wrong? For instance, you can write letters, sign petitions, call political representatives, raise funds, or pass information along to others to expose unfairness. It is up to you how you do it, but find a cause that is important to you, and use your personal power to begin to change the outcome of that issue.

An exercise in popular thought

The media has great control over how we as a society view different world events and groups of people. To understand the negative messages that you might be getting from sources such as magazines, advertising, news programs, and TV shows, I would like you to watch some TV news programs for one hour every day this week. Write down each of the top stories of the day. For each one, what is the message of the story? Did you feel that the newscaster had any particular slant one way or the other? How many stories were "good" news? How many were "bad"? What messages are you being given about the state of the world? What messages are you being given about the behavior or beliefs of certain racial, cultural or religious groups? How about what is considered "normal" by society?

Watch each of the commercials carefully. How are different groups of people portrayed in advertising? What messages do you receive about what is "normal"? What physical attributes or actions are celebrated positively? What negative messages do you notice?

By doing this exercise, you will quickly become aware that for every hour of TV that you watch, you are inundated with thousands of messages about public opinion and popular thought. Further, you are given an enormous amount of frightening images that are designed to cause you to believe a certain school of thought. The more that you see these stories and opinions, the more you take these perspectives on as truth. Once you are subconsciously programmed with all of these beliefs, you then begin to seek experiences that flow with that energy, for good or for ill. Because of this, there is simply no question that it is absolutely essential that you become vigilant about that which you take on as a belief.

Anytime that you are feeling the pressure to conform to popular thought, go back to Principle 5 and reread it. Reconnect with the reality that the only opinion of your life that matters is your own. Truly accept your personal authority, and choose to make **only** the very best beliefs **your** most popular thoughts!

Your family, you, and the "symbols of survival"

What are the "symbols of survival"?

They are the physical indications of how well a person or group is surviving in this world: such "symbols" as money, shelter, clothing, and food.

As you now know, while each symbol seems very physical (and is, in a way), each really simply represents a certain energy frequency, or wave-archetype. They become symbols of the group's beliefs about their ability to not only survive, but **thrive**. Just as your level of self-esteem tunes you into positive or negative experiences, your group's collective level of "group-esteem" tunes your group into success or failure, depending on the frequency.

If your group has a negative vision of itself (something that you will have identified in the "mission" section above), it will tune into the experiences of lack of funding, failed enterprises, broken-down homes, and an inability to achieve its goals in any way. However, if your group flows with a positive vision, it will tune into great success, financial ease, and perfect satisfaction with life.

Many of your beliefs about your ability to create group success were set in your childhood through your experience with your primary family. In fact, a good part of your family's identity was tied up in how well the group manifested these symbols of survival. For instance, the house that you lived in was a physical manifestation of how you felt about yourselves as a group. If your family had low "group-esteem," your family home may have been messy and uncared for, exhibiting the group feeling that you were not worth much. Your experience of lack and dissatisfaction was likely increased as you compared yourself to other kids— especially if some of your friends lived in beautiful, opulent, and well-cared for houses. This would have been made worse if your group beliefs tuned you into an experience of poverty, where you had to wear the same clothes to school every day, or did not have money for lunch. If other kids made fun of you for your family's lack, you will still have fears about your own ability to create prosperity and abundance. Due to these preprogrammed presets, you may tune into negative group experiences now, for instance, you may have difficulty providing for your own family, or might end up associated with a failing business or other organization.

In fact, unless you have consciously chosen to retune negative group beliefs from your childhood, they are still programmed into your mind—and are still causing you loads of difficulty. By retuning these problem presets, you can create prosperity with all the symbols of survival in all of your groups!

Questions

1. What were your family's beliefs about money? Were you financially well-off as a child? Were you poor? What were you taught about your own ability to make money?

Retuning statement: "I am allowed to be successful. I am allowed to create my own relationship with wealth."

2. Have you done better financially than others in your family? Do you feel conflicted about this?
3. What is your family's relationship to food? How do your traditional foods identify the group that you belong to? Do you have behavior patterns associated with your relationship to food, for instance, cleaning your plate or cooking certain foods for the holidays? Do you notice that your eating patterns are different when you are with your family? Do you choose to eat very differently from your family (for instance, being a vegetarian)? Is this accepted? Was food hard to come by when you were a child? Do you hoard food now?

Retuning statement: "I have a positive relationship with food. I have more than enough."

4. Are there acceptable and unacceptable careers in the eyes of your family? Do you feel pressure to go into the family business or follow in a parent's footsteps? If you do not do this, what are the likely consequences? If you decide to acquiesce, what are the consequences to you, your happiness, and your health?

Retuning statement: "I have a right to choose a life that meets my needs. When I create happiness in myself, I create happiness for others."

5. What kind of home did you have as a child? What did it say about your group identity? Do you believe that you must replay that reality and group identity in your life now? What kind of home would you like to have? Do you feel conflicted about your right or ability to have this home, when compared with your family home?

Retuning statement: "I deserve to create in a way that I desire. I can move beyond my family's experience of the world. I am safe."

6. What kinds of clothing did you have as a child? Did you have all designer brands, or did you have only hand-me-downs? What did this tell you about your family's ability to survive in the world? What did it tell others about you and your family's identity? Can you see that you now have the choice to create your experience of life any way that you want—that you can have your own flowing experience with all of the symbols of survival? If not, why not? What beliefs are holding you back?

Retuning statement: "I am able to thrive in the world. I easily create all that I could possibly need and want."

7. Please go through the above questions for other groups that you are part of now, especially those that are failing or doing badly financially. What negative group beliefs do you have in these groups? What does the group believe about itself and its identity? How can you help to retune any negative frequencies? In the same way that "I am" creates a moment that immediately retunes your personal identity into a new reality, use "we are" with a positive phrase, for instance, "We are winners," or "We are successful." Use the Principle of Repetition, repeating this retuning statement as much as possible with the difficult group.

Retuning statement: "We can create a positive collective experience."

Station 1: Body language

From genetic disease to a properly functioning immune system, this Station is essential for your overall health.

Just as the groups in your life are supposed to support and protect you, your immune system is designed to do the same. When it functions well, it successfully fights off invaders and keeps you in perfect health. However, your immune function will be compromised when you flow with negative group beliefs and experiences, especially when you feel that the group is turning against you. For instance, you may get a cold or virus right after you have had an argument or difference of opinion with some primary group in your life—perhaps you tried to stand up for yourself with your family, and the entire family turned against you. Or, perhaps you are accused of disloyalty by your parents, when all that you were doing is trying to work out an equitable split for the holidays with your in-laws (and, by the way, this is why so many people get sick during the holidays—it is caused by the pressure of dealing with competing families). However it plays out for you, the stress of going against group thought will often compromise your

171

immune system, making you vulnerable to sickness.

And, while you may believe that germs are contagious, what is really contagious is the belief in it. For instance, when everyone that you know is saying that "everyone at work (or school, or church, etc.) is getting the flu," you are sure to resonate with the experience of the flu—and you might just tune into this frequency.

Disease in Station 1 can manifest in other ways as well. If you were taught that "you don't move away from home," you may experience pain or disease in the legs, hips, and knees if you decide to move away. After all, the function of your legs is not only to stabilize you; it is also to carry you forward in life. If you feel guilt about moving forward into a new life that is far away from your family home, this can tune you into disease in this Station. Further, if you choose to stay in a group situation out of obligation, you may either have pain in your hips, or you might develop varicose veins; this is due to the fact that you are literally stopping the flow of life (blood), and choosing to create obstacles with your inability to move forward or stand up for yourself.

Whatever the issue, first find out the function of the affected body part—what does the body part do for your body? Then write down a description of the disease—how it progresses, what it does, what is malfunctioning now. Look at what you have written. How can you relate the description of the disease and the proper functioning of the body part with the issues of this Station? Look at the language that you have used to find clues for the issue.

Questions:

1. Does your family have any beliefs about genetic diseases? For instance, "All the men in our family have bad hearts," "We all get diabetes," or "We're just big people. There's nothing we can do about it." Do you find yourself tuning into this reality?

Retuning statement: "I create my own health. I believe in my personal power."

2. Notice the body language that is used by others in your groups. Do you move in the same ways that they do? Did you take on the mannerisms of one or both of your parents? Do you have any secret handshakes or signs that show you as one of that group?

Action plan for resetting Station 1:

✓ Select 2-3 retuning statements to reset your preset.
✓ Go to page 409 and take the Reality Type Test, if you have not already done so.
✓ Select 4 Reality Type exercises, and do these for 40 days.
✓ Become aware of the dynamics that you are manifesting in your groups.
✓ Do not allow yourself to automatically follow the group. Make sure that you agree with the direction that they are going **before** you go along for the ride.
✓ Believe that you deserve unconditional love and respect in all of your groups.
✓ View all life as one.
✓ Believe in your ability to create positive group experiences.
✓ Accept and love yourself first—only then can you choose to be part of groups that are unconditionally accepting and loving.
✓ Do not believe that you are limited because of the way that you grew up. Believe in your ability to create the life that you desire.

STATION 2

The Energy of Individual Dynamics and Creative Power

Station Motto: I have the ability to be a great life-creator for myself.

Location of Station: Lower belly

Problem Playlist: If you are preset with negative Station 2 beliefs, you will find that you have some of these behavior patterns and difficulties:

- Being in relationships where you feel powerless and unable to stand up for yourself, such as emotionally or physically abusive relationships, or co-dependent relationships.
- Bullying others, or feeling a need to always control other people
- Never finding lovers, friends, or business partners that truly meet your needs.
- Difficulty or fear about birthing your creative ideas.

175

- Having others take your ideas as their own.
- Being in relationships where fighting is the norm, not the exception.
- Having stifled creativity, which causes problems ranging from an inability to close new sales or grow your business, to writer's block and an extreme fear of rejection.
- Finding it difficult to meet your personal needs—for instance, being unable to make money, get the raise that you deserve, own the cars or homes that you desire, or create the opportunities necessary to attain any other material goods that you desire.
- Having a conflicted relationship with food—for instance, eating for emotional reasons, or always cleaning your plate, even if you are full.
- Having negative or unfulfilling sexual encounters.

Station 2 Body Issues: If you are tuning into negativity here, you will find that you have disease, pain, or extra weight in these areas:

- lower vertebrae
- pelvis
- sexual organs
- bladder
- large intestine
- hip
- buttocks

Attention, please: Relationships should not be hard work!

It is not "normal" to have difficult, unsatisfying relationships, no matter what anyone has told you. In fact, if your relationships **are** hard work, it indicates that you have negative beliefs that are tuning you into patterns of fighting, struggle, power plays, and annoyance. Worse yet, these patterns are likely repeating throughout your life, causing you to live the same issues over and over again.

After all, how many times have you had the exact same problems in different relationships? Maybe you repeatedly choose the emotionally or physically abusive person, ending up playing out the same power dynamic time and time again. Or, you move from job to job with the exact same kind of controlling, micromanaging boss, each time feeling that you are unappreciated for the work that you are doing. Perhaps, no matter how many people that you meet, you always end up becoming friends with people who take advantage of you, asking you to put aside your personal needs in order to fulfill theirs.

And, once you have managed to get yourself in the same bad relationship once again, you likely throw your hands up in despair, crying out to the Source, "How did I manage to get myself in this situation again? What have I done to deserve this?"

You now know that you haven't done **anything** to deserve the streak of bad relationships that plague your life. Rather, you keep choosing the same relationships because that is what is programmed into your mind as what you deserve and are expecting; it is simply a preset that is tuning you into the same experiences over and over. Because of this, it does not matter who the individual is **physically**; it is more important to view each person in your life as a **specific energetic frequency** that you repeatedly tune into due to your preset expectations. Since you always choose the energy that matches yours, for each difficult relationship in your life, ask yourself, "What negative beliefs do I now hold that is tuning me into this type of experience?" Answer **that** question and you will know the key to getting rid of that pattern from your life for good.

To begin the process of reprogramming your limiting relationship beliefs, choose first to believe with your whole body, mind, and spirit that you **have the power** to create the best, most fulfilling relationships for you. To fully tune into this power, you must be willing to take responsibility for your part in creating the dynamic of every relationship. Additionally, once you are conscious of the underlying issues that are causing you to seek the same patterns again and again, you must be willing to change those patterns, **even if it means releasing some of these relationships from your life.**

Are you ready to use your personal creative power to fix your relationship "flow"? You can start by evaluating every relationship in your life in terms of these three basic power dynamics:

Major Dynamic 1: You are the authority in the relationship, drawing power from the other person.

This relationship is built on your need to control others, perhaps out of a fear of abandonment, or perhaps it makes you feel powerful to force others to prove themselves to you. In this relationship, you detach yourself from the best, most loving relationships by asking others to meet your expectations of them, resulting in dissatisfaction on both sides. Resentment, anger, disappointment, and passive aggressive behavior are common here.

Major Dynamic 2: The other person is the authority, and draws power from you.

This relationship is built on your belief that you must prove yourself worthy of love and respect. In this dynamic, you believe that you are not good enough just as you are, and therefore, you do not deserve better. Due to that fact, you often give up who you truly are in order to please the other person—or to fit into **their** mold of who they expect you to be.

Major Dynamic 3: You have a balanced and harmonious relationship, where each individual is exactly who they are without compromise.

This relationship is built on both your belief that you can love all

178

beings unconditionally, and your true desire to express your Source-power in authentic, loving partnership with another spirit. This is co-creation at its best and most limitless.

Which one of these dynamics do most of your relationships fit into?

While many of your relationships likely fit into Dynamics 1 and 2, the reality is that every relationship in your life can and should flow with Dynamic 3. The truth is that you should never have to control another person or give up who you truly are in order to keep a relationship going. You should never be afraid of another person, and there is no need for fighting and anger. You should not feel exhausted, depressed, belittled, taken advantage of, betrayed, disrespected, or unloved in a relationship with **anyone**.

So, believe in your ability to create Dynamic 3 relationships! No matter how long you have suffered from frustrating relationships, you can stop the madness now. The truth is that you have **every ability** to create wonderful, easy, flowing relationships in work, love, friendship, or any other relationship.

Are you beginning to believe this? I hope so. In the upcoming sections, you will learn about several relationship sub-dynamics that typify how these power plays manifest. As you go through these sections, you will likely start to recognize the dynamic at play in various relationships in your life. When you do, jot down the names of the people involved. After identifying which power balance each of your relationships match, you will get a specific retuning statement in the "questions" section that follows, which will reset that preset to create flowing relationships in every area of your life.

Let's get to work!

Sub-dynamic 1: The parental repeat dynamic

Do you believe that you will marry a man just like your father? Or, if you are a man, a woman just like your mother?

If so, you will have relationships that mimic your parents' relationship exactly.

This is a tremendously common belief—so much so that I see people replaying their parents' relationship everywhere that I go. More disturbing, people who are in these relationships either think that this is a "normal" relationship, and therefore do nothing to change even the most dysfunctional situation, or they are completely unaware that this is what they are tuning into, causing both parties to react out of unconscious habit, rather than a real response based on their personal needs and desires. Either way, both parties are frustrated and unfulfilled, but neither knows how to do anything different.

Of course, if you are one of the lucky ones whose parents had a "Dynamic 3" relationship—one where both people are able to be who they are as individuals, and who respect each other's needs and desires—then, by all means, replicate this relationship in your own life, if you choose. However, if you witnessed dysfunction, control, antiquated notions of gender roles, limitation, abuse, fighting, disrespect, or any of the other ways that the negative dynamics can manifest, evaluate whether this is an experience that you really want to repeat in your own life.

To increase your consciousness about your own presets, become aware of how and why you are reacting in a certain way. Do you begin to notice that you react to issues within your relationship in the same ways that your mother or father did? Do you expect the exact same things from your spouse that your parents did from each other? Do you believe that you must replay your parents' dynamic? Do you believe that there are specific roles that each of you should play? Do you become angry when your partner refuses to fill that role?

Then, the next time that you feel yourself becoming angry, stressed out, or irritable about something that your partner is doing, stop and ask yourself, "Am I truly feeling this way? Or is this reaction simply an old preset learned from my parents' relationship?" If you realize that it is not an authentic reaction from who you are, then release the patterned response, and change your reaction to one that is in alignment with who **you** really are.

Use your personal power to choose your **own** love relationship for your **own** reasons, and discontinue believing in preset notions of how marriage or love "should" be—or what is "normal" to those around you. After all, if every one of us believed in our own power to choose a **personally** fulfilling relationship, there would be far less fighting, dissatisfaction, and divorce—and better yet, every child would be raised in an environment where they had respectful, unlimited love relationships modeled for them. Now, **that** could truly change the world!

Break the negative pattern now. Choose to use your creative Source-power to create truly loving, supportive relationships that allow you to be true to yourself!

Sub-dynamic 2: The god complex dynamic

Do you have people in your life that tell you, "It's my way or the highway"?

Do **you** demand that others bend to your will?

In the "god complex dynamic," one person is the absolute authority in the relationship (playing the part of "god") and the other plays the totally submissive role (becoming the "follower"), going along with the orders of the "god" exactly, either because they feel that they have no choice, are afraid of losing the relationship, or do not trust their own personal authority at all.

As described in Principle 5, the person with absolute authority can be your religious teacher, doctor, friend, parents, boss, coach, or even co-workers, just to name a few of the possibilities. Regardless of who plays the "god" in your relationships, you are in a relationship that negates your personal power and weakens you.

If you play the "follower" in this dynamic, then you are preset with a belief that you do not trust yourself to make good decisions on your own, or to even navigate life itself with your own instincts. Because you don't trust your creative power or feel yourself worthy of the love and admiration of others, you **need** a leader or mentor to guide you—and, by choosing to be totally in their power, you "earn" the "god's" love and approval. As a side bonus of this dynamic, you may feel a strange sense of freedom by following an authority completely, as it releases you from having to take responsibility for yourself, your decisions, or your actions. However, the downside of this is extreme; by giving away your personal power, you will only create the life that the other person wants, never living in a way that is in any way authentic to you.

On the other hand, you may be playing the role of "god" in your relationships. If so, you are preset with the belief that you must control others in order to feel good about yourself. In this case, because you believe that you are unlovable for who you are, you overpower people in order to gain respect—a word that, in your mind, is synonymous with "love." Due to the fact that this subconscious desire for respect and "love" is so strong, you may blow up any time that someone questions you or your ultimate control. While undesirable, this kind of reaction is actually caused by a tremendous fear of being powerless and alone—after all, without "followers," you cannot be a "god."

When this dynamic is pushed to its worst potential, it manifests as physical and emotional abuse. In this case, the "god" fears losing the "love" of the "follower" so intensely that they must do whatever they can to ensure that the person never leaves them, and increasing the control by physical and mental intimidation and brainwashing is the only way that they know how. Unfortunately, the dynamic is such that the person receiving the abuse has been trained by their abuser (usually for years) that they are unlovable, so they believe that they deserve this mistreatment, and, more often than not, just give in and stay.

Whether you play the part of the "follower" or the "god," release this dynamic. As outlined in Principle 5, you are the only authority over your life—and you are the authority over your own life **only**. You have the ability to create flowing, beautiful relationships where you are loved and respected for who you are, and you can extend this love and respect to all that you are with. Trust yourself to create the love and respect that you desire, without a need to control or be controlled.

Sub-dynamic 3: The blackmail dynamic

Have you ever gone along with someone's demands just to stop the feelings of guilt and intimidation that accompanied the request? Have ever you gone against your own needs and personal ethics to fill another person's need? Have you ever given in, simply because you are afraid of standing up for yourself?

If you answered "yes" to any of these questions, then you have been energetically blackmailed of your power, and that needs to stop!

The blackmail dynamic can be an extension of both the "parental repeat" and the "god-complex" dynamic, or it can stand alone. Regardless, you will know that the blackmail dynamic is at play when someone uses fear, guilt, intimidation, and obligation to force you to do their bidding, causing you to feel that it would just be better to give in to their needs, rather than standing up for yourself and saying "no."

Make no mistake: the "blackmailer" is powerful—he or she knows just how to push your buttons to trigger you to react a certain way. For instance, maybe your fiancé knows that you try to be a giving, kind person. All he has to do is call you "selfish," and you will automatically give in to his requests, just to prove what an unselfish person that you really are. Perhaps your dad knows that you always put family first (a button he programmed himself when you were a child), so all he has to do to get you to cancel plans with your friends and help him work on his car is to say, "I thought that you cared about your family. I guess not." Or, your boss knows that you are a perfectionist about your work. To get you to take on more work, even when you **really** want to spend more time with your family, she just needs to say, "I noticed that your last couple of reports had a few errors. I thought that you cared more about the quality of your work. You need to prove to me that you can handle this project."

In each case, you will give in to the blackmailer's requests simply because your triggers tune you into a habitual reaction. Although you know that you are going against what is best for you, you will convince yourself that giving in to this **one** request is not that big of a deal; however, the truth is that it is a huge deal. Every single time that you go against what is best for you, you tune into the "I'm not important or powerful" frequency, and that tunes you into more experiences where everyone else is more powerful than you. Worse, it completely negates your ability to create the best life for yourself; rather, you will always be limited to creating experiences that fulfill others needs, not your own. Inevitably, you will begin to resent the "blackmailer," resulting in frustration and anger at both the "blackmailer" **and** at yourself for giving in to him or her time and time again.

In contrast, **you** can play the part of "blackmailer" in your relationships, using fear, obligation, intimidation, and guilt to force others to do what you want. For instance, to make sure that your girlfriend does not leave you, you tell her that you will go back to drinking or kill yourself if she does. Maybe you want your adult kids to spend more time with you, so you mention that you "won't be around forever" to get them to acquiesce to your desires.

Becoming the "blackmailer" may get you what you want temporarily, but it never allows you to get what you truly need: the joy and fulfillment that comes from relationships where people give to you freely out of true love and respect. Even worse, being the "blackmailer" robs you of your ability to use your creative power in a positive way, creating many experiences where you will feel disappointed and unfulfilled when others do not give in to your pressure.

If you feel that you have "The Blackmail Dynamic" as a pattern in your life, I highly recommend that you read *Emotional Blackmail: When the People in Your Life Use Fear, Obligation, and Guilt to Manipulate You*, by Susan Forward, Ph.D. In this book, she explains not only the many ways that this dynamic plays out, but gives you a concrete plan of action to stand up to your blackmailers and take back your power.

Sub-dynamic 4: The helper dynamic

This could also be called the "I-pick-up-every-broken-winged-bird-dynamic," because that is certainly how it manifests itself. Over and over again, you will find yourself becoming the caretaker, fixer-upper, knight-in-shining-armor for the person in distress. On one hand, this plays to your ego—you become powerful by being the one with all the solutions. On the other, it shows that you have a preset belief that you do not deserve to have an equal give and take in a relationship—instead, you **prove** that you are lovable by helping this helpless soul.

Of course, **you** could play the part of the broken-winged bird, getting all that you want by allowing others to take care of you. If you find yourself engaging in this kind of expression, it is likely that you got what you wanted as a child when you acted sick, sad, or played into someone's need to be a caretaker. Truthfully, whoever played the part of "fixer-upper" in your life needed the dynamic as much as you did—your neediness made him or her feel needed and valuable.

Either way, this dynamic robs both of you of your personal power, and of a truly loving relationship. If you are the "fixer-upper," then you only get love if you fix or save the other person from whatever ails them (this is very conditional love, obviously). If you are the "broken-winged bird," then you never get the satisfaction of using your creative Source-power to create the best life for **yourself**.

Sub-dynamic 5: The suffering martyr dynamic

This one can be an extension of any of the above dynamics. In this case, you are fully aware that you are in a relationship with a person who is abusive, unreasonable, and unchangeable, but you stay in the relationship to show the world what a good, holy, or caring person that you are. Doing this allows you to get attention, admiration, and sympathy from others, making you "powerful."

You are a "suffering martyr" if you command every conversation with tales of how difficult the other person is, or how much effort you have made to make things work. Moreover, if others frequently say to you, "Oh, you poor thing—after all you have done for him," or "I just don't know how you put up with her behavior. You are a much better person than I," then this is absolutely a dynamic that is playing out in your life and relationships.

Many times this dynamic is encouraged by the religious tradition that you believe in. Sometimes, divorce is seen as a blasphemy against the Source; other times, you will be told that a wife must hold together the marriage, no matter what. By staying in a bad relationship, you not only show yourself as good enough for the Source's love, but you also get approval from others in your church—both desirable rewards.

The problem is that this is a total misuse of your power and a misinterpretation of the Source's desire for you. You **always** have the right to leave a bad relationship—after all, the entire purpose for your existence is to create life in alignment with the highest frequencies, and I am certain that staying in a bad relationship is a low frequency existence.

Beyond just the religious underpinnings of the marriage relationship, you can choose to be "the martyr" in **any** other relationship, using your suffering to gain power in the rest of your life. For instance, perhaps your boss takes advantage of you, yelling at you and overworking you for little pay. You certainly have the choice to leave, but if you stay, you can command the attention of friends and family who feel sorry for your plight. This gives you tremendous power, allowing you to control conversations with tales of the horrors that you endure, gaining admiration for being a good and devoted person by staying "despite it all." The "suffering martyr" card allows you to turn the lack of control that you have in one relationship into major control in others.

However this dynamic manifests in your life, it is never the best use of your Source-power. Why not get attention by doing some truly good things for yourself and others? Why not command respect by taking control of your life, and using your Source-power to create the exact life that you desire? Of course, people won't feel sorry for you anymore, but you will get something even better: respect and admiration for **yourself**!

Sub-dynamic 6: The "gotta go it alone" dynamic

Do you tend to do everything yourself because you believe that "if you want something done right, you've got to do it yourself"?

If so, you believe that no one could possibly do anything up to your standards, and so, you "gotta go it alone." Because of this belief, you will either totally avoid entering into individual relationships because you assume you will be disappointed, or when you do, you'll have a pattern of dealing with others who do not come through for you. For instance, you'll hire a graphic designer who cannot understand your vision and does the opposite of what you want, causing you to have to do the graphics yourself. Or, you'll have a business partner who never does anything that he says that he will, leaving you holding the bag with clients. Maybe you'll have employees that continuously mess up and never do what you ask of them, causing you to have to cover their work. However this dynamic manifests, the end result will be the same— you will deal with the same let downs and disappointments time and time again.

This dynamic may come from your fear of being controlled— especially if you have seen others in your life be controlled by their significant others or other authority figures. It may come from an inherently independent streak, and your desire to never owe anyone anything. It might also be because you hate asking others for help, feeling that you look weak or needy if you do. It certainly can come from a desire to appear perfect and fully capable in every situation and with everyone.

I truly understand, as I have had to battle this dynamic (and the set of negative beliefs causing it) myself. However, when you open your heart to the possibility of finding others that can and will bring your vision into being and truly be fulfilling and helpful to you, you will create experiences where the power of co-creation creates something better than either of you could do alone. When you keep your intention to finding a flowing and balanced relationship with someone that fills your needs exactly, you will flow with this experience— leaving your fears of control and loss of independence behind.

What a relief it is to feel you can count on someone else to help you! Release your fears, and allow a true partnership to form with someone who complements you exactly.

Sub-dynamic 7: The wish-fulfillment dynamic

Do you expect someone else to make you happy?

Are you in a relationship with someone who expects **you** to be the sole provider of their personal fulfillment?

If so, you are tuning into this dynamic.

I cannot tell you how common this dynamic is—or how detrimental to everyone involved. If you are the one who expects others to make you happy, then you have a preset belief that you are restricted in your ability to get what you want in life, so you choose relationships with others based on what you believe that they can provide for you. For instance, you might marry for money, or become friends with people who you feel would advance your career.

On the other hand, if you are the one that consistently chooses people who depend upon you for their happiness, you are flowing with the belief that you are responsible for others' wish-fulfillment (likely something that you learned as a child). Further, you believe that you must **earn** love by granting other people's wishes, instead of deserving love simply for being who you are. In this case, you might have a spouse that pressures you to provide everything that they desire, whether it is more money, jewelry, cars, or a certain lifestyle.

Whichever part you play, this dynamic never leads to true happiness and love. When one person is totally dependent upon the other person to provide their desires, it is just a matter of time until the "wish-fulfiller" crumbles under the weight of this responsibility. Additionally, the burden of each person trying to be what the other wants is exhausting, resulting in resentment, disappointment, fighting, and possibly the termination of the relationship. Of course, when this happens, it may **seem** that the other person has changed, but the truth is that they were going against their authentic self to try to be what you desired, building a relationship on a false foundation.

As with any of these dynamics, the energy of "wish-fulfillment" can show up in any of your relationships—work, family, friendships, and others—and you can play either role. For instance, you may play the "wish-fulfiller" with your mother when you have a baby because she thinks that becoming a grandmother will make **her** happy. Or, you may play the opposite role, requiring that your mother fulfill **your** happiness by having her purchase you the things that you want, such as make-up, jewelry, or even providing a down payment on a house.

Either way, you will know that you are in a "wish-fulfillment dynamic," if you entered into the relationship expecting to mold or change this person into what you truly desired. If that is the case, then you never loved the person for who they really are, but for the potential that you saw in them to be who you wanted them to be. Perhaps you are the one that was to be changed or molded? You are not being loved for who you are, but what you can provide.

The main problem with this kind of relationship is that you are looking outside yourself for happiness, when it is an **internal** creation. In this way, you have bought into the romantic notion that someone else completes you—when that is never true. You are who you are—and fully complete—**as you are**, as is the other person. When you love yourself and know who you are and what you want, you can then choose a person who does not complete you so much as allow you to be exactly who you are, without restriction or expectation. Because of a true respect for each other, you will work in flowing partnership to co-create a life together, where each person is both totally authentic to who he or she is, **and** is totally committed to the collective vision of the relationship, because the relationship allows each of you to enhance and express your innate "you-ness."

Understand that you create your life and no one else's. You are not responsible for someone else's happiness, and they are not responsible for yours. You must make choices that allow you to grant your own wishes and live the most unlimited life possible, and it is the other person's responsibility to do the same.

Sub-dynamic 8: The unconditional love dynamic

This is a sub-dynamic of "Major Dynamic 3" from above, and it is the ultimate relationship experience that you could possibly have. In this dynamic, two spirits work together with unconditional love, both for each other **and** for themselves as individuals. It is a relationship that is filled with ease and joy, where every moment of the relationship feels completely balanced and respectful.

In this dynamic, neither person expects anything from the other, and each person is exactly who they are without fear or reservation. In fact, when this kind of relationship is at its best, each individual is free to become **more** of who they are—to express themselves in a way that is totally consistent with what each wants and needs as an individual. Each person gives freely of themselves—not because they have to—but because they **want** to.

It almost goes without saying that all communication in this relationship is loving, respectful, and filled with compassion. Each person can express himself or herself with openness and honesty, and the other will always receive it with openness and honesty. There is no manipulation. There is no need to control. There is no concern that the other will do or say something willingly mean or hurtful. There is only total unconditional love.

This is the relationship that you should have with every person that you meet. This is the ultimate expression of who you are in the world, and who you can be in relationship with another.

I can speak from experience here, because I am lucky enough to have this relationship with my husband. Neither of us is ever anything other than exactly who we are. We never fight—not because we are holding back—but because we are so respectful of each other's thoughts, feelings, and personal position on any issue that there is just no need. Our relationship is not in **any** way hard work—rather, it is a delight that grows and tends to itself. We love our life together and unconditionally support each other in everything that we do, but we are each responsible for our own happiness. We make time for each other, not out of obligation, but out of a true desire to be with each other.

It is my experience with my husband that taught me how fantastic all relationships can and should be when you know who you are, and you refuse to settle for people who do not match you. Every relationship that you have—whether in work, love, friendship, or family—should flow with ease and joy, and you should always be able to be who you are without restriction. If you cannot be, then you are tuning into one of the problem dynamics above.

Be unconditionally loving to all beings—**including yourself**—and you will begin to tune into unconditional love in all your relationships.

Questions:

1. Write down the name of every person with whom you have a personal relationship now. Beside each name, indicate whether you are in control of the relationship (Major Dynamic 1), the other person is in control (Major Dynamic 2), or you are balanced and flowing (Major Dynamic 3).
2. Look through the sub-dynamics above. For each relationship, write down which sub-dynamic that you feel

is going on, and why you feel this. Are you re-creating former relationships in your life? What beliefs do you have about your personal authority in each relationship? What are you getting from being in the relationship? Do you have to compromise yourself to maintain each relationship? Why do you feel that you need to compromise yourself? What would happen if you decided to stand up for yourself or just leave the relationship?

3. Do you have any unconditionally loving relationships? What is that experience like as opposed to the difficult relationships?

4. Do you choose relationships that match your parents' dynamic exactly? Do you want this dynamic to be true for you? Can you see that you have the ability to define the relationship that you desire, and that you are neither fated nor required to mimic your parents' relationship? Do you have any fears about breaking this dynamic? How do you react in the same ways as your parents did to your spouse or partner?

Retuning statement: "I am free to create the life and relationships that I desire for myself. I am not fated to live as my parents do (or did)."

5. Do you find yourself choosing relationships where you are belittled, controlled, or abused? Does someone else have absolute authority over you? Do you feel blackmailed into doing what others want? Where did you get the belief that you were unlovable? Did you grow up in a home where you saw this dynamic play out? Can you see that you no longer need to repeat this pattern? Are you afraid of changing this dynamic, because you may have to lose the relationship? What can you do today to show love for yourself?

Retuning statement: "I am lovable just as I am right now. I deserve respect, and I create relationships where we can both be loved and respected."

6. Do you find yourself getting into relationships for what the other person can do for you? Do you knowingly use others to get what you want? Do you feel that others need to make you happy? Is your love or friendship conditional—as in, "If you do this for me, I will love you"? Why do you feel that you do not have the power to create the life that you desire for yourself?

Retuning statement: "I have the authority to create the life that I desire for myself. I am powerful. I am creative."

7. Are you in relationships where you are trying to be what the other person wants you to be, even though it is against who you really are? Are you tired of this? Do you feel resentment toward the other person? How did you see other people in your life play out this dynamic? What can you do today to begin to create the life and relationship that you truly desire?

Retuning statement: "I am responsible for my own happiness. I create my own life to fulfill me."

8. Do you get attention by playing the "suffering martyr" in any of your relationships? How does this get you what you want? How difficult would it be for you to release this pattern and empower yourself to be a powerful life-creator for yourself?

Retuning statement: "I choose to empower myself to use my own creative power to create the best life for myself."

9. Are you afraid of losing your personal identity or freedom by being in a relationship? Do you feel the desire to "go it alone"? Have you seen other relationships where people gave up their rights or

personal identity to be in the relationship? Please note: there is absolutely nothing wrong with being independent or single, if that is what you wish. It is only a problem if you reject good relationships because you are afraid of losing who you are.

Retuning statement: "I attract relationships that allow me to be fully me, without restriction. I enjoy relating to others from a place of personal power and mutual sharing."

10. Are there other patterns that you see in your life? What would you name these dynamics? What beliefs have created these dynamics? How have you injured yourself or others in this dynamic?

Whatever these issues are for you, please design your own retuning statement to reset your preset.

Creating the partner of your dreams

Whether it is in love, work, friends, or family, there is a perfect partner out there for you—you just need to identify what you really want and need, focus your creative power on that goal, and watch this person appear out of the Source-hologram.

To start, write down each area of life where you desire better individual relationships. Maybe you are looking for the love of your life. Perhaps you are trying to build a business, and need to attract the right people to co-create your vision. Maybe you just want some friends that let you be just who you are. Whatever it is, write this intention down on the top of the page. Of course, make the intention in the positive and present—for example, "I attract my soul mate," or "I easily find the people who are best for my business."

Now, write down everything that you want this person to be. Write about who you are and how this person would compliment your innate abilities. Imagine how you would feel upon meeting this person, and write down those observations. Be very specific—you can specify things such as height, body type, personality, knowledge base, and personal philosophy. You can also search magazines to find pictures that seem to typify what you are describing.

Go to the "4 for 40" section of the book, and choose your exercises based on your personal strengths. Use this list of qualities along with the 4 for 40 system to connect with the exact person that you are seeking. Be grateful for this person coming into being, even before you physically see them.

Remember, the list that you have written down is exactly what you believe that you need and want in a partner. Do not settle for less. For instance, if you meet someone who has 10 out of 15 of the qualities, and think that you just might be able to mold them into the other 5, do not give in to this thought. When you refuse to settle, you will meet the person that matches you in the best possible ways, and you will have relationships that flow with love, respect, and joy. Believe in your power to create just what you need. When you meet this person, you will **know** that they are the right one—and that will be one of the best moments of your life.

You can retune any relationship right now

While there is no question that you can choose flowing and unlimited relationships, there may be relationships in your life now that are blocked, difficult, and stuck in an unhealthy power dynamic. I could certainly tell you to get rid of all of these relationships, but the reality is that many of them are with people who you feel that you cannot or do not want to leave, such as parents, siblings, friends, and business partners.

What to do? Obviously, it is not a positive use of your power to continue re-creating the same dynamic over and over with the same people. Because of this, I wanted to give two methods for keeping the relationship, but changing the dynamic. The great thing is that you can use these exercises in any and all experiences in order to retune the way that you are interacting with anyone— from a close friend to a potential client, or even a total stranger.

By using your personal power in this way, you can create flowing moments for yourself in even the most difficult relationships or experiences.

Exercise 1: Instant power transformation

Perhaps you are giving a brilliant presentation, when one of the audience members decides to go after you, attacking you and your ideas. Maybe you're at the ticket counter asking for an upgraded seat, when the employee decides to give you serious attitude. Or, your spouse comes home from work in a terrible mood, and decides to take it out on you.

Do you match the other person's attitude with more attitude? Or do you decide to take a different tact, choosing to respond with understanding and patience instead? If you're smart, you will do the latter, because giving attitude back will only escalate the situation, aggravating and enraging both of you.

Why is this so? Remember, when two matching waves meet up, they add their frequencies together and create a wave with double the intensity. So, when you meet resistance with resistance, all that you will accomplish is to **double the resistance**, which is why so many difficult situations escalate so quickly. After all, have you ever solved a problem by getting angry, bullying people, or giving someone attitude? Even if the situation resolved itself in your favor, you will have left the situation tuned into this frequency, which is hurting you in the long run. It belittles you and it belittles the people that you are dealing with. There has to be a better way.

Thankfully there is, and it has to do with the Principle of Resonance. Resonance is a scientific principle most easily explained by using musical strings as a model. A musical string can vibrate at almost any frequency, but it is usually tuned to a set frequency, such as the note of middle C. If you have two instruments near each other—let's say a piano and a guitar—and each have a string tuned to middle C, when you hit the middle C key on the piano, you will cause the guitar string to vibrate at the same frequency—even though you have not plucked that string.

Let's take this to the human level. If you view each of us as a musical instrument with an infinite number of possible vibrations, you will see that when one person is playing the vibration of "aggression," the other person may tune into that frequency, and begin acting and speaking in aggressive ways. Because these are matching-frequency vibrations, this increases the energy given to the "aggression" vibration, and doubles the aggression in the room.

However, every person **also** has the vibration of "peace," "joy," "respect," "understanding," and "co-creation" available as a possible frequency. When you choose to change your vibration to one that flows with any of these positive frequencies, you are causing the other person's personal "instrument" to begin to vibrate at that frequency as well. At this point, you increase the vibration to one of collective co-creation at the highest level— literally changing the reaction and eventual outcome of the situation by simply choosing to send out a positive signal. I guarantee you can and will leave the situation in a win-win mode, leaving everyone the better for it.

How do you use the Principle of Resonance to retune any experience right now? First, become aware of the energy being played by the other person (or people) in the situation. If it is angry, difficult, manipulative, or aggressive, take a moment to focus your mind on the vibrationally opposite thoughts. Bring your attention to your own energy and physical reactions, and breathe deeply to release any tension or anger that you feel. As you breathe deeply, imagine that you are sending the other person the energy of peace, joy, understanding, or whatever you desire. Allow yourself to feel your connection to this person, and choose to speak in ways that convey your understanding and true intention to create a positive experience for both of you.

This may seem over-simplified, but it really works. I have been at meetings where we were negotiating the purchase of one business by another business, and believe me, there was a lot of ego-based fear and anger at the table. As I felt the anger rise, I started to focus my mind on the idea of connectivity. In my mind, I repeated the words "love" and "oneness," breathing in deeply and allowing my body to become a conductor of these frequencies. Suddenly, the energy at the table changed, and the two people started talking about common ground and complimenting each other's businesses. Finally, the two sides came to an agreement that was equitable in every way to everyone.

Try this simple exercise any time that you sense that someone is coming at you from a place of anger or aggressiveness. You will be amazed at your ability to retune all experiences and relationships into true win-win situations, where understanding and joy is the **norm**, not the exception.

Exercise 2: Meeting new people every day

Are there some people in your life that frustrate the heck out of you, no matter what you do or say?

I am guessing that there are. However, you can change this relationship now to a more positive one, just by imagining that you are meeting this person for the first time.

I know this sounds silly, but the truth is that you are stuck in your current perception and expectations of everyone in your life—and most especially those that give you difficulty. In order to become aware of the preset expectations that you have of the difficult people in your life, start to notice how you talk about each of these people. What are the words that you use to describe him or her? Do you say that he or she is crazy, annoying, lazy, overbearing, manipulative, egotistical, a pain in the butt, or any other negative terminology? If so, you are expecting that this person is **always** going to be this way, and you will get just what you expect.

You can open your mind and choose to observe people for who

they really are, not who you expect them to be. Further, by retuning your expectations of each person in your life, you will begin to change the outcome of your interactions with them to be more in the flow with what you desire. To do this, release your predisposed ideas of everyone that you know. Instead, each time that you are with them, take the time to view them as if you were meeting them for the first time. Ask questions of him or her as if you have just met. Find out something new about their childhood, where they grew up, their thoughts on the issues of the day, or their hopes and dreams. Really listen. Listen with a totally open mind and heart. Choose not to judge this person for their words or viewpoint on anything—just connect with each one as a completely new being in your life.

What do you learn from this exercise? Do you have more in common with this "difficult" person than you thought? How are they different from who you predetermined them to be?

By repetitively choosing to imagine each person in your life as a completely new being each time that you meet, you will be amazed at the improvement in your relationships. However, do not just do this with your difficult relationships—choose to do this with everyone in your life. By viewing **everyone** with fresh eyes and fresh expectations, you will constantly reconnect with those that you love, co-creating flowing and satisfying relationships.

What are you birthing?

While Station 6 helps you to flow with the creative ideas and mental solutions that you need for your life, **this** Station deals with your ability to physically birth those ideas—to create physical form from the waves of potential all around you. Because of this, Station 2 deals with the issues of conception, gestation, labor, and birth, as it relates to not only a physical child, but also to a creative or business endeavor. Depending on your personal presets, each phase of the creative process can be flowing and easy, or it can have a pattern of difficulties specific to that phase. In order to birth any creative venture or project from its inception as a simple idea to the final physical reality, you must reset any negative presets to allow the process to go smoothly at every phase.

Phase 1: Conception

If you have heard the phrase, "before you were a twinkle in your mom or dad's eye," then you understand the first phase of physical creation. The "twinkle" is that first thought that you would like to bring some new aspect of your life into being—whether it is a child, a business, a piece of art, a book, a new sale, or any other project. At this point, it is just **mental** creativity (Station 6).

Just as it is with an actual baby, you must be open to allowing this idea to take seed and form into a **physical creation**—to take the desire that you feel and transform it into the action that begins the actual development of the idea—and this is where the difficulty begins. If you have a negative preset about your right to bring your ideas and thoughts out into the physical world, you may continuously shoot down your ideas as "impossible," or say that you've got a "great idea, but it will never work!" The result will be many ideas that never get a good start.

In contrast, you may be what people call a "great starter." Because of your fertile imagination and passionate energy, you may start many projects, but never complete any. If so, you need to explore why you are afraid of completing your projects—are you afraid that your creation will be judged? Do you fear that you do not have the skills to see it all the way through?

Phase 2: Gestation

In this phase, you've conceived the idea, and it is taking form. It is at this point that you may see the most significant patterns emerging.

Just as it is with a physical child, this is the phase where you take care of all the details to form your idea into a real creative venture—one with all its "fingers and toes," so to speak. In this phase, you come up with business plans, decide what color your storefront will be, secure financing, and generally do everything that needs to be done to assure that everything is in place for the final launch of your business or creation.

If you have fears about your ability to be a "good parent" of this idea—to nurture and lead this venture to success—then you will see a pattern of many businesses and creative projects being miscarried throughout your life. If this is a negative preset for you, you might start out on your career to be a dancer or an actor, but although you are completely prepared, you end up blowing every audition. Or, you put together an unbelievable business plan, but you cannot get the financing that you need to go forward. Maybe you write a terrific novel, but cannot get an agent to pick it up. No matter how you see it play out in your life, the key with creative miscarriage is that this business or project's failure seems to be unintentional (and consciously, it will be), but the truth is that you are tuning into this experience because you are preset to believe that you are not worthy of the success and recognition that comes with a successful creation.

The energy of abortion is similar, although in this case, you knowingly and willingly terminated the project. If this is an issue for you, you will notice a pattern of many experiences in your life where you started out well, but then decided that you could not make the venture a success—usually citing the many reasons why it was totally impossible for you to go forward. Perhaps you felt that people were criticizing your work. Maybe you worried that you just did not have what it takes. Perhaps a nasty fear of failure crept in and messed with you, and you decided to end your venture before you embarrassed yourself by failing. In any case, you felt that you could not bring that venture into being successfully at that time, and you let it go.

A final issue in this phase is the concern that there will be a "birth defect" in your creation. If this is an issue for you, you will find yourself pouring over every little detail to make **certain** that there is nothing that you missed that will cause catastrophic problems when the business or idea is birthed. A fear of failure and a lot of perfectionism is usually seen in people who get stuck in this phase of development. In addition, if you are dealing with issues here, you will constantly worry that you are doing something wrong in the way that you are forming your idea—and that this error will cause long-term issues with your creation.

Phase 3: Labor and birth

Do you believe that labor and delivery are difficult? Are you afraid of launching your business or project because of the effort that you must put forth, or the change that it will mean for your life?

Our culture is saturated with the idea that giving birth to **anything** is a very difficult, painful process—often needing miracles, drugs, and a lot of luck. However, this does not have to be true for you—giving birth to anything can be easy and flowing.

Once your creation is ready to go—for instance, you are ready to open your doors for business, launch your website or book, or present your art at a gallery opening—you are in the labor and birth phase. At this point, your idea is fully formed into physical reality, and it just awaits your "go ahead" to come out to the world. Because of this, this phase can be filled with fears of being a "good parent" of your creation as well, or with extreme fears about how your life is going to change when your "baby" is born.

If these fears are true for you, then you will labor longer than necessary—you will put off the final birth of your project by attending **one more** seminar, getting **one more** certification, looking for **a bit more** information, or reading **one more** book before you can actually birth your creation. Additionally, you may encounter last-minute problems that hold up the delivery—your website will crash, your partner will leave, or you will injure yourself just before your big debut.

Listen, **you deserve to bring your creations into being.** Yes, your life will change (sometimes radically) when your "baby" is born, but when you flow with the best frequencies of life, these changes will be very positive and fulfilling to you. As long as you are creating this business or project because you want to—not because you have to—your life will be enriched by its birth. In fact, you will wonder how you ever lived without it!

Even knowing this, you may face another significant fear in this phase. Just as it is with a real child, you may realize that once the idea or business is born, you will not be able to always protect it from criticism or harm by others. While I truly understand how difficult this can be, you must trust that you have done all that you can do to make a good product or create a great business, and believe that it will be received well by all who encounter it. Intend that your creation is for the best purpose that it can be, and you will attract the best frequencies to both of you.

Also, realize that you cannot please all the people all the time, and frankly, you shouldn't even try. If you have created something that is truly authentic to you and that you are proud of, then that is all that matters. Trust life to greet this new "baby" with open arms—and believe that you will be showered with gifts and praise for bringing it into being.

Finally, do not become a "smother mother" of your idea, trying to keep control of every aspect and owning it. Give your creation lots of leash, and be open to others who want to help it grow into the very best it can be.

Questions and exercises:

1. Do you have many mental ideas that never take form? Do you tend to think of great new solutions or business ideas, but immediately drop them because "they'll never work"? Do you worry about the ideas that you did not let take root? Are you a "great starter"—starting tons of projects, but never seeing any through to completion?

Retuning statement: "I allow all ideas to flow to me with ease. I allow the ideas that are for my best to take seed and grow within me."

2. Are you afraid of being able to handle all the details to make sure that your idea comes into form in the right way? Do you have a pattern of miscarrying or aborting projects, businesses, and creative ventures? Are you afraid that you will not be a good parent of your "baby"? Are you afraid of failing? Are you afraid of a "birth defect" in your creation that will cause issues in the long run? Have you learned these fears from others in your life? What repeating patterns do you notice?

Retuning statement: "I am a good parent of this _____ (insert your particular creation here). I allow it to develop fully and completely, and I trust that I will bring it into being in the right way at the right time."

3. Are you afraid to give birth to your creation? What are your main fears? Do you find a pattern where you labor longer than necessary, avoiding the actual launch of your venture because of these fears? Are you afraid that your "baby" will be criticized or treated badly once born? Do you have a pattern of negative experiences happening at the last minute—just as you are ready to give birth—that delay or stop your creation?

Retuning statement: "I easily give birth to _____ (insert your creation here). I trust that it will be received with love by all who encounter it, and I know that my life and the lives of others will be enriched by its existence. I release it to the world now."

What's your creation worth?

Maybe you are in the conception phase and are working on bringing your physical creation into being, but you do not know how to make the money that you need to survive. Perhaps you are already in a job that you love, but are not getting paid what you deserve. Maybe you have started a business, and it is not doing well financially.

In any case, you'd like money.

The good news is that money is very easy to attain, once you understand a few basic principles:

1. Income is always coming in—if you let it.

Are you truly open to allowing money to come to you?

While you may be screaming "yes!", hold your horses. Just like the personal relationships above, you have a personal relationship with money, and any of the above dynamics can be (and likely are) played out: money can control you, you can control money, or you can have a balanced and flowing relationship with it, allowing it to come in and out of your life with love and trust.

That said, while you may **say** that you are absolutely open to having money, your beliefs about money may tell a very different story. In fact, you may have an internal conflict raging within you—on one hand, seeing money as evil or bad, and on the other, seeing it as your very life-blood to achieve what you desire in life. You fear both having too much, believing that you must do something unethical to earn it—or having too little, fearing an unfulfilling, impoverished existence. It really is a mess—and it absolutely blocks your ability to allow money to flow to you easily.

If you allow money to control you, you will do almost anything to get it, often going against common sense and your personal morals to make money. You can easily see examples of money controlling people on many of the reality TV shows—I am always

205

amazed at the amount of humiliation that someone will endure for a very small amount of money. Understandably, when you see the effects of money controlling people—manifesting in people prostituting themselves (energetically or physically), stealing, and even killing for it—it seems to prove that money **is** bad or evil. However, like anything else, money is not inherently good or bad—as always, it is your **expectation** of what you must do in order to get the desired money that creates negative, imbalanced experiences.

Even so, your fears of money being evil or bad may cause you to be afraid of earning enough for you to be fulfilled. Because of this fear, you try to control money, creating many experiences where you allow money to slip through your fingers, or where you do work for almost nothing. You may also give away all of your money out of guilt for earning more than others in your life— feeling that having less money makes you a better person.

On the other hand, the need to control money may manifest in a very different way. If you have a fear about never having enough, you may find yourself hoarding it, becoming a miser and never giving money to anyone. Even if you have lots of money, you'll never let any of it go, causing you to be the person that stiffs the waitress or valet, or who sees a homeless person and refuses to give him a dime. You may also try to control others with your money, feeding your ego and getting what you desire—buying people that will never leave you. Of course, if the money ever leaves you, you will feel that you are no longer worth anything as a human being, as your entire identity was tied up with the money that you once had.

However, if you have a balanced relationship with money, you will find that it flows easily into and out of your life, appearing in mysterious and unexpected ways. For instance, you might get a letter in the mail telling you that there is a sum of money that you forgot about in an old bank account. Later that day, you might be approached by a co-worker who asks you to sponsor her for a charity run. You do so without reservation because you know that there is more than enough to go around—and you are happy to keep the positive flow of money going.

206

Like anything else, money itself is never good or bad, it is neutral. It is simply a physical manifestation of your expectation about it, no more, no less. Begin to see all money as just energy—and view it as an abundant stream coming in to you from everyone and everywhere. Change your perception of what it takes to make money (or to keep it). Nothing outside of you makes you money—**you** "make" money with your beliefs and expectations about it, creating it from the waves of potential that compose all life.

Choose to keep your mindset in a place that sees money as energy coming in to you in the best and most positive ways. After all, they don't call it an **income** for nothing! Money is always incoming—allow it to flow to you (and away from you) with ease.

2. Money doesn't buy happiness, but happiness just might buy money.

You may have heard the phrase "Do what you love, and the money will follow."

Of course, when you are in a job that you hate, or just barely struggling to keep food on the table, this seems like an impossibility. How in the world are you supposed to do what you love, when you would risk everything to do so? After all, you have so little now!

I know it is scary, but there are ways to make a transition to loving your work and making more money an easy and painless process.

A major roadblock to doing what you love is the common belief that work should be hard and dissatisfying. After all, if you hate your job, it makes it okay to be paid well for it, right?

Wrong. You can love your work and make a good living doing so—in fact, you **should** be doing this. Best of all, you can start this process now with your current job, and then allow yourself to easily flow into a new job, if that is what you desire.

First, start to see your current job as what you make of it. Do you go to work each day expecting to have an awful day with a terrible boss and horrible customers? Most of us do, but this is obviously not going to create a job that is even mildly enjoyable for you. Instead, I would like you to use the Art of Connecting each morning to visualize the kind of day that you would like to have. Imagine what the day would be like if you had an absolutely amazing, fulfilling day. How different do you feel at that moment, in that kind of day, than you normally do? Connect with this positive feeling, and stay with it all day. If you begin to find yourself falling back into your old way of feeling about work, take a minute or two to close your eyes and reconnect with the positive feeling. You will be literally amazed at how much better your day will be if you begin to cultivate this little practice each morning. You might just find that while it may not be the job of your dreams, it **is** a job that you can enjoy.

Now that you have a positive feeling about work, begin to take a real look at your options with this particular job, and what you truly want to do in life. To your surprise, you may have found that when you change your expectations about your current job, you actually have such a positive experience during work that you truly do love it. If so, you can make the decision to stay—you are in a good situation that is fulfilling to you. You will likely begin to have more and more positive experiences that will bring you all that you desire from your work, including more money and even promotions, if that is what you desire.

However, you may have found that this job just truly does not fit either who you are as a human being, or your dreams and desires for yourself. By observing this job from a new attitude, you may have realized that you are compromising yourself and your beliefs by doing the work that you do. At this point, it is time to leave this job. Remember, if you live to 80 years of age, you only live 29,200 days. Why waste any more of them in a job that you hate? Of course, you certainly **can** make the decision to stay, but you will likely be doing so out of fear or obligation, and that will repetitively send a signal to your mind that you are expecting more of the same—and more of the same will flow to you, depleting both your energy and your creative self.

You truly do deserve better. I know that the immediate

response might be fear—fear of the unknown, fear of how to get a better job, fear of the effect that this decision will have on others. Just put that aside for a moment. Ask yourself: What kind of job have you always dreamed of? What kind of job has called to you? What do you love doing? Put together a clear picture of what you think that you would like to do for work. Just like creating a perfect partner, write down a list of what would make a perfect job for you, and believe that you can bring that job into being. As always, refuse to settle for less than what you truly desire.

How would you feel each day if you had a job that fulfilled you like this? Connect with that feeling, and know that a job matching this feeling is flowing to you now, and with it, all the money that you desire.

3. Make yourself valuable.

Because you are!

Maybe you have decided that you would like to create art in one form or another. Perhaps you would like to be a speaker or a business consultant. Maybe you are a graphic designer, or own your own business.

Are you making the money that you would like? Or are you taking lots of pro-bono work, or making far less than others in your field?

If you do not value what you do as valuable to others, it will not be. You must make yourself worthy of asking for the money that you truly deserve for the good service that you are performing.

When I first started doing workshops, this was an enormous struggle for me. I feared that I did not have much to say to others, or that I did not have the right experience in the field to command a fair price for what I was doing. Consequently, I was always getting offers to speak for free, or for so little money that by the time that I had put the work in needed to create the presentation, I was making far less than minimum wage for all my effort.

Each time that I accepted these experiences, I sent another

strong message to my mind that I was not worthy of being treated better than that by life, and I flowed with that thought again and again. Frankly, I would really like to save you the trouble of dealing with this issue yourself.

To that end, please understand that you deserve to be paid fairly for what you do, but until you believe that, you will never have the experience of making good money in exchange for your creative effort. Choose to believe that what you are doing is valuable, and that it is not only good enough, but desirable to others. Do not believe that you need to prove yourself to anyone in order to make the money that you desire—**you are good enough as you are.** Do not believe that you are not experienced enough to advance in your job. If you truly need more schooling, then go and get it—believe that you have the time and money to get the schooling that you need, and you **will have** the time and money necessary.

Begin to act and speak in ways consistent with a successful experience. Never say that you don't have enough customers, or that you don't have enough to make the rent. Don't say you never have "two pennies to rub together," or that you are "not good enough to make money yet." By doing this, you are not only devaluing yourself and your creative effort with all that you meet, but you are also reinforcing this reality in your mind and using the Principle of Repetition to tune you into those exact experiences.

Trust me when I tell you that there is always someone who will value what you are creating. After all, I am sure that you have seen art that is distasteful to you, but that is selling for top dollar. Or, maybe you know of a song that you think is just awful, but that has just gone platinum. Believe me, if you look around, you will find many people making a very good income doing something that you do not find valuable.

However, don't just sit there and talk about how you are better than that person! Go out and create that life for yourself, and allow the money that you deserve to flow to you. Act and speak as if you have all the money that you need. Put a high value on yourself and that which you create, and you will find yourself in a truly prosperous life.

4. Focus on yourself, not on your competition.

In fact, do not even believe that there is such a thing as competition.

I know that I just drew your attention to other creations that you might rate as not as good as what you can do, but that is exactly as much as I would like you to focus on supposed "competitors." As I went over in Principle 3 with the video game example, there is no such thing as competition. You are not trying to beat out anyone else for the money that you want and need for your life. You do not have to be better than anyone else in order to get the life that you desire.

You simply need to be authentically you, and to focus only on your own creation and your own life.

I know that this is hard, especially in a world so saturated with the idea of win-lose and dog-eat-dog. This viewpoint comes out all the time in those that I work with when I tell them to chase their dreams and create the money that they desire. Many, many times a client will have realized what they truly want to do and be in life, but they will object to going after their dreams, saying, "But I can't make a living doing that!" My response is always the same: *"Why not?"*

Usually, the answers are: "No one makes money doing that anymore," "The market isn't there for my product," or "There are already so many other people doing that. How will I ever make money?" You may believe similar things about your chosen profession, but it does not have to be true. Whatever you are doing, whatever you are selling, there is always a market for it, and there is always someone making money at it. For example, I know many realtors who will say that they cannot make money in the current market, but there are still many that are making tons of money. There are countless coffee houses and clothing stores in every city and town, and yet there is always room for more. There are an amazing amount of CDs, video games, websites, and books coming out all the time, and yet there are more flooding the market every day.

What is the difference between those that succeed in the supposedly challenging markets and those that do not? The ones that succeed believe that they have the ability to make it and are constantly looking for proof that this is true. They are open to the flow of life, and always aware that opportunities are literally always knocking. They know how to focus on themselves and their own goals, without worrying about another's success.

This last part is critical, because when you focus on your "competitors," you are taking mental and energetic power away from yourself and your creation and giving it to the object of your focus, **empowering their success with your energy.** By becoming concerned and jealous of a "competitor," you only tune yourself into more experiences of lack, and watch as they tune into more experiences of prosperity. In fact, the next time that you find yourself worrying about a supposed competitor or becoming jealous of their success, I would like you to visualize that you have 100 one-dollar bills in your pocket. Each time that you think about your competitor, imagine that you hand him or her one dollar out of your pocket. Each time that you focus on yourself and your own success, imagine that the Source gives **you** a dollar bill. How wealthy is your competitor at the end of the day? Do you have any dollar bills left?

It may seem like just a mental exercise, but it is **exactly** what you are doing when you focus on your "competition." Every time that you think or speak about your competitors, you are taking time and energy away from creating your own success. Never let another person define who you are, or how your creation comes into being. Do not talk negatively about your "competitors"—you only tune yourself into a negative frequency, where you are judged as well. Always do things because they are authentic to you, and because they are in alignment with the life that you choose to lead.

Do not even believe in the notion of competition. Don't worry about how you will create success—as long as you focus on the end result, the "how" will take care of itself. We all are connected to an endless supply of abundance, and can use our personal Source-power to create more than enough for every one of us. Instead of competitors, expect that everyone that you meet is there to help you, and to provide you with something that you need, whether it is a change in perspective, a boost in confidence, or an opportunity that you did not even expect. By doing this, you will watch your creation blossom into a prosperous, flowing source of power and fulfillment—and your life will be abundant beyond your wildest dreams.

Questions:

1. Do you view money as evil or bad? Where did you learn that from? Do you believe that you must do unethical things to become wealthy? Have you ever done something to earn money that you are ashamed of? Why did you feel that you had to do that?

Retuning statement: "Money comes to me easily. When I am true to my best self, I have an abundant life."

2. Do you fear having money so much that you try to control it by not having any for yourself? Why do you feel guilt over having enough money to make you feel fulfilled?

Retuning statement: "I deserve to have the money that I desire. I am a good person, and money is good."

3. Are you afraid of being poor? Were you poor as a child, and want to make sure that you do not repeat that experience? Do you hoard money, even when you have more than enough?

Retuning statement: "I am prosperous in every way. The more that I share with others, the more prosperous I am."

4. Are you in a job that you hate? Do you believe that

work must be difficult and tiring? Where did this belief come from? What is the first thing that comes to your mind when you think about your current job? What kind of job would you like to do? Use the exercises above to create a job you love.

Retuning statement: "I love my work. I have a job that fulfills me in every way."

5. Do you value yourself highly? If not, why do you feel that you are not worthy of success and prosperity? What fears do you have about being successful? Where did these come from?

Retuning statement: "I deserve success and prosperity. I am worthy."

6. How often do you focus on your competition? Do you do things in reaction to what they are doing? Do you feel that you are going to be chased out of business, or not make enough money because of them? Where did you get this perspective?

Retuning statement: "I create an abundant, successful life. Everyone is there to do me good."

Releasing the need for greed

You don't just have a relationship with money—you also have a relationship with all the material goods of life: food, clothing, houses, cars, jewelry, and everything else. Just as it is with any other relationship, material goods can control you, you can control them, or you can have a positive and flowing relationship with them, allowing goods to move into and out of your life with ease.

If you allow your need for material goods to control you, you will compromise who you are in order to get them, going against your personal ethics to attain what you want. This comes from a preset belief that you do not have the power or ability to create more positive opportunities to get these desirable objects.

If you want to control material goods, you may become greedy. While greed is certainly an undesirable quality, it comes from a preset belief in a limited life, which is coupled with a significant fear that you might lose what you have. You might have developed this belief from growing up in poverty, or by losing everything because of a bad business deal or a down economy. Because of these negative experiences, you think that by controlling all the material goods that you can, you will have the power and safety that you may have lacked previously.

The need to gather and hoard as much of these goods as possible can become an all-out obsession, **especially** if you feel that you have little power in the rest of your life. For instance, you may begin to overeat; stuffing yourself for fear that you will not have enough. You may become a hoarder, keeping everything that comes into your possession until you have no more space in your home. You may become addicted to online shopping or the home shopping channel, as each purchase proves that you are no longer the poor kid that you once were, or gives you a little hit of pleasure and a feeling of safety.

This same need to control material goods can manifest in just the opposite way—you may be so afraid of having material goods that you give away everything that you have. This fear may either come from religious teachings about the spoils of success, or it may come from a belief that you are a bad person if you have too much wealth, but either way, it results in a negative relationship with all material goods. For instance, you may restrict your eating as a penance for having so much prosperity, or refuse to buy anything new for yourself because you believe that you should give more away to others.

However it manifests in your life, fears about the material goods of life result in a dysfunctional relationship with **all** of life. It truly does not have to be this way—you can have a flowing, unconditionally loving relationship with all material goods. To do

215

so, recognize all experiences as energy that is easily and consciously flowing into and out of your life. Develop the ability to view food, drink, clothing, furniture, paintings, jewelry and any other material goods as simply energy that matches your beliefs now. Release negative beliefs about these material goods, and know that you can create more than enough for yourself in all ways. Align your mind with the knowledge that you keep an easy flow of goods coming in and going out—and become open to offering others to partake of your personal creation by giving to charity, sharing your meal, giving away clothes and furniture to the needy, and offering your talents to the world without restriction.

By doing this, you will always be provided with all that you need and more. Better yet, you will feel a real sense of control over your life—because you will know that you truly have an unlimited and abundant life.

Questions:

1. Evaluate your personal relationship with cars, food, jewelry, and other material goods in terms of control. Do any material goods control you? Do you try to control them? Or, do you have a flowing relationship with them, allowing energy to come and go in your life with ease? What level of material goods would be fulfilling to you?

Retuning statement: "I have an abundant life. Material goods come and go from my life with ease."

2. Do you hoard any material goods? Have others called you greedy? Do you take money or goods from others in unethical ways? Are you obsessed with collecting anything? Do you feel safer when you have your collection around you? Are you afraid of not having enough, so you either stuff yourself full of food, or your

house full of things, to guarantee that you always have enough?

Retuning statement: "I am safe in all ways. I allow material goods to flow freely in my life."

3. Do you only feel real pleasure when you acquire more goods—for instance, cars, jewelry, watches, or even food? Where do you think that this relationship of new goods to pleasure comes from? Were you denied these things as a child?

Retuning statement: "I take pleasure from all of life. Every moment is filled with joy and happiness."

Let's talk about sex.

I have yet to meet a person who does not have an enormous conflict raging within them about their own sexual needs and desires. I am willing to bet that the mere mention of sex starts questions swirling in your head: Is it okay to want sex? Are fantasies normal? Are my personal sexual needs and desires okay? What is okay to do? What is not? Where is the line drawn? Am I allowed to enjoy sex? Is sex only for procreation?

Let's just clear up any misconceptions that you may have been given by well-meaning (or not so well-meaning) authorities in your life: **Sex is good.** It is good when you intend to create life, and it is good when you are just interested in a physical connection with another human being. You are allowed to take great pleasure in your sexual self—and you are invited to enjoy this beautiful act— free of guilt, fear, and shame.

I cannot emphasize strongly enough that sexual repression and conscious disconnection with this important aspect of the human existence is ridiculous. The Source is not judging your sexual acts—*you* are. In fact, the sexual act is the most literal expression

217

of your Source-power, as it can result in a child—certainly the greatest creation of all. If the Source has given you this act to co-create life, then how in the world can sex be viewed as dirty or bad?

I know there are many religions that seek to control your sexuality by setting forth rules on how and why you can have sex. Again, if that is how you choose to believe, by all means, do so. But be aware—these religious beliefs can cause an environment where the energy of Station 2 becomes blocked or constricted, resulting in STDs, ovarian cysts, tumors, and even impotence. Self-hatred over your own sexual desires and rebellion against this control can result in sexual addiction and dangerous sexual acts. As with anything else, you are connected to the Source and infused with the Source-power. This power is unlimited—you are trusted on every level to use this power as you choose, and create whatever life suits you. By connecting fully with your sexuality, you are opening yourself up to take full responsibility of your life-creation abilities. Do not disconnect from this part of yourself— **embrace it**, and use this power to create beautiful moments for yourself and your partner.

Open yourself to allowing your sexual energy to flow. Do not believe that enjoyment of sex is dirty or bad. After all, if you were not to enjoy sex, would the Source have created parts of the body whose entire purpose was to create a pleasurable experience? It would be a fairly big waste of energy if you were not to fully use these parts of you.

All of that said, you do need to realize that the relationship dynamics described above apply to sex as well, and by assessing any of your sexual relationships (past, present, and future) in terms of the dynamic at play, you can easily identify any negative patterns in your sexual encounters. For each sexual relationship, ask yourself these three key questions: Do you feel controlled by the other person, acting in ways that are meeting their needs, but are ignoring or disrespecting yours? Are you the one in control, asserting your sexuality over your partner? Or, are you in an unconditionally loving and consensual relationship, where sex is an expression of love and respect?

218

As you answer these questions, you may begin to understand where your own negative and limiting beliefs about sex came from. If you are a woman, you may begin to be aware of the conflicting messages that you have received—on one hand, there is the expectation that you should be sexy and "hot" for your lover, on the other, there is the requirement that you should deny your sexual feelings; if you don't, you may be labeled a "whore" or "slut." Due to this conflicting programming, you might find that even when in a committed relationship, you may be so afraid of expressing your own sexual response that you cannot ask for what you need, even from your partner. Unfortunately, this fear can cause you to block your orgasmic response, which creates serious blockages in your creative and sexual energy.

If you are a man, you may have been programmed to believe that you must "sow your wild oats" by having sex with many partners in order to prove your manhood. Or, you might have been programmed with such fears over "performing well" in bed that you end up undermining your own sexual energy, causing physical issues such as impotence and premature ejaculation. In addition, you have likely been given such conflicted messages over the "manly" way to express yourself sexually that although you really desire a more tender sexual relationship, you are afraid to ask for it, less you be called a "sissy." However it plays out for you, this kind of negative programming—especially that which causes you to act in ways inconsistent with who you really are—causes a real energy imbalance in your system.

For either gender, many fears come from the very nakedness of the act. After all, you are never more exposed than you are during sex, and that opens you to the possibility of being emotionally and even physically injured. Because you fear this loss of control, you may try to control your sexual encounters and detach from your feelings, never truly opening yourself up to the full experience. This fear can be increased substantially if you have ever had a lover cheat on you. The hurt that you feel in the situation may cause you to question your feminine or masculine power, and you may either go wild, trying to prove your desirability by racking up many sexual encounters, or you may shut down, refusing to open yourself to loving anyone again. If you continue to hold on to this emotional wound, you can develop cysts and tumors from the emotional scarring.

If you are in a relationship where the dynamic is such that your partner has total control over you, you may perform sexual acts that go against who you are just to fulfill the other's needs, fearful that you will lose your partner if you don't. The next day (and perhaps many after that), you will not respect yourself, causing you to eventually tune into experiences in the rest of your life where you are treated with disrespect.

Certainly, if you have ever been raped or sexually abused, you may be afraid of unleashing your own sexual power, either because you feel somehow responsible for what happened to you, or because you fear the negative uses of sexual power. If you cannot heal from this experience, the imbalance that it causes in your energy in this Station can result in serious issues in your reproductive system, ranging from an inability to orgasm to cysts and tumors.

Any of these negative experiences can create a total lack of trust in others, which results in the belief that you must "go it alone." If this is true for you, you may find that you can orgasm very easily on your own, but you have a total inability to do so with a partner. Until you open yourself up to trusting another person to respect you and provide you with what you need, you will never have a satisfying relationship, or for that matter, a satisfying life.

Sex should not be a constant tug of war between controlling others and controlling yourself. As with all other relationships, the ultimate sexual relationship is one that is unconditionally loving, unconditionally respectful, and that allows each person to be exactly who you are as individuals. It is filled with open communication about each of your sexual needs, and there is **never** any question that you are both safe. At its best, the sexual relationship allows each of you to have a wonderful way to connect with your partner and co-create a powerful physical experience.

No matter what, it is always important to understand that no sexual act is inherently bad, as long as there is agreement of your intentional act of creation, and mutual consent that both parties are comfortable. Like anything else, you must evaluate any sexual encounter in the same way that you do with any decision—simply decide if this is how you want to use your power. Ask yourself, "Is this a moment that flows with what I desire for my life and who I am, or will it send out a signal of disrespect and tune me into the opposite of my desires?"

You and you alone can answer that question. Choose to express your sexuality in ways that honor who you really are, and you are always assured of creating the best for yourself and for your partner.

Questions:

1. What do you believe about your sexuality? Are you ashamed of your sexual expression? Are you ashamed of your "private parts"?

Retuning statement: "I am a sexual being, and I love and approve of myself. My needs and desires are appropriate for me."

2. Are you in a relationship where you engage in sexual acts that you do not agree with? Do you feel that you need to do this in order to please the other person, or to ensure that you do not lose him or her? Have you had other relationships where this dynamic played out? Why do you feel the need to earn this person's approval?

Retuning statement: "I deserve to be treated with respect in all ways. I deserve love and approval for who I am."

3. Do you use your sexuality to control others? Do you withhold sex to get your way? Do you force others to

do what you want? Do you get a sense of power from this?

Retuning statement: "I deserve love and respect because I give love and respect. I open myself to unconditional love."

4. Have you ever been sexually abused or raped? Do you fear that you did something to deserve these acts? Have you ever told anyone? If yes, how did the person react? Did you get justice? If no, why did you feel you needed to hide this? Out of shame or fear? Are you afraid of opening yourself up to a free expression of your sexual self? If this is an issue for you, I highly recommend that you seek help to deal with the emotional and physical violation that you have endured, and to understand that you did nothing to deserve any of this. Please see the "Resources" page for a list of helpful resources.

Retuning statement: "I am sexually powerful. I attract only loving sexual relationships to my life."

5. What have you been taught by your religion about your sexuality? Do you want this to continue to create your experience of sex?

If this is an issue for you, please use the retuning statement: "I am allowed to express my sexuality and to take pleasure in my body."

6. Do you have difficulty achieving orgasm? What beliefs do you have about your ability to enjoy life, and to take pleasure from experiences? Do you feel that you are allowed to communicate what you need to your partner? Does your partner listen to your needs with respect and love?

Retuning statement: "I allow myself to experience pleasure. I am fully open and present for the sexual experience."

Station 2: Body language

Since Station 2 is such an active area for physical life-creation, it is also one of the most likely to tune into the negative energy that results in disease. For instance, if you feel totally controlled and demeaned by a horrible boss, your loss of creative power may develop issues of impotence or infertility. If you lose all your money to a failed business, you may feel emasculated, resulting in issues such as prostate cancer. If you fear that you will never make the money that you need to sustain yourself, you may develop pain and disease in your lower back and hips. If you are afraid of your creative power as a woman, you may become infertile. If you restrict your personal creativity, energy blockages may show up as cysts, fibroids, and tumors. If you are afraid of letting anything go, you may become constipated.

Whatever the issue, first find out the function of the affected body part—what does the body part do for your body? How does it function when healthy? Then write down a description of the disease—how it progresses, what it does, what is malfunctioning now. Look at what you have written. How can you relate the description of the disease and the proper functioning of the body part with the issues of this Station? Look at the language that you have used to find clues for the issue.

Action plan for resetting Station 2:

- ✓ Select 2-3 retuning statements to reset your preset.
- ✓ Go to page 409 and take the Reality Type Test, if you have not already done so.
- ✓ Select 4 Reality Type exercises, and do these for 40 days.
- ✓ Become aware of the dynamics that you are manifesting in your relationships.
- ✓ When you notice a button being pushed, stop and choose to do something different.

- ✓ Believe that you deserve unconditional love and respect in all relationships.
- ✓ Allow your ideas to take hold, and believe in your right to birth those ideas.
- ✓ Open yourself up to a flowing relationship with money.
- ✓ Make yourself valuable. Make yourself worthy of success.
- ✓ Do not focus on your competitors. Focus only on yourself.
- ✓ Define what you want and need in your sexual relationships, and be open to experiencing that with your partner.

STATION 3

The Force of Positive Self-Image

Station Motto: I worry that I am not good enough.

Location of Station: Solar plexus

Problem Playlist: If you are preset with negative Station 3 beliefs, you will find that you have some of these behavior patterns and difficulties:

- Continuous feelings of low self-worth.
- Never being good enough.
- Being in relationships where the person puts you or your dreams down.
- Facing criticism for your personal beliefs or opinions.
- Never having anyone listen to your feelings about anything.
- Hiding your true feelings from others for fear of being put down or criticized for your beliefs and thoughts.

- Being arrogant, angry, and over-powering.
- Expecting others to always agree with you or to acquiesce to your way of doing things.
- Feeling that your way is always right.
- Feeling that your way is always wrong.
- Difficulty making decisions.
- Not trusting yourself, your beliefs, or your gut instincts.
- Feeling in your gut that you should do a certain thing, and then not following through or going the opposite direction.
- Not knowing who you are.
- Not being authentic to yourself.
- Not standing up for yourself.
- Not taking care of yourself.
- Having addictive problems, such as alcoholism, smoking, obsessive-compulsive disorder, drug addiction, compulsive shopping, and gambling addictions.

Station 3 Body Issues: If you are tuning into negativity here, you will find that you have disease, pain, or extra weight in these areas:

- Liver
- Pancreas
- Stomach
- Upper intestines
- Kidneys
- Adrenals
- Middle spine
- Gallbladder
- The core of the body

You love you

In the first two Stations, you'll learn about how you deal with your relationship to all of the external people and things in your life, and the beliefs and thoughts that go along with that. Station 3 shifts that focus to the quality of the relationship that you have with yourself. You may not think that you have a relationship with yourself, but trust me, you do—and in many ways it is the most important relationship that you could possibly have. Feeling that you admire and respect yourself is the most essential factor in your ability to choose the experiences you desire—after all, if you do not believe in your personal power or do not trust yourself to use your power wisely, you will continue to tune into self-defeating and self-sabotaging experiences.

To make the best use of your creative power, you must love yourself completely and unconditionally—which is certainly a tremendous challenge for most of us! A further challenge is to be able to hold your own truths and desires without worrying about what others think, how they view you, or how they feel that you should be living. Because of this, it is very likely that the work needed in this Station will challenge you to the core of your being.

As you start this workbook section, keep this question in mind: Are you capable of expressing love to yourself?

How Do You *Really* Feel About Yourself?

Imagine that you have searched and searched for the perfect outfit or suit and tie for a high school reunion or an important business appointment—somewhere that you want to dress to impress. After looking and looking, you find a fabulous dress or suit—and it is just your style! You put it on, and feel wonderful wearing it. You head out for your reunion or appointment beaming with confidence. Upon arriving at your destination, you notice that people are looking at you. This bolsters your confidence a bit more—they are obviously noticing your wonderful attire. However, as you are walking around, you overhear a couple of people making fun of the way that you look. Then, a friend or associate comes up and makes a crack on your outfit. In fact, it seems that everywhere you go you hear negative talk about what you are wearing.

Do you still feel good about yourself? Do you **still** feel confident?

Probably not, and that's okay. This is a normal response to being ridiculed or criticized—even I had a knot in the pit of my stomach as I wrote this little story. Take a breath and look at the story again. What do you notice? You were wearing something of your choosing that matched your style, and that you really felt confident in. It made you feel good when you put it on. So what made you feel so bad?

The outfit had not changed. You had not changed. The only thing that changed was other people's **reactions** to your attire.

Other people's reactions (or worry about what others' reactions might be) drive even the most confident of us to go against our inner desires and instincts and avoid life experiences that we truly desire. It is this exact same phenomenon that causes you to second-guess your decisions or to feel guilt or worry about taking an action that is true to you, especially when someone that you care about and respect has told you that they disapprove of what you are doing, wearing, or even thinking. Because of this, when faced with a decision to either follow your personal truth or to go along with what others think is right, you'll find yourself wavering on what you should do, even when you know in your gut what is right for **you**. Of course, these decisions can be anything in your life, from your job and career choices to your choice of spouse, place of residence, child-rearing decisions, and much more. **Any** decision— big or small—is open to criticism and ridicule from others—and even the possibility of such reactions is enough to make most of us choose the easy (read: **accepted**) path instead of the right one.

Take a look at your own life to see where this dynamic might play out. For instance, maybe you decide that you want to make a complete career change to do the work of your dreams, but everyone around you begins complaining about the sacrifice it would mean for them, or telling you why it is a "ridiculous" idea. Or, maybe you decide that your current church no longer serves your needs, but suddenly your church "friends" (and maybe even your family) threaten to ostracize you if you leave, or simply put pressure on you to stay there. Or, perhaps you decide to go on a diet, workout plan, or success program (or maybe even follow the suggestions in this book!), but when you excitedly tell your friends and family about your new plan for success, everyone around you seems to be discouraging your efforts, either telling you why it won't work, or subtly undermining your efforts as you go along—perhaps by bringing cake over to your cubicle, putting pressure on you to go out when you truly want to go to the gym, or otherwise distracting you from your goals.

Now ask yourself: In the face of this adversity, do you **still** change careers, move churches, or start on your life improvement program? Or, as so often happens, would you let others' opinions of you and your decisions keep you from experiencing things that are in alignment with who you really are and really want to be?

If you are like most of us, you will be able to identify many experiences in your life where you have given up on your dreams due to outside pressure. In fact, all too often others' opinions and criticisms cause you to give up on what you truly want in order to avoid the possibility of being ridiculed, criticized, or riddled with guilt.

That's going to end right here! This workbook section is designed to give you the confidence to always follow **your** right path, no matter what others think about you or your decisions. You know in your gut that in order to be truly powerful and flow with the life of your dreams, you must develop the ability to be able to feel good about yourself and your decisions **regardless** of what other people's reactions might be. By working through this Station, you will become confident that your feelings, your desires, your beliefs, and your needs are completely appropriate for you—and acceptable for your life.

By developing true personal power, an entire room of people could be making fun of you, and you would be unaffected. You would still be perfectly okay with yourself, and you would move forward making decisions that were in alignment with your personal truth.

I know this sounds impossible—even total lunacy—but it is

not. By the time that you are done with this Station, you really are going to love yourself, and that will give you the ability to flow with the confidence, charisma, and strength necessary to tune into the life of your dreams.

Isn't that what you **really** want?

Questions:

1. Can you remember a time when you felt humiliated because of your decisions? What happened? How do you feel about this experience now? Do you make decisions now to avoid experiencing this kind of humiliation again?

2. Have you avoided taking the steps necessary to live a truly authentic, empowered life, simply because you are afraid of others' reactions to your decisions? What small steps could you take **today** to start in the directions of your dreams?

Retuning statement: "I trust myself to make decisions that are appropriate for me. Others offer me support and love in all my endeavors."

3. Are you authentic to yourself? Are there situations where you are not authentic to yourself? Look at these situations—why are you denying your personal truth here?

Retuning statement: "I have the power to be authentic to myself. I choose experiences because they bring me joy and fulfillment."

What's not to love?

I know you likely hate parts of yourself right now, but stop and really think about this:

You are a complete miracle! Your very existence was molded out of little particles of energy that were once stars and supernovas and trees and mountains. Your body works in miraculous ways, heart pumping, lungs taking in oxygen and releasing carbon dioxide. Your brain operates in such a complex way that even the most brilliant scientists can only guess at the many functions and inner workings of this bunch of little gray cells. Everything about you is amazing, gorgeous, and wonderful.

At one point, you believed this. As a baby, you loved everything about yourself. In fact, if you were like me, you may have even streaked through rooms wearing nothing but your birthday suit. You didn't worry about the size or look of your butt, tummy, nose, legs, or anything else. In your eyes, you were a fantastic creature, and indeed, you were.

So what happened? As you grew, you were inundated with opinions on everything about you. You watched commercials and TV programs that told you what was acceptable and attractive, and what was to be changed or disliked. Your church likely taught you that there were bad, dirty or sinful parts of you. You heard your parents criticize things about themselves, and in turn, you learned to criticize yourself in the same way.

Even your personality came under scrutiny, as you may have been ridiculed for personal qualities or traits. You may have had teachers criticize you for being too much of a clown or a talker, or conversely, for being shy and sensitive. You may even now have co-workers and friends that criticize you for aspects of yourself and your personality, making you feel that you are worthless and unlovable.

All of this is nonsense. **You** are lovable. **You** are perfect just as you are, and there is nothing bad, dirty, or sinful about you.

The parts of your body that you have been taught to believe are "bad" or "dirty" are necessary for your survival. After all, if you

231

did not have a bottom to sit on, you wouldn't be too comfortable. If you did not have sexual organs, you could neither receive the pleasure of making love, nor create life (the biggest miracle of all!). If you did not have intestines to move waste out of your body, you wouldn't live for long.

Furthermore, it just doesn't make sense that any part of your body could be bad, because after all, the Source created every part of your body. If that is the case, and you follow the logic that parts of your body are bad, dirty, or sinful, then the Source must be bad, dirty, or sinful to have created these parts.

Are **you** going to be the one to tell the Source that He or She messed up?

I didn't think so. Instead of criticizing that which composes you and your body, choose to love all of it as a beautiful representation of the Source. Love every bit for the wonder and miracle that it is, not for the criticisms and non-truths that you have been taught.

To choose the life that you truly want to live, you need to be able to love yourself right now, as you are. You cannot keep putting conditions on **when** you will love yourself, such as: "Well, if I get a breast enhancement, I will love myself then!" or, "I can't love myself until I lose 30 pounds." By putting these kinds of conditions on **when** you will love yourself, you are telling the Source that you desire experiences where you have to meet certain requirements in order to achieve your goals, which will keep the life of your dreams just out of your reach. Because of this, you will neither achieve your goals, nor learn to love yourself.

However, when you choose to love yourself right now, **just as you are**, you add that frequency to your you-hologram, which tells the Source that you deserve the life of your dreams right now—and the life of your dreams will flow to you.

As you can see, it really would be best if you give in and decide that you love who and what you are right now!

This does not mean that you cannot change things about yourself that you are not happy with—it simply means that there is no reason to criticize or hate yourself for what and who you are now. Don't hate yourself for being a procrastinator or a smoker, or overweight, shy, smart, old, young, or anything else. You are who you are now because of the experiences and lessons of your life up to this point. Choose to love this current self, and work on non-critically reprogramming yourself to be what you desire. For example, you might dislike yourself now for procrastinating on important actions. Recognize this as something that you would like to change, and use the retuning statement, "I love who I am now. I now choose to be proactive in every way." Or, maybe you feel unhealthy at your current weight. Don't judge your body, flowing with the frequency of hate and criticism. Instead, say, "I love my body. My body allows me to see and feel the world in wondrous ways. I now choose to be fit and toned, happy and healthy. I now create this reality."

Remember, criticizing yourself only tunes you into criticism and dissatisfaction. By choosing to focus on the positive, you are retuning your mind to seek the life of your dreams now, allowing your mind, body, and life to flow with power and love in the present moment.

Love yourself unconditionally. It is the only way to true happiness and freedom!

Questions:

1. What conditions do you put on yourself? What do you dislike about yourself? Make a list of all the things that you dislike about yourself. Pick the top five things that you really don't like (or even hate!). Write these down as "I love" statements. For example, maybe you really hate your thighs. Write down, "I love my thighs!" Then, at least 4 times a day for the next week, please say these 5 positive statements to yourself in the mirror. Let me just state: this may be very, very hard at first. Just keep doing it. Before you know it, you **will** love these things—and you may even decide that you don't need to change any of them.

2. Why do you hate certain aspects of yourself? Do you believe that you deserve the life of your dreams without changing anything about yourself now? If not, why not? Can you remember when you started feeling this way? Who told or taught you that you needed to change to be more deserving?

Retuning statement: "I deserve all that I desire, right here, right now, right as I am."

3. Make a list of the personality traits that you find undesirable, or that others have criticized you for. Do some research and find celebrities, famous people, scientists, visionaries, or even just those that you admire that have this very trait. How has this trait assisted them in their life? Can you see that you admire others that have the very same traits that you do? Can you see how special you really are? Everything about you is an asset—you just need to view it as such. Put pictures of these people all over your personal space. Write on the back of each one what the attribute is, and how it has served that person and even humanity. For example, perhaps you feel that you are too shy. In researching famous people that were shy, you might come across Emily Dickinson. How was her shyness an asset? It allowed her to write amazing poems known the world over for their beauty. Do this for each "undesirable" that trait you might have. You will be surprised what an asset each aspect of yourself really is!

Who told you that you weren't good enough?

What is the most embarrassing picture that you have of yourself as a child? Are you in plaid pants with a matching bow tie? Perhaps you look prim and proper in a ridiculous amount of ruffles with a terrible bow affixed unnaturally to your head. Or perhaps yours is something worse than even these indignities.

Whatever your most embarrassing picture is, I am willing to bet that you have **sworn** that you will never dress your children in such a humiliating way. I hate to tell you this, but you will (and might have already), and your children will have exactly the same amount of say in their attire as you did, which is to say, no say at all.

As a child, you truly had no say in how you dressed, thought, or acted. Your parents or elders were the final authority on everything, and, though you might have thrown a temper tantrum, you still ended up in the ridiculous clothes that they wanted you to wear. More than just clothes, your parents and elders taught you what they thought that you should know about the world, your part in it, and what they felt that you should believe. Some of these beliefs might be completely ridiculous, but as a child, you accepted them because you had no choice.

Now you are all grown up. Do you still allow your parents to put you in clothes that you do not like? I would bet that you don't.

But—do you still let them dress you in their beliefs?

I am guessing that you just might.

You have certainly outgrown some beliefs that you were taught as a child. Unfortunately, because of your early experience and training, you are likely operating on the idea that you must just "put up" with their expectations of you, or that "it will just be easier" if you go along with what they want for you or your life.

It's simply not true. If you are going against what you truly believe is right for your life, then it is **never** easier. Every moment of every day will feel like you are wearing that pair of old, itchy wool pants that your mom was so fond of, but that gave you a terrible rash. By living out of the flow with your personal truth— even when you have a choice to do otherwise—you will be tuning into irritation and a life that feels truly unfulfilling.

You now have the power and right to stand up and say **"NO!"** People that **were** the authority figures in your life as you grew up are no longer the infallible forces that you once believed that they were. Remember, no matter how much they might represent their opinions and teaching as truth, **the truth of the matter is that**

none of it *is* the truth of the matter. You don't have to keep wearing destructive beliefs about yourself. No one can make you believe that you are not good enough, smart enough, kind enough, or anything else. You do not have to keep making amends for mistakes that you made years ago or for not living up to someone else's standards for you. In short, you have permission to take off all the "I'm not good enough" clothes, and replace them with beliefs that exactly suit you and your desires.

You now have the ultimate choice in the matter. You can choose to believe that you **are** good enough in every possible way, because you really are.

Your mind may be resisting this truth, coming up with reasons why you simply aren't good enough. For instance, you might think, "But I have done bad things," or "I don't really have any talents." Maybe you think, "I never finish anything," or "I am really not very smart." Try to put these thoughts aside for now. It really does not matter what you think that you've done or not done, what you look like, or how you think and feel. Whatever it is, it is enough. **You** are good enough, just as you are. In fact, right now, you are **everything** that you want to be—everything else is just old negative programming. Let it go.

To help you believe this, remember that you are made of the same particles as everyone and everything else—even people that you admire and who you perceive as better than you. In addition, your particles were once part of everything that you see in the entire universe—so whatever you want to be, and anything you want to do, some of your particles have done it before. Once you really understand that, you will see that the criticisms of others have no power to create you anymore. They are only words, and they are in the past. The past no longer exists, so it is time to create a new day—and a new you that is truly **you.**

As an exercise, I would like you to write down everyone else's expectations of you. If you have an old t-shirt, go get it, and write all of this down right on the shirt. If not, just write it out on a piece of paper. Write about what **they** want you to be. Jot down everything about where they expect you to be, in your life, in your decisions, even just on Sunday afternoons or Monday mornings.

What do they expect that you must do for them to earn their love? Write down all the things that you should be doing, but aren't; then write down the things that you **are** doing, but don't want to be. Write down every criticism of you that they utter. Write everything that they say to get you to comply to their wishes, even when you are struggling not to. Take your time—write it all out.

Are you finished? If you have written this on a t-shirt, I want you to put the t-shirt on for a moment. Imagine that you have literally been carrying all of this around with you all the time (you have, you know!). Now, take the t-shirt off, saying to yourself, "I now understand that I do not need to carry your expectations of me anymore. I am going to take you off, and figure out what **I** want for my life, what **I** believe, and who **I** believe myself to be." Hang this t-shirt up in a closet or put it away in a drawer that you don't use—somewhere out of sight. If you have written all of this on a piece of paper, I want you to put this list in an envelope or a box—somewhere where it is closed away. Put it aside—and say to yourself, "I don't need to deal with you just now. You are not me; you are not my dreams for myself. I am putting you to the side." Literally push it away from yourself.

You now understand that it is your **choice** to either take on these beliefs about yourself, or to decide to throw them away. You are now free.

How do you feel after doing this little exercise? Unburdened? Lighter? It is amazing how much stuff you carry around with you all the time! You can never know yourself or develop real self-esteem if you are always dragging all of this along with you. Just for now, you are putting it aside to take a look at what you really feel about yourself, your life, and your dreams.

It may be difficult as you start to realize how much of your self and your life you have sacrificed to negative thinking that was not even yours, and likely was not even true. However, try not to feel bad that you have taken on all of these negative messages about yourself—it really couldn't be helped. **Everyone** has been given messages that told them that they were not good enough. I've certainly received my fair share. These messages and experiences dig deep within you, where they become part of your you-hologram. The words that others used to criticize you become the words that you think to yourself about your perceived failings. The expectations that others placed upon you become synonymous with what you think you want for yourself—so much so that you cannot even tell what is your dream, and what is someone else's dream that was imposed upon you.

Look at these non-truths, and let them go. Live up to your own expectations, and no one else's—and be your very best every single day!

Questions:

1. Do you find that the things that you say about yourself are the same as the things that you used to hear as criticisms of you? Can you see that you can release these negative beliefs and non-truths and replace them with your own empowering truths?

Retuning statement: "I release all negativity. I am good enough in every way."

2. What were the most surprising revelations that came out of doing the t-shirt exercise? How much have you been living your life by others' thoughts and expectations? Which observations shocked you the most? Who did these come from? Can you now release these beliefs and replace them with your own expectations of yourself?

Retuning statement: "I am responsible for my own happiness, and everyone else is responsible for theirs. I live my life by my rules, and no one else's."

Identify yourself!

Who are you?

I know, I know—this is a big, complicated question, but in order to live the most fulfilling and unlimited life, it is a question that **must** be answered. After all, if you don't know who you really are, you cannot possibly know what you really want. If you don't know what you want, you cannot possibly tune into the life of your dreams.

It is really quite a conundrum, and it has been made more complicated by all of the "authorities" in your life that have convinced you that you are who **they** say that you are, whether or not you truly are this identity. For instance, perhaps your father always told you that you were a failure. It isn't true, but because you believe it is, you will create experiences that prove this true. Or maybe a teacher told you that you would not amount to anything. Because you believe this, you will have great difficulty achieving *anything* that you desire.

You have been labeled by other people's opinions of who you are, and those labels are limiting both what you can create, and which experiences are appropriate for a person "like you." Truly, the more that I work with people to release the limiting beliefs that they have around their own identity, the more that I think that most of us see life as some sort of bizarre carnival that only allows you to have tokens for certain experiences based on the identity labels that you have accepted as who you are. At this carnival, instead of a name tag that says, "Hi, I'm Joe," you'd have a label that declares, "Hi, I'm a responsibility sponge!" or, "Hello, I'm a former anorexic that still lacks self confidence!" To gain entrance to certain events, you would step up to the front door, and the person giving out the tokens would review your identity labels and remark, "So... you're a high school drop-out with a failed marriage. Your tokens allow you to go to the beer table and apply for a job in construction or secretarial work. You'd like to own your own business? No, no—I'm afraid you can't have access to those experiences." Then, another person would step up, hand the token-giver their list of identifiers, and he would comment, "Ah, you're beautiful and stick-thin. Okay, here's the tokens for modeling…that's about all you are qualified for."

This may seem rather humorous, but the sad thing is that this is very likely **exactly** what you are doing to yourself right now. Since you have been taught that you shouldn't aim too high for a person "like you," you mentally give yourself tokens that allow you to try for only certain goals and experiences. Because of this, you avoid experiences that could be very fulfilling, because you "shouldn't," "can't," or "won't" do that sort of thing. Worse, you decline these experiences without even being conscious that you are turning them down based on an identity that may not even be who you actually are!

This is a real problem because it means that you are limiting your life to only the kinds of success and joy that **you** think you deserve based on your own (and others') perceptions of what is right for the type of person that you are. As this thinking has been forced into your mind for so long, it is very difficult for you to understand that by simply changing the way you identify yourself, you can begin living a limitless existence that you may have never dared dream of before.

Nevertheless, it is true—you can be whoever you choose to be, and you can experience whatever you choose to experience. As you know, you contain the entire Source-hologram within you. Because of this, you are literally every identity label that you can dream of right now. It is your choice how you want to manifest yourself and your life.

You've likely been taught that you're just born a certain way, making aspects of your personality inherited and unchangeable, but it isn't true. It is true that you **are** born with a you-hologram that contains genetic information and all of the wave information from your spirit, and this information creates the physical and mental "you" that you experience. However, none of this is unchangeable—you are **not** stuck with being painfully shy, bad at math, unsuccessful, overweight, or anything else that you might believe was genetically programmed into your being. Actually, you have already made many, many changes to the original you-hologram in the process of simply living your life and taking on new beliefs and expectations. After all, you are likely very different now than you were ten years ago, and you are certainly different than you were when you were born, but you are still "you."

I will agree that some identity labels (such as your gender or race) do **seem** unchangeable, but the truth is that even these identity labels are just an illusion created by your perception. No matter how you perceive yourself, you are not just one gender or race or anything else—you have particles that were once everything in the entire universe, so, in a very real way, you are both male **and** female, white **and** black, straight **and** gay, or any other set of opposite labels that you might like to insert here. And, while you may not be able to change some of your intrinsic genetic manifestations, you can change the way that you **define** this identifier. For instance, you may be a woman, but how you **define** being a woman can be very different from how others choose to define this gender. **You define the identity label; the identity label does not define you.**

How do you want to define yourself? It is up to you. Never again allow yourself to believe "I am who I am, and that is all that I am," or feel victimized by an identity that is different than you desire. Instead, you must begin a new mantra: "I am who I am because that is **who I have chosen to be.**"

Questions:

1. So who are you? Make a list of the identity labels that you currently wear, starting with the phrase, "I am." For instance, you might say: "I am a doctor," "I am a wife," "I am a woman," "I am a kind person," "I am a nature-lover," etc. Write down as many identity labels that describe you as you can.
2. Please take a look at your list of "I am" statements. As you review this inventory of who you are, I would like for you to think about what it means to be a person with

each quality. What experiences are allowed for a person who chooses this identity? For instance, in order to take on the identity label "I am a kind person," you must act in kind ways, and make life choices in alignment with what a kind person would do. Or, if one of your labels is "I am a successful person," then there are experiences that you are allowed to have as a successful person: you can have successful businesses, drive cars that say to you "success," eat at the top restaurants, and so forth. However, what would happen if you identified yourself with the statement, "I am a failure"? You would absolutely not make the choices that a successful person does—rather, you would be limited to the experiences of failure—nothing would ever seem to work out the right way for you. Remember, the experiences that are "allowed" for a person with that identity label are based on your own definition of what it means to be each quality.

3. Please go back through the list once again. What experiences are "off limits" in order to choose to identify yourself with that label? For instance, if you said, "I am successful," then you would not be able to tune into problems and issues that would keep you from success. I would like you to do this for every one of the identity labels that you have noted. What ways are you limited by each label? Please note: being limited is not a good or a bad thing, it just is. For me, I am perfectly okay with labeling myself as a "nature-lover," and knowing that this limits some of my experiences. For instance, I cannot just toss trash out my car window or ignore environmental issues if I want to choose this identity. Go through your list carefully, noting what experiences you will miss out on if you choose that label.

4. Look at your entire list, with each set of experiences that you can and cannot have for each identifier. Circle the identifiers that you would like to associate yourself

with, and cross out the ones that do not fit who you choose to be.

5. What do you desire for your life? What kind of person do you need to be in order to match these goals? For instance, if you want to be a successful artist, you need to identify yourself in statements such as: "I am talented," "I create art that is desirable," and "I am confident in my abilities." Make a list of identity labels and statements that match who you need to be to be in the flow with all that you desire.

6. Are any of the identity labels inconsistent with the life that you desire? For instance, perhaps you want a very expensive car or big house, but currently have the identity label of "middle-class." The label that you might want to take on would be "I am wealthy." Cross any labels off the list that are inconsistent with the life of your dreams.

7. Create a list of the identifying labels that you have chosen as "who you are." Make several copies of this list, and read it aloud, post it in your workspace, place it on your bedside table, and stick it on your mirror. Read it several times each day. When you are faced with decisions, go to your list and ask yourself which choice would be in alignment with your identity. Do not make choices that are outside of who you are, unless you are choosing to change that label.

8. Look back over your entire life. What experiences have you turned down because they were not right for a person "like you"? Where have you limited yourself or your thinking because you believed that a person like you did not deserve that experience or material object?

9. Play a little matching game with your chosen identity labels. Ask yourself what a person with each identity label might drive, what kind of spouse they might have, or where they might work. You can even cut out pictures or make drawings to reinforce the life that you are choosing for yourself now.

10. Look at your original list again. How many of your original "I am" statements were identity labels given to you by other people? How many of these were negative or limiting? How have you limited your life because of these experiences? Do you now see that these labels are not you— instead, they are simply who you believed yourself to be at one time? You can choose to take those labels off right now!

Come out of the closet

Are you under the impression that you are not in one?

Sorry, but you are.

The phrase "come out of the closet" is most often associated with homosexual individuals choosing to stop hiding their true selves by telling those that they love who they really are. It is often both a terrifying and liberating experience, as by declaring their personal truth, they are taking a real chance that the people that they love are going to reject them, ridicule them, or worse.

What you may not realize is that, homosexual or not, **you** are hiding who you really are from the people that you love, too.

Don't think so? Ask yourself these questions: Do you truly act like yourself with everyone that you know? Are you authentically you, or do you hide aspects of yourself?

I imagine that the truth is that there are few (if any) people with whom you are truly yourself.

Why do you hide who you are from so many people? Maybe you are afraid that people will either laugh at you or shun you. Perhaps you have been repeatedly made to feel that parts of you are bad, sinful, or shameful. Maybe this belief was even reinforced by experiences where you opened yourself up to someone, only to have them turn on you, yell at you, or even use this information against you. In reaction to this betrayal, you slammed your closet door closed, frightened to ever let anyone see the real you again.

This could not be a more human reaction, but here's the problem: when you refuse to bring your true self out into the light, you are using an enormous amount of energy to keep that closet door shut. After all, you have to be very guarded about everything that you say or do, less someone figures out who you really are. Not only is that a lot of mental energy, it also sends out a frequency to the Source that you are ashamed and embarrassed by who you are. Obviously, you can never tune into the life of your dreams with this kind of frequency.

It is **exhausting** to have to try to be something that you aren't in order to earn or keep someone's love and respect. But, is it really love if they don't know the real you? If they choose to reject you or deny you love because they will not accept aspects of who you are, then they were not offering love in the first place. Instead, they may have "loved" you for what you could do for them, and that is not love at all.

You deserve to be loved for all that you are, not for what you do for someone, the role that you will play in his or her life, or for conditions that you must meet for love to be offered. Always remember, love is love. It is completely unconditional. It is totally accepting. Unconditional love is not only what you deserve, but what you should offer to all life as well.

Please understand—this does not mean that the people in your life have to agree with you or your choices. They don't. The key is that you can be who you are and the other person can be who he or she is, and you are both treated with acceptance, respect, and love.

Stop hiding in the closet! You have just defined who you are and what you want to be in life. Be authentic to this truth, and discontinue relationships where you are not true to this vision of you. Simply **be** who you are in action and word. Be confident in yourself. And finally, love yourself—the more that you are authentically you, the more that you create a world that is authentically fulfilling.

Questions:

1. Think about all the people in your life. Do you change

who you are around certain people? What reactions are you afraid of? If you are not authentically you with some people, why are you still in a relationship with them?

Retuning statement: "I am who I am, and I love me. I am treated with acceptance and respect by others."

2. Are there people in your life with whom you **can** be authentically you? Why do you feel safe with these people? What is different about the love and acceptance that they give you compared to the conditional love given by others?
3. Of all your identity labels, what are the aspects of who you are that you most expect others to reject? To make yourself feel more powerful, I would like you to act out (in private) a recent interaction or experience where you felt that you hid parts of yourself. I'd like you to replay the events, this time acting in a way authentic to who you are, and letting the other person have their own reactions while you remain calm. How liberated do you feel? How frightened? Do this little exercise every time you have an experience where you feel that you are not true to yourself. By doing so, you will literally rewrite the experience to be in alignment with your true self and desired reactions.
4. Imagine that one of the people that you love told you something about himself or herself that you found difficult to accept. Would you still love this person? If not, why not? Have you ever chosen to revoke love from someone because they told you something about themselves that you did not or could not accept? Can you try to offer each person unconditional love, allowing them to be who they are without having to meet your standards or requirements?

Retuning statement: "I accept myself, and I accept others."

Reality check

If I asked you to take a good hard look at yourself, would it cause you stress?

I imagine that it might.

The process of self-evaluation is often avoided, because most of us are sure that we are terrible people, failed miserably in life, and barely deserve to live. Most of us avoid thinking too much about who we are, what we want, and what we choose to believe because we are certain that in doing this, we will just feel worse about ourselves.

However, that is just not true. You are much better than you think you are—you just need to change the way that you look at your accomplishments.

This negative perception of yourself is fueled by an all-out focus on to-do lists and "success measures" such as money made, promotions earned, and goals achieved. Chasing these things, you attempt to get a zillion things done each day at a pace that approaches the speed of light. "To-do" lists are often in the double-digits, and checking one or two things off that list hardly seems like a dent has been made. When you review your accomplishments for the day, you end up feeling like a failure because you seemingly got so little done.

You can feel like a success each day—you just need to shift your focus from what you didn't get done to what **you did.** By changing the way that you evaluate your accomplishments, you will instantly feel like a real winner in every area of your life.

The reality is that you are a great success in many areas of your life. To give yourself this wake up call, list everything that you did yesterday. When I say everything, I mean **everything**. How many times were you kind to someone? Did you help anyone? Were you a great mom or dad? Did you take your dog for an extra-long walk? What did you learn yesterday? Did you teach yourself a new skill, figure out new software, or make a new recipe for dinner?

Now think about the last week. How did you help others? What things did you do to contribute to your spouse, your friends, your family, your company, or others?

How about in the last month? The last year?

Look over the list of everything that you have accomplished. How do you feel about yourself now?

You do a lot more than you think you do. Reframe your focus to view your **real** accomplishments in life.

Questions:

1. In doing this exercise, how different was your perception of your achievements from what you actually achieved? Do you feel a new sense of yourself as a valuable person?

Retuning statement: "I am good enough. I am proud of who I am."

2. Cultivate the practice of reassessing your day in this way every day. Keep this ongoing list somewhere where you can review it on days when you are feeling down about yourself or your accomplishments.

Rejection's not so bad, and frankly, neither is failure

I know that this sounds crazy, but bear with me.

Think about being rejected for a moment. Imagine having your dearest dream fail. How do you feel? Breathless? Panicky? Scared out of your mind? Ready to drown your sorrows in a bottle?

I am not going to say that those reactions are good, but they **are** pretty normal. Just the thought of rejection or failure is enough to paralyze even the boldest of us with fear—and will absolutely stop you from going after the life of your dreams. Faced with the possibility of failing, all the frightening "what ifs" crop up: "What if I fail?" "What if I do the wrong thing?" "What if I cause the entire world to explode?" That last one may be an exaggeration, but you get the point. Faced with these fears, you avoid taking risks, opting for the "safe" or "guaranteed." You may know what you really desire, but a nagging terror in your gut keeps you from going after it. For instance, perhaps you would like to start a business, or hit a higher sales goal. If you fear rejection, you will never even pick up the phone to get that small business loan or call prospective clients. Maybe you would like to go back to school, but are older and fear the ridicule of younger students. Perhaps you dream of a loving, fulfilling relationship, but are afraid of leaving the average, slightly unhappy one that you have. After all, isn't it better to deal with the devil that you know?

In order to succeed wildly and take the steps necessary to bring your dreams into reality, you must view rejection and failure from a different perspective, and reprogram your mind with these three truths:

1. You do not need to prove yourself to anyone.

I know, I know, you have been programmed to believe that winning and success prove your worth—and maybe even that you must earn love—but it is just not true.

If this book has taught you nothing else, I hope it is that you are good enough just as you are, and that you deserve to succeed because you are a wonderful, talented co-creator of life.

If that is true, where does this feeling that you must prove yourself come from?

Years of training, my friend.

Think about how many times you were told by your parents you needed to "earn their trust" or "gain their respect." By winning awards and trophies, you proved that you were lovable—you were likely given accolades from parents and peers alike. You started dating and learned that the more desirable people are either the best athletes or those in prestigious careers—supposedly making them a better "catch." Because of this programming, you learned to try to collect the spoils of success—the expensive cars, large houses, and shiny jewels—to show others that you are a desirable, accomplished, important person.

When you are programmed with the need to prove your worth to others, each success becomes a new award to hang around your neck that screams, "Love me! I have earned it! I am good enough!"

By believing this, your self-worth is tied to what others think of you. Desperate to prove that you are worthy of love, you continue acquiring material things to keep getting that ego hit—that sweet moment when another person admires you for the spoils of your success. You might even think that you are gaining someone's love by showing off all of these riches. Sadly, this puts everyone else in control of your self-worth, which will never allow you to create the life of your dreams.

As you learned earlier in the book, no one else's perspective of you matters—**the only person that you have to prove yourself to is you**. You must admire yourself for who you are by taking the steps necessary to live a life in alignment with your deepest desires and goals. When you release the need to earn love by racking up successes, you will truly embrace the truth that you don't need someone else's approval of what you do, you don't need to prove what you can accomplish, and you don't need to show that you can meet some absurd set of standards that are not even yours.

Do you feel it? Rejection and failure have absolutely nothing to do with your self-worth, and so, do not need to be feared.

On to the next fear-of-failure-busting truth!

2. Neither failure nor success is personal.

Imagine this scenario: You go to a prospective client and sell your heart out. You look good, sound good, and are prepared beyond reason. You ask for the sale, and low and behold, the prospective client remains just that—*prospective*.

You leave, feeling like you are less of a person. You wonder what you did wrong. You search each moment of the meeting for your mess up, your screw up, your mistakes.

In short, you assume that the person was personally rejecting you, saying that **you** were not just good enough—that **you** didn't make the cut.

It's just not true. This is not a blow against you personally. It just is what it is, and nothing more. The person may have been having a bad day. They might have a friend that they would like to give the account to. It just may have not been the right fit for you.

Unfortunately, in our society, who you are is often defined by what you have, what you have done, and how you looked while doing it. Your goals and achievements become synonymous with "you"—so, if you fail or are rejected, you feel this as a blow against your ego, calling your very identity into question.

However, you are quite different from your goals. You have an identity (the one you just identified) that has nothing to do with whether or not you succeed or fail. Look at all the "I am" statements that you put down describing who you are. They are likely things such as, "I am kind," "I am intelligent," and "I am hard-working."

Please understand, you **are** this identity whether or not you ever meet your personal goals. This is who you are, and no one can ever take that away from you.

Now think about some goal-statements. These might read something like, "I want to earn $200,000 this year," "I would like to marry the woman of my dreams," or "I want to win the sales contest at work." What is the difference? While all the identity statements are a declaration of who you are as a **person** right now (I am), these statements are **action** statements (I want, I will, I would like). The goal statements are things that you would like to have—things to be acquired—while the identity statements are who you are inside, right now.

That being true, a rejection or failure is simply a bump on the path to connect with your ultimate goals. It is outside of you, and separate from you. It is not an identifier, and is never a blow against who you are, unless **you allow it to be**.

And for that matter, success isn't an identifier either. Your personal successes are not who you are, they are goals that you are accomplishing. They are simply manifestations of how you are choosing to create right now.

And finally,

3. Failure can be for your best.

Seriously.

I know that I am showing a blatant disregard for conventional thought, but here goes...

What shows itself as failure or rejection in your life may simply be an experience that was moved out of your way so that you can connect with one that is better for you. It is not failure—it is simply connection with a better success.

A friend of mine is a perfect example of how "failure" really can be for your best. He was married, somewhat happily, for several years. He had accepted the usual fights and difficulties as part of a normal relationship. One day, he came home to find out that not only had his wife been having a long-term affair, but she was leaving him. He was understandably devastated. However, a few months later, he met the woman of his dreams—one who fulfills him in every way, and who is a joy to be around. They are now married, and I have never seen him happier.

What would have happened if his wife had never left him? He would have stayed in a lackluster marriage, never being able to have the experience that would truly make him happy.

It is no different in your life. Throughout this book, you have worked on fine-tuning your beliefs and intentions to be at the frequency of the experiences that you want to tune into. By doing this, you can know that you will only tune into experiences that match these frequencies—and that are for your best. This means that you may not get the sale that you wanted, simply because you have a more prosperous, enjoyable one that you are supposed to tune into. You may lose one friend and gain ten that meet your exact needs.

Failure and rejection can be a show of your success in changing yourself, rather than an indication that you are worthless or a loser.

How do you know whether you are experiencing failure that is "in the flow" or failure that is an indication of negativity and being "out of the flow"? First, check in with yourself. Have you been doing your 4 for 40? Have you been working on thinking positively? Do you feel authentic to yourself? If all of these things are in place, then you must trust that you are tuning into an experience that is disguised as "failure" because you are ready for something better.

If you find you have not been doing your inner work, or are feeling afraid or apprehensive, then you may have tuned into this because you still do not believe that you deserve all that you desire. Do not berate yourself. Step back. Look at the experience for the lesson to be learned. See if you can identify the negative belief that is causing the problem. Reassess, and then work on trusting that you are bringing into being experience which are only for your best.

If you are finding that this is difficult for you, please go to the detachment section of Station 6 (actually all of Station 6 will work wonders for you!).

You are responsible for creating your experiences and the quality of them. When you keep your intentions in frequency with the very best in life, you will get the best in life. There's no reason to fear failure or rejection—after all, they could be indications that you are succeeding at getting in The Flow!

Questions:

1. What experiences have you avoided due to a fear of failure? Have you put off starting on important goals due to this fear? What steps can you take today to begin going after the life of your dreams?

Retuning statement: "I easily flow with success. I am confident in myself in all situations."

Become your own bodyguard

I am not suggesting that you become a black belt in martial arts, or even bulk up with weights (although that's certainly an option, if you like).

What I mean is that you must love yourself enough to know how to protect yourself in thought, word, and deed in order to truly have a positive flow in this Station. Let's take a look at the three ways that you can cultivate true personal strength:

1. You create your own security and peace of mind.

Perhaps the greatest stress that you will ever face is the impression that you cannot protect yourself from life itself.

I have certainly had moments like this. A few years ago my husband and I went through two hurricanes, completing renovations on our house, putting it on the market, a cross-country move, and the death of my beloved grandmother all in a four week period (actually, all but one hurricane happened in one **week**). I have never been so stressed out in my life, and I began to notice that I was constantly looking over my shoulder, waiting for the next disaster to happen. To top it off, I found I had gained about ten pounds in a week, although I hadn't eaten a thing in days.

I felt exposed and unable to protect myself, and this frequency began to create the physical reactions that I was having. My fight or flight response was so overstimulated that my adrenal glands burned out. My mind was saturated with the idea that life was unsafe, so I manifested padding all over my body to at least soften the energetic blows.

If you carry excess weight in your mid-section, ask yourself why you feel unsafe. Very often, you will feel the answer in your gut immediately. Perhaps you have been hurt by someone close to you, and you are afraid of being hurt again. Maybe you are afraid of being rejected for who you are. Or, perhaps you are at a point of chaos in your life, and you feel that the blows will never stop. Any threat against your physical, emotional, or spiritual self can trigger an imbalance in this Station.

While you may feel that you cannot protect yourself, this is never true. As the co-creator of your life, you have the ability to create your own security and your own safe space, even in threatening situations. After all, the more that you identify a particular situation (or all of life) with the expectation, "I am not safe," the more that you will trigger a fight or flight response in your body. Instead, when you find yourself feeling that you are being threatened in any way, bring your awareness to your breath. You will likely notice that you are either holding your breath or it is speeding up, so choose instead to take deep, slow breaths. By doing this, you communicate to your mind that you are calm—and your body remains calm. Then, in this calm state, repeat to yourself the new expectation, "I create my own security. I am safe. I am protected." If you would like to, you can place your hand over your stomach as you do this, further reprogramming your mind to connect your physical state with your mental reality.

If you have specific fears and phobias, use this practice coupled with the Art of Connecting and Principle of Repetition to retune your reaction to the experience. The object or experience that you are afraid of is simply a "trigger" for you right now—the instant that you see or even think about the experience, it triggers the physical responses of fear. At some point in your life, you learned to associate this experience with pain or panic, and you need to retune the memory-hologram surrounding that trigger. Begin by using the Art of Connecting to visualize yourself in a phobic situation, but see yourself reacting with calm. Breathe deeply to allow your physical self to feel safe. Repeat this practice over and over until you can do it without any feelings of fear. If possible, allow yourself to be in the presence of the phobic thing or experience, and continue to breathe calmly, just as you did in the visualization. By doing this over and over again, you will be able to use the Principle of Repetition to create a new hologram that tunes you into a positive, calm, and safe experience when presented with the specific trigger.

This simple practice will not only tune your you-hologram into better (and happier) experiences for you, but it will allow you to see that you always have the power to create a safe space even in threatening situations, just by choosing to set your expectations in a positive way. Try this practice every single day and your life (and your body) will be safe and happy!

2. You deserve to take care of yourself.

Have you ever wished that you had a definite sense of how to protect yourself in every situation?

The good news is that you do—it is a little thing known as your physical intuition, or more commonly, your "gut instinct."

While you have mental intuition (Station 6), **this** Station represents your mind's connection to your **body**, and it is this connection that allows the varying physical responses that you feel in different situations—responses such as a queasy stomach or tingling feeling when you are in danger. When you become aware of the subtle (and not so subtle) ways that your gut instinct speaks to you, you will have a very reliable tool to keep you away from experiences that are not in alignment with your highest self.

Developing this ability to connect with, respect, and listen to your own intuition is the greatest act of self love that you can take, but it may be the last thing that you do. How many times have you gone against your gut instinct simply because you were worried about hurting someone's feelings, disappointing them, or disagreeing with them? How many times have you ignored your gut instinct simply because you were afraid to trust yourself? Probably too many to even count, and that's a problem. When you choose experiences in opposition to what your gut tells you, you not only negate your personal worth, but you create a dysfunctional relationship with yourself. After all, would **you** be happy in a relationship with someone who never listened to you, never protected you, and paid no attention to your feelings? When you ignore your gut instinct, you are doing just that to yourself, which not only undermines your personal worth, but it dulls your ability to protect yourself.

Send a little love note to yourself by becoming respectful of your instincts. To increase your experience of your physical intuition, become aware of your center, or hara. Hara, as defined in the practices of Tai Chi and Aikido, is the energetic center of your body, but it is also the physical center of your body and the location of Station 3. By bringing awareness to this important part of your body and energetic system, you will develop personal strength and confidence in yourself and your instincts—and your instincts will be stronger than ever.

To develop this awareness, place your hand over your belly, approximately two inches below your navel. As you inhale, imagine a light radiating in that spot. As you exhale, imagine that light radiates in a circle around your center. Inhale again, and watch as the energy pulls back into a ball of light in your center. Exhale again, and see this energy reach farther away from you. Continue to do this as long as you like.

After doing this, how do you feel? Calmer? More at peace with yourself? I would highly suggest doing this simple exercise every single day, and especially anytime that you begin to feel nervous or stressed. The more that you do this, the more aware you will become of your own instinct about each situation and every person you meet. For instance, you may notice the tension in the air when you arrive at work one day and know to stay out of the boss's way. Or, you will feel an instinct to not walk into a bank or store, only to find out later that a hold-up occurred minutes after you walked by.

You will also have a reliable tool to allow you to be authentic to yourself in every situation, and especially in conflict situations. When you begin to feel anger, fear, or panic arise when dealing with a difficult person, choose to bring your awareness to your center. Breathe deeply, allowing yourself to bring your energy and awareness into your gut. In this centered state, not only will you feel much calmer, you will also know how to respond to any situation in such a way that you not only diffuse the anger, but also stay true to yourself.

Take time to be aware of your gut instincts. The more that you listen to them, the more powerful you'll become. The more powerful you become, the more confident you are—and that is always for your best!

3. You do not need to be perfect to be worthy.

Are you a perfectionist?

A lot of us are, and that's not a good thing.

When you hold yourself up to a perfect ideal, you are telling life that you do not deserve love, respect, or any other good thing **unless you meet that ideal**. Of course, it is impossible to be perfect, so you end up feeling like a failure because you never get what you want.

Perfectionism is also at the root of most addiction. Anorexics think that they will be lovable if they are thin. Alcoholics and drug addicts fear that they will never be as perfect as they think they need to be, so they drown this hurt and pain in the bottle or with pills—at least this way, they can have a reason why they are not living up to the ideal. Workaholics are always striving to prove themselves worthy of their jobs, love, and the respect of others by working themselves into the ground. Overeaters are often so frustrated at feeling that they will never measure up to the ideal body that they just eat—this way, they have control over **how** they failed. Plastic surgery addicts are chasing their individual belief of the perfect body, believing that attaining it will earn them love and approval.

Perfectionism is a nasty thing, because it never allows you to be good enough, lovable enough, or just **enough.** A perfectionist could do an absolutely perfect job, but they will only see the little flaws that no one would ever notice. Happiness is elusive for a perfectionist, because there is always something **more** that can be done to make their work, life, or body better.

This way of life will literally eat you alive. It is self-hatred, plain and simple. To live up to some fictionalized ideal, you will restrict eating, exercise excessively, and work until you have pushed way beyond your limits. You will beat yourself up for every single slight, mistake, or imperfection, and make yourself sick with worry that someone will find out that you are not as great as everyone thinks that you are. By making the ideal more important than you and your heath, your body will get the message that you do not really care about yourself, often resulting in disorders such as chronic fatigue and mononucleosis.

Stop abusing yourself! It's time to start taking care of yourself, and learn to accept yourself as you are now. Understand that no matter what messages you have received on what makes someone perfect, none of it is true. There is no ideal—there is no perfect person. You are perfect as you are right now. After all, you are one with the Source. How much more perfect could you possibly be?

Choose to connect with your inner beauty and truly love yourself for being you. Choose to be authentic to yourself, your instincts, and your needs. When you make a little mistake, take a deep breath and say "So what?" Everyone is entitled to make mistakes. Instead of seeing your "flaws," realize that these very flaws are what make you unique and desirable. After all, Cindy Crawford could have seen the mole on her lip as a flaw, but it became a real asset for her career—a desirable beauty mark.

You are just as beautiful. Feel it in your spirit. Accept it in your soul.

Questions:

1. When have you felt that you were not safe? Do you feel that you are unprotected now? What are you afraid of?

Retuning statement: "I am safe. I create my own security."

2. Do you think that you have a strong physical connection to your intuition? Do you get gut instincts? What has happened when you did not follow your gut instincts?

Retuning statement: "I trust myself and my instincts. I am grateful for this ability."

3. To further develop your connection between your mental and physical intuition, first ask yourself a question that you'd like the answer to, and then journal about the issue without stopping or filtering out your thoughts. Write everything that comes into your head, whether or not it seems like it has anything to do with the question at hand. Be aware of your physical reactions as you are writing. Do certain words or phrases elicit different responses in your body? When you are finished, read over what you have written. You will be shocked at how clear the answer usually is!

4. If you are a perfectionist, why do you feel that you need to be perfect? Are you afraid of not measuring up? Not being loveable? Not being accepted? Were you raised in a family where every little slight, action, or word was analyzed and blown up to massive proportions? Do you still fear that one word or phrase will cause a catastrophic response? How often do you push yourself beyond your limits to chase an ideal? Where did the ideal come from? Can you make yourself worthy of taking care of yourself?

Retuning statement: "I love myself. I am good enough in every way. I am perfect just as I am."

Are you a trustworthy leader?

And now I come to that over-analyzed but essential concept: **self-esteem**. Of course, it makes sense that good self-esteem is a major requirement for getting "in the flow"—after all, the whole book is about taking back your power and feeling good about your life and decisions. However, developing self-esteem seems to prove a terrible challenge for most of us. How in the world do you develop true, powerful, and flowing self-esteem?

Quite simply, you become a great leader of you.

This may not make sense at first, but I assure you, this is the path to truly feeling great about yourself.

Think about the qualities that make up truly great leaders. Great leaders earn your respect by doing what they say they will do. Without question, you will follow great leaders because they think through their decisions and have a clear, focused plan of action. Great leaders always take responsibility for themselves; they do not blame others for their mistakes. Finally, the greatest leaders inspire you to become more than you thought you could, inspiring groups of people to work together to create more than any one person could do alone.

On the opposite end, you likely also know some very bad leaders—perhaps your manager, a former boss, a corrupt church leader, or an unethical politician. Bad leaders do not do the research it takes to understand the decisions that they are making. They will often pass the buck when things go wrong, and they will be unfocused—changing goals with the whims of their mind. They'll demand your respect, but they do not earn it.

Do you follow the orders of this kind of leader? Do you hold someone like this in high esteem?

Of course you don't.

You have learned in this book that you are the one and only "leader" of your mind, body and spirit. You are responsible for coming up with the game plans, issuing the orders, and programming all your Stations. You decide what you want to come into your life, and you are responsible for seeing it through.

Do you think that your mind is going to be willing (or able) to bring into being what you want if you keep criticizing yourself, doubting your abilities, and changing your focus? If someone did this to you, would **you** do what they asked of you?

Not likely—and you certainly would not respect this person.

The key to feeling self-respect and self-esteem is to hold yourself in high regard. You must talk to yourself kindly and be willing to learn everything necessary to make good decisions. **Do what you say that you are going to do**—even if it is only little things at first (if taking appropriate action is difficult for you, please see Station 5). Each time that you prove yourself to be a good leader of your life and mind you will be rewarded by a mind that follows your directives and brings you what you desire.

Questions:

1. Do you feel that you are a good leader? Do you follow through on what you say that you are going to do for yourself? Do you feel that you should trust yourself? If not, why not?

Retuning statement: "I trust myself to know what is best for me. I am a good leader."

2. Who are the people that you most admire? What are the qualities that cause you to hold them in high esteem? Do you have these qualities? If not, how can you work on developing these qualities?

In order to develop the qualities that you admire, make a list of these qualities, and put "I am" in front of these. For example, perhaps you admire intelligence—a good affirmation would be: "I am intelligent."

262

3. As an exercise, write down all of the things that you admire about yourself right now. What are your good qualities? What might others admire about you? What compliments have you heard about yourself? If you have people that you trust, ask them to tell you what they admire about you. Write all of this down, and then put this list on your mirror or in your day planner. Make sure to reread this list every day (adding to it as some more good qualities come to you). You will be surprised at how much there is to admire about you!

4. Do you feel that you deserve respect? Say aloud, "I respect myself and my opinions." How do you feel? Notice if you feel nausea, sense nervousness, or feel muscles tighten up. Write down your observations. Continue saying this until you release the negative reactions from your body. This may take a little while—just keep at it. If it at first it is too difficult, just be gentle with yourself, starting again slowly each day until you can do this confidently.

Put your best self forward

Is the way that you dress now consistent with who you are or want to be?

If not, it needs to be.

Many people think that it is irrelevant how you dress, but the truth is that it is extremely important. The way that you dress says a great deal about not only what kind of person you are, but how you feel about yourself in general. After all, if you felt the same in a t-shirt and sweatpants as you do in a business suit, it wouldn't matter if you showed up to an important meeting in sweats. But it **does** matter—because you not only feel better in a suit, you project a very different image.

When you don't dress and groom yourself in a way that is consistent with who you want to be, you are sending a strong signal to your mind that you don't deserve to take the time to make yourself important, and that translates to a belief that you do not deserve positive experiences. In contrast, by choosing to take the time to make yourself important to **you**—to get a great haircut, to put on clothes that make you feel good, to select cologne or perfume that makes you smell good—you send a strong signal to life that you are not only important, but also *worthy* of every success and fulfillment that you desire. When you take the time to do the things that are important to you, you take better care of everyone else.

You are important. Choose to attire yourself in a way that says, "I love you!" to you!

Questions:

1. If you were to be the person that you desire to be— healthy, successful, happy, loved—what would you look like? What would you wear? Look through magazines to find pictures of people that have what you desire. How do they dress? Make an effort to find clothes for yourself that match the image that you want to project. Keep a scrapbook of pictures of people that are dressed in a way that matches what you desire for yourself.

2. Do you take care of your hair? What kind of haircut would you have if you were projecting the image that you are what you want to be? Find some pictures and a good hairstylist, and get a cut that matches who you desire to be.

3. If you are a woman, what makeup do you wear? Notice other women that you admire. How do they look? If you are unsure how to put on makeup or what colors would look best on you, schedule a makeover or two at a makeup counter.

4. Look through your closet. Which clothes do not make

you feel good? Which ones do not match who you want to be? Which ones remind you of bad experiences? Give all of these clothes away to a charity.

5. This week, make time to go to a mall and try on lots of clothes that are of a different style than what you would normally wear. How do you feel in each? What image do you project? Why have you been choosing the clothes that you do? Do you find that some of these new clothes actually make you feel better about yourself? If so, buy them immediately!

6. Do you feel that you deserve to look attractive? What fears do you have about dressing in a way that is authentic to you and that makes you happy?

Retuning statement: "I deserve to look and feel good. I am worthy of attention."

Station 3: Body language

If you are having disease in one of the body parts of Station 3, first, find out how the body part should be functioning if healthy. Then, find out what has gone wrong to create the disease that you are experiencing. For example, let's say that you are having an issue with your liver. What is the function of the liver? It detoxifies the body, removing waste from your system. What could this tell you about the beliefs that you hold that are causing this disease? Are you having a hard time releasing negative beliefs about yourself? Are you holding toxic thoughts about your self-worth? If you are overflowing with toxic thoughts, you could vibrate at a frequency that causes this dysfunction of the liver. Based on what you discover about the energetic cause of the disease that you are manifesting, compose a retuning statement specific to that issue. For the liver, it might be, "I flow with thoughts of my self worth, and allow all negativity to be easily released."

What I want is for you to learn to use your inner wisdom to understand the diseases and pain that you are experiencing in this Station. The more that you feel that you have the power to understand your own circumstances, the more that you can take control of your life—and truly believe that you have the power to change any negative or difficult experiences.

Action Plan for resetting Station 3

- ✓ Select 2-3 retuning statements to reset your preset.
- ✓ Go to page 409 and take the Reality Type Test, if you have not already done so.
- ✓ Select 4 Reality Type exercises, and do these for 40 days.
- ✓ Believe in your self-worth.
- ✓ Evaluate every choice for whether it is in alignment with the "real you."
- ✓ Choose to be authentically yourself in all experiences and with all people.
- ✓ Love yourself right now, as you are.
- ✓ Do not judge anything about yourself.
- ✓ Decide who you want to be, and be that every minute of every day.
- ✓ Be confident in yourself.
- ✓ Become a great leader of you.
- ✓ Listen to your gut instinct.
- ✓ Dress and act in ways that show the world who you truly are.
- ✓ Be proud of yourself and your accomplishments!

STATION 4

The Emotional Connection to Life

Station Motto: I feel all of life completely.

Location of Station: Heart

Problem Playlist: If you are preset with negative Station 4 beliefs, you will find that you have some of these behavior patterns and difficulties:

- Over-expressing your emotions (for instance, being a drama queen, a "bridezilla," or an anger-management candidate).
- Flying off the handle at little annoyances, or screaming at co-workers, spouse, or friends.
- Repressing emotions.
- Feeling numb—having an inability to feel anything for anyone.
- Holding grudges long after the issue is past.
- Being unable to forgive others for their actions against you.

- Being unable forgive yourself for mistakes that you have made.
- Playing and replaying difficult or painful incidents over in your mind.
- Being unable to heal from chronic pain or illness.
- Extreme attachment to the material things in life (such as the corner office, the expensive car, the great handbag), and a fear of losing your sense of self if you lost these "toys."
- Extreme attachment to your job or job title (people with this issue often have heart attacks, respiratory problems, or hyperventilation if they are laid off).
- Feeling broken-hearted over a lost love or failure, even years after it has occurred.
- Denying your feelings—being afraid to accept that you feel anger, envy, rage, or any other "bad" feeling.
- Having an inability to feel unconditional love.
- Being unable to feel joy about life.

Station 4 Body Issues: Finally, if you are tuning into negativity here, you will find that you will carry extra weight or have pain or disease in these areas:

- Heart
- Ribcage
- Lungs
- Respiratory system
- Breasts
- Circulatory system
- Shoulders
- Collarbones
- Arms
- Wrists
- Hands and Fingers
- Thymus Gland
- Thoracic Spine

Feeling the flow...

If you have been through any of the workbook sections for Stations 1, 2, or 3, then you have learned that these sections focus on how you **think** about yourself, your relationships, and the experiences in your life. However, in Station 4 you are going to be asked to understand how you **feel** about all of life—and your ability to connect emotionally with other people, experiences, and all that you desire to bring into being. When you emotionally connect to life and release destructive emotions, you will transform your life in truly radical ways—and enjoy all experiences more than you ever thought possible.

As was discussed in Principle 3, emotion is the key to not only life transformation, but perfect health. Every memory-hologram of any experience in your life is composed of not only all the sensory information of the experience, but also the thoughts that you had coupled with the emotional responses that you felt at the time. If the original experience was soothing or calming to you, then you will have a positive physical and emotional response anytime that you encounter any aspect of the experience now. In the same way, if the experience was particularly traumatic or fearful, the memory-hologram is coded with this emotion, and you will respond with the same exact feelings each time that you encounter any frequency matching any aspect of the original event. This being the case, the key to living a truly flowing life is to rewrite all negative memory-holograms to tune your emotional response to one that is positive and life-giving at every moment.

To do this, you will work through not only understanding your emotions, but allowing yourself to feel all emotions fully—to not block yourself from anything. This means learning how to express every emotion—especially those that you have blocked—in a positive, healthy manner. Once you have been able to do this, you will be able to forgive all those who have hurt you, and further, forgive **yourself** for anything that you feel that you have done. While forgiveness is often a difficult process, this Station is designed to make it much easier for you. Making it as easy as possible is important, because offering true forgiveness to yourself and to others is the fastest way to transform your life and your health.

Finally, you will learn to retune your "triggers" to be able to tap into the awesome power of emotion and tune into your desires with ease. When you complete this Station, you will be able to connect with all the most positive emotions of joy, compassion, and faith—and your life will be truly **transformed**!

The good, the bad, and the human

Let me ask you a few questions:

Is anger good or bad?

How about fear?

What about love?

Are your instincts to label hate and anger as "bad," and love as "good"? If you are like most of us, I am guessing this is just how you see it. In fact, you have likely been told that there are "good" and "bad" emotions, and were taught that, due to this fact, you needed to hold in or block "bad" or "negative" feelings. For instance, you may have been told that "nice girls don't get angry," so you automatically bottle up angry feelings, even when you have every right to be upset. Or, you might have been told that "crying is for babies," causing you to refuse to express sadness even in the most difficult of circumstances.

While many of these messages are spoken outright, just as many come from the positive reinforcement that you received when you held in "bad" emotions as a young child. For instance, when you held in tears or made nice with others, you may have learned that you were given love, admiration, or even toys and treats. Perhaps you found that when you acted fearless or denied pain, you were given a better spot on an athletic team, or were praised by your coach for your strength and devotion to the sport.

No matter how it played out for you, the message was clear: controlling your emotions and the responses that they evoke is favored; allowing free-feeling and expression of emotions is not. You have likely taken this message into adulthood, holding in or denying "bad" emotions in order to subconsciously seek rewards from others or to prove yourself "good," "strong," or "enlightened."

It's time for a little tough love...

Blocking yourself from feeling or expressing an emotion does **not** make you stronger or more in control of yourself. It does **not** make you more enlightened to refuse to feel the emotions that you deem negative. It does **not** make you more spiritual or religious or good.

What it makes you is sick.

When you block yourself from feeling any emotions not deemed nice, good, or spiritual, they end up being bottled up with no outlet for expression. Eventually, the frequency that you have manifested creates blockages in your energy system that show up as breathing problems, blockages in arteries, shoulder pain, and even breast and lung cancer. The cycle continues as you encounter more experiences that evoke the same emotional response. When you block those feelings once again, you create additional backups that tune you into more health issues, thus continuing a nasty and wholly unnecessary cycle.

In one sense, what you have been taught about emotions is a very human response; surely most of us would prefer to block or avoid pain and allow only pleasure. As you well know, anger, sadness, hate, guilt, and despair can cause very uncomfortable (even quite painful) feelings, and that does seem less than desirable. In contrast, love, joy, excitement, peace, and confidence bring to mind quite pleasurable experiences—obviously something that one would want to cultivate.

I can't argue with this logic; seeking ease and happiness is what this book is all about. However, I do take contention with the notion that you cannot enjoy the experience of the more difficult emotions, or that they are not good for you. In truth, with awareness and the right attitude, much can be learned from difficult emotions, and when viewed in the best light, these feelings can bring you to a renewed sense of life and a change for the better in all that you do.

Understand that regardless of how it may appear, there are no truly "good" or "bad" emotions. Since everything is a creation of the Source, then even the emotions that you would deem the least desirable are still creations of the divine force. Remember, everything is one, and all of it springs forth from the quantum level, meaning that anything in existence **is** the Source; nothing can exist and be otherwise. Nothing—and I do mean **nothing**—can be non-Source.

This means that although we as humans judge hate as "evil" and love as "divine," that cannot be true. Like it or not, everything is divine. Nothing is disconnected from the Source, and so, nothing can really be judged as good or bad or anything else for that matter.

I know that I have explained that there are higher frequency emotions—love being one, certainly—and lower frequency emotions like hate. While "higher" and "lower" might be equated in your mind with "good" and "bad," that is not the case. It is not about good or bad; it is only about what you want to bring into your life. If you are looking for a life of struggle and difficulty, you can choose to act in alignment with lower frequency emotions. If you are looking for ease and happiness, you must make the choice to speak, think, and act in alignment with the higher frequency emotions.

Oh, the humanity

The first step to allowing your life to flow with the best emotions (and therefore, the best experiences) is to allow yourself to simply feel every emotion in life without judgment or reservation. The more open you are to feeling the full range of emotions, the more unlimited your life will be. After all, all emotions flow from the endless potential of the Source. You are Source in physical form. When you close yourself off from feeling certain emotions, you attempt to control the flow of experiences coming to you—and trying to control **anything** in life is never going to tune you into the life of your dreams.

As a human, you have the unique opportunity to not only create any experience of life that you desire, but also to feel all emotions. By opening yourself to every emotion, you not only give respect to your humanity, you also allow yourself to be open to the abundance of life, which makes you **more** spiritual and enlightened, not less. The most enlightened people understand that simply feeling a "bad" emotion does not make you less divine—but blocking yourself from your own humanity by judging or denying your feelings just might.

By believing that you are not allowed to feel or express certain emotions, you are holding yourself up to an unrealistic and seriously flawed standard. In reality, it is not so important what emotion you are feeling, but rather, what you **choose to do with that feeling**; for instance, what actions you take because of it, or how you express it. The feeling itself is not positive or negative, but the expression of it is.

Take the emotion of anger as an example. Anger is often seen as a bad emotion—one that many people are taught that they must block in order to be considered "nice," "enlightened," or "spiritual," causing people to neither allow themselves to feel anger, nor to express it. However, when both felt freely and expressed properly, anger becomes a **catalyst to positive change**. For example, let's say that you are in a bad relationship; one that is limiting to you and exhausts you physically and emotionally. In the middle of yet another argument, you become aware that the anger you are feeling is an indication that you are tuning into a bad pattern, and that you need to end this relationship. Armed with this knowledge, you choose to express the anger not by yelling, but by talking with your partner from a place of personal power, breaking it off in the best possible way. By bringing your awareness to the feeling of anger and taking the time to understand it, you are not only able to express the anger in a positive way, but you are also able to break a negative pattern, opening yourself up for a new, more fulfilling relationship to flow to you. Obviously, this is a good choice in expression, and a great catalyst to move you to flow with a better life ahead.

However, instead of using anger in a positive way, you **could** respond by expressing it in a negative and frightening way, perhaps by yelling, hitting, or throwing things. Or, you could decide that it was unenlightened to feel anger and choose to bottle it up, not only continuing to take abuse from your partner, but also unknowingly choosing to take the anger out on others in your life. In either case, the belief that you do not deserve to either feel or positively express your anger would cause you to remain stuck in a debilitating experience, tuning your Stations into a cycle of repeating this experience again and again in all your one-on-one relationships. Clearly, this is a negative choice to make in response to the feeling of anger.

I said it before, and I will say it again: it is never negative or positive to simply **feel** an emotion, but you do make negative or positive choices in how you **express** the emotion. When you allow yourself to fully feel all emotions you become **more** enlightened, conscious, and powerful, because you grow in self-awareness. In fact, regardless of what is commonly thought, blocking your emotions **does not** give you control over them—allowing yourself to flow with a feeling and then consciously choosing the most positive way of expressing it, is **true control**.

When awareness is brought to an emotion, power is brought to your life.

Understanding this premise and making choices to express emotions in the best possible ways results in a positive flow for you, your energetic system, and your impact on the rest of the universe. Even better, "negative" emotions, when felt freely and expressed in alignment with your best life, are important catalysts for positive change. Keeping your eyes and system open as emotions come and go in your day assures that you are ready, aware, and willing to allow these positive changes to happen.

The next time that you sense yourself beginning to feel a "bad" emotion, just allow yourself to feel it. Don't put a wall up; don't try to control it. Become aware of why you are feeling it, and note the physical reaction that it causes. Work on being totally non-judgmental of the emotion itself. Consciously choose a positive way of expressing this emotion. Finally, be grateful for your humanity—and your ability to experience all emotions.

Questions:

1. Were you taught that there were emotions that were better than others? Did you see authority figures in your life who held in emotions? Did you admire this control?
2. Please look at this list of emotions. Identify whether you view each one as good or bad. Add any other emotions you desire to the list.
   Anger   Sadness   Happiness   Jealousy   Betrayal Guilt   Fear   Joy   Contentment   Peace   Anxiety Apprehension   Worry   Excitement   Faith   Hope
3. Can you remember when you learned that some emotions were good or bad? Can you remember specific messages given to you by your parents or other authority figures about the appropriate ways to deal with your emotions? Do you still operate on these messages today?
4. List some ways that you can positively express "bad" emotions. How have you expressed them in negative ways before? How do you feel about those experiences now? Did you learn anything from these experiences? Did you have negative consequences in your life because of this? If so, is there anything that you can do now to remedy the situation?

Let them go...

Your emotions, I mean.

In the upcoming sections, you are going to need to dig deep

into feelings that may have been clogging up your system for a while, which means that not only are you going to be asked to express these blocked emotions, but you are also going to need to let them go once and for all. While this is absolutely a liberating process, it can be a difficult one as well. When looking at these emotions, you may realize that they have become synonymous with "who you are." Because of this, it may be scary and challenging to let these aspects go for fear of losing parts of you. In addition, if you have been blocking painful emotions for a long time (sometimes an entire lifetime) it can take both great courage and great compassion with yourself to move through the feelings that are surfacing.

I was reminded of the difficulty of this process by a client who was finally confronting some blocked memories from his childhood. In the process of working through some of the reasons for his emotions, he finally remembered events that he had blocked due to their painful nature. Courageously, instead of putting up a mental wall against these feelings as he had done for his entire life, he chose to allow himself to feel the waves of sadness and anger that flowed over him due to these memories. While this was a scary and confusing process to go through, he ended up being able to release a great deal of the anger and grief that he had held for 30 years, and is now living life from a place of joy that he had not felt before. By feeling his bottled up emotions, he was able to release the frequency of burdensome sadness, which allowed him to move through to forgiveness, and finally to self-confidence and joy.

Needless to say, it can be hard to open yourself up to allowing painful emotions to flow freely, **especially** if you have blocked them for years. If you find yourself having difficulty with this, remind yourself that by choosing to let this negativity go, you are tuning into the life of your dreams. Make certain that you take time for yourself. Take a break when it gets to be too much. Allow yourself to go for a walk, or do anything else that is comforting to you. Do not feel that you need to push yourself through this process at any particular pace—do this in the timeframe that you feel you can, and above all, take care of yourself.

You may get to a point where all the hard work that you are doing does not seem to be doing much good. If so, try imagining the process of expressing emotions like logs in a fire. Remember that when you hold unexpressed emotions, they become solid particles, clogging up your arteries, increasing your stress levels, causing you to develop asthma, breast cancer, and heart palpitations (among other issues). However, when you choose to release these emotions out of your system, you are releasing these solid emotion-particles back into energy, just like lighting a fire and watching the logs turn into heat energy. As you express difficult emotions, imagine that you have lit them on fire, and watch them go off as smoke. Even when it is hard for you to express old emotions, remember—by not expressing them, you are clogging up your system. Instead, burn them off—and allow them to become energy that floats off and becomes something that you or someone else really wants (remember the big energy swap meet in Principle 2!).

As you go through releasing these different emotions, realize that all emotions are inter-related—and one can lead to another. For instance, betrayal can cause you to feel anger, or it can cause you to feel sadness. Hatred can be born from fear—especially if your survival is being threatened by someone or something, you may develop hatred of that person or thing to cover the fear that you feel. In truth, you will likely find that you have a range of emotions that are all connected around one issue or event. Allow yourself to intuitively deal with all of those emotions in a cohesive way.

Do not be afraid that expressing your emotions will cause you to lose control, go crazy, or sink into some manic-depressive state. Remember, **you control your emotions**, not the other way around—and believe me, it is **always** worse to repress your feelings. If you do find yourself feeling overwhelmed by the feelings that you are expressing, remember that you can (and potentially should) seek out a trusted advisor or psychologist to help you to deal with the issues that this process may bring up. There is no weakness in needing help or support, so please do anything that you need to for your own health and well-being.

Now that I have your attention (and potentially scared the heck out of you), let's get to it!

"Negative" emotion #1: Sadness

When is the last time that you had a good cry? Do you allow yourself to cry when you feel sadness?

I know that crying doesn't sound like all that good of an idea, especially when it holds such a social stigma. Children learn quickly that if a boy cries, he is told that "men don't cry," or is called "girly." If a girl cries, she may be called "overly sensitive" or "a cry-baby." As you grow up, this becomes even more deeply ingrained; men who cry are often put in a position of feeling that they are not strong enough for the women around them, and women who cry are frequently accused of using tears to manipulate situations to their bidding (such as getting out of a speeding ticket). Worse, women who show tears in business situations are passed over for promotions due to being labeled "too emotional" for leadership roles.

Due to this relentless conditioning, you may fear expressing the authentic emotion of sadness, preferring instead to block it and hide your true feelings, even if it means that you make yourself sick by bottling it up. You may have been taught that by holding back tears, you show strength, courage, or a "stiff upper lip," which is undeniably positive reinforcement for this behavior. This, along with any other messages that you may have received, will cause you to hold your sadness in, even when every fiber of your being wants to express it.

All of this conditioning is wrong. There is nothing cowardly or weak about expressing sadness or grief, and it does not make you a better or stronger person to hold it in. In truth, it makes you a person that others don't want to be around, since continuously blocking the expression of sadness leads to such undesirable traits as depression, dissatisfaction with life, and even total emotional numbness. Hating yourself for feeling sadness makes it even worse.

Still, there is no doubt it seems less desirable to feel sadness than to feel joy. While this is true, it is good to remember that even sadness, when expressed in a positive way, can lead you to a new place in life that is wonderful and limitless. After all, some of the greatest songs, poems, and works of art have been born from the feelings of despair and sadness of their creators—by allowing themselves to tap into the raw emotion of sadness, they created beauty from the pain. In contrast, when the same sadness is blocked or expressed in a negative way, it can cause people to harm themselves, drink or gamble excessively (this, from the avoidance of the feeling), or even commit suicide.

Again, **feeling** the emotion is not positive or negative—the way you **express** it is. Choosing to repress an emotion is **always** negative to your life and health.

Be aware that sadness is often wrapped up with grief, although grief is more specific to a sense of loss. While you can feel sad over many issues and events in life—things like not getting a promotion or having someone be unkind to you—grief deals with the sadness that you feel over the **loss** of a loved person or thing. Because grief is such a powerful emotion, unexpressed grief is one of the most detrimental emotions for your well-being. When you do not express grief, it can envelop you (sometimes for years) as it is combined with feelings of guilt over both the loss itself **and** your perceived personal responsibility for that loss. By refusing to deal with these feelings, you may develop an increased sense that you "should have" or "could have" done something to prevent the loss, which then limits your life to seeking experiences where you somehow think that you will "make it up" or "make it right." Unfortunately, this leaves your self-esteem crushed and your spirit weak, as that is an endless and impossible pursuit. Physical ailments are sure to result from the burden of this frequency, often due to the fact that you now feel that you deserve bad things to happen to you as some sort of punishment for living.

Grief is most often associated with the loss of a loved one, but it can also be felt over the loss of material things, such as houses, cars, or pieces of jewelry—or it can be felt over the loss of your social or financial standing, or even your career. While you are often told that it is not okay or appropriate to express your sadness over such changes in life, it is not only appropriate, it is necessary for your well-being.

The loss of **anything** that you hold dear may cause grief, which includes the grief that you will likely feel at the loss of who you are now as you transition to the new, more powerful you. Yes, this transition is a positive one, but you may still feel a sense of loss about the familiar circumstances, experiences, and thoughts that are comfortable and known as "you" now. While few people allow themselves time to feel the sense of loss that accompanies this change, it is an important one to express. The reality is that by choosing to empower yourself—and take charge of this transition—you will never again be who you are right at this moment. A total life transformation also means a total "you" transformation—so, if you find that you need to, allow yourself to grieve over the loss of the "old you."

Whatever it is that makes you feel sadness and grief, open yourself to the feeling. When you feel an inner resistance to letting these feelings flow, say to yourself (loudly, if necessary), "I am empowering myself to get the very best out of life!" By allowing these feelings of grief and sadness now, you are consciously sending out a signal to life declaring that you respect and love yourself enough to both feel emotions and to learn from them, matching the reality of your desires with the "you" that you truly want to be.

Questions:

1. Write down the words "sadness" and "grief." What do you associate with those words? Allow yourself to free-journal anything that comes to mind about sadness for 5—10 minutes. In looking back over your notes, what strikes you as important about your thoughts and experience of sadness or grief?

2. How did the authority figures in your life express sadness? Do you find yourself expressing or repressing sadness in the same ways? Were you taught that you could express your sad feelings, or did you have to hold them in? Have you ever been criticized or yelled at for expressing sadness? How did that make you feel? How do you think that your life would have been different if you were encouraged to feel and express sadness in good, open ways?

Retuning statement: "I choose to express sadness in positive ways for my own good. I release others' patterns and use my own power to create my best emotional life."

3. Write down some of times in your life where you felt the greatest sadness or grief. Did you fully express the sadness at the time, or did you hold it in? If you repressed the sadness, why did you feel that you had to do this? What effect has this repressed sadness had on you emotionally, physically, and mentally?

Retuning statement: "I allow myself to feel sadness, grief, and all emotions fully."

4. For any of the experiences listed above, how do you think that you could express that sadness now? Is there something that you would like to say to someone but never had the chance, perhaps because they are deceased or no longer in your life? Write a letter to that person expressing everything that you would have liked to express. Put that letter in a special place—perhaps a box or hidden drawer. You could also listen to music that reminds you of that person or of the experience, or rent a sad movie. Imagine yourself as the character in the movie, and allow the tears to flow—expressing the sadness and grief that you have held in for too long.

5. As you transform to the new you, what do you think

that you will miss most about the "you" that you are today? Write out all of these things and grieve for them; light a little fire and burn them, or do a small ceremony to say goodbye to these aspects of yourself.

"Negative" emotion number 2: Anger

Ah, anger. Without question, it is an extremely difficult emotion, and one that gets a bad rap, in many cases, for good reason. Anger, when expressed in a negative way, can do incredible harm—the many people that have been killed in war can certainly attest to this fact. More than just war, anger is responsible for splits in families, domestic violence, rape, and murder, to name just a few of its nasty consequences.

However, anger can also have very positive consequences. It can give you the push needed to move into a better phase of your life. It can tell you when you have changed from a pattern of just passively accepting someone's bad behavior to finally feeling the anger signaling that you are ready to stand up for yourself. Because of this, you should actually be **glad** when you feel anger—it is very often an indication that you are not willing to take behavior or experiences that you once thought that you had no power to change.

That said, keep in mind that anger directed at yourself can be very misplaced. Self-directed anger is usually a learned response to not living up to someone else's standards that you mistakenly think are yours. For instance, I know that I get very angry with myself when I feel tired and cannot push myself to finish a project by whatever self-imposed deadline that I have set. Of course, being angry at myself because I am human and need rest like any other person is **ridiculous**. However, this anger manifests in me because I was programmed from a young age that I should be able to pull off super-human feats, and I was particularly rewarded for pushing beyond my physical limits and putting my health second to completing whatever project I was faced with. It is such a deep-seated issue that I still struggle with it today.

You may have the same kinds of feelings about yourself, or certainly about your own ability to feel and express anger. You may have been yelled at when you expressed anger as a child, or, if you were like me, because you felt that it was not nice to feel anger (and you were, after all, a nice girl!), you found ways to redirect that anger, such as by exercising excessively or overeating. While there are many ways to positively express anger (and exercise is certainly one of those methods), if you never confront your anger or the person or experience that has made you angry, then you never reprogram the corresponding Station into a new reality, and you live the same frequency of experience over and over again.

If you are accustomed to holding in your anger, it will be a great challenge to allow this to flow through you. Without doubt, if you are a person who has seen the ill-effects of anger in your childhood—perhaps by witnessing domestic violence or having abuse turned on you—you may be terrified of allowing yourself to even **feel** anger, less you express it in these frightening ways.

However, for your own health and best life, you must challenge these long-standing messages and beliefs and learn to feel, express, and release anger in your life in the most positive ways. Choose to take on the new belief that feeling anger does not make you a bad or mean person, and it most certainly does not make you unenlightened. It is an authentic feeling that can be used positively to retune your Stations to flow with the life of your dreams when given its proper place.

To that end, these questions and exercises are designed to help you both understand your anger *and* find ways to positively express this anger—both to yourself, and to anyone that you are angry with. By doing this, you become the truly enlightened person that you are on a quest to be, and you become **lightened** from the burden of this difficult emotion in the process.

Questions:

1. Write down the word "anger." What do you associate with this word? Allow yourself to free-journal anything that comes to mind about anger for 5—10 minutes. In looking back over your notes, what strikes you as important about your thoughts and experience of anger?
2. How did your parents and other authority figures deal with anger as you grew up? Was anger directed at you? How has this affected you? Do you find yourself repeating their expression of anger in your own life? What did they teach you about your right or ability to feel and express anger?

Retuning statement: "I choose to express anger in positive ways for my own good. I release all learned patterns and use my own power to create my best emotional life."

3. Think of moments in your life when you felt the most anger. Did you express or repress the anger? In imagining each moment now, do you still feel the same physical reactions linked to anger that you did during the actual event? Can you identify the underlying issue in each moment that caused you to feel anger? Are there similarities? If you have repressed anger in a situation, write that situation out completely—including everything that you felt at the moment, and what you wished that you had said or done. How has this experience(s) had an influence on your life? Have you had positive or negative changes because of it?

Retuning statement: "I allow myself to feel anger fully, and I make choices to positively express it in my life. I am worth defending!"

4. If you have experiences in your life where you have

repressed anger, choose to express it now. Write a letter to the person, saying everything that you wish you had said—but do not send it—instead cut it up, shred it, or burn it. Punch pillows and scream at the top of your lungs. Take a boxing class, and dedicate that class to the expression and release of your anger from this experience. Do whatever occurs to you as the right expression of this anger, but do express it in safe, healthy ways—get this out of your system right now! After you are done, make sure to journal about your experience.

"Negative" Emotion Number 3: Jealousy

Have you ever had someone do something hurtful to you only to watch them go on with their life as if nothing has happened? It's not too fun, is it?

Or, perhaps you know someone who operates terribly unethically, but who is rewarded with all the spoils of success, while you plod along day after day with half as much as they have. Maybe you find yourself envious of the soccer mom that goes on and on about all her diamond rings, expensive cars, or luxury vacations that she and her husband go on, when you and your husband cannot afford those things.

Experiences like these can certainly make you feel jealous of what someone else has that you don't. Faced with these situations, your life may pale in comparison, and you find yourself not only preoccupied with thoughts of what your life lacks, but also focused on how you might get back at the object of your envy. Caught up in a jealous fit, you may do things that are totally against who you are as a person, such as spreading rumors about how the person **really** got their riches, or finding yourself selling out your personal ethics to get the money or objects that you desire.

Jealousy is a nasty emotion—causing you to expend time and energy on obsessive thoughts that are not going to do you any good, and that might even make you sick (ever heard the term "green with envy"?).

What to do with this emotion? You cannot let it bottle up and cause you to get ill. How can you express it effectively, using it as a catalyst to get all you truly want?

First, you learn about your personal power, and then you use that power to help you live well (since you are already doing that, you are halfway there!). As you now know, anything that you repeat—either in thoughts or words—tunes you more strongly into whatever frequency is represented. When you speak unkindly about a person for whom you feel envy, you are really hurting yourself by manifesting the frequency of unkindness in your life. Worse yet, each time that you think about the other person's success, you are creating a frequency of lack in **your** life and giving energy to **theirs**.

Use a simple image to break your own pattern of jealousy (if you have been through Station 2, you will recognize this exercise). Imagine that you have a pocketful of dollar bills, and each time that you think about the object of your envy, you hand him or her a dollar bill, creating more wealth and ease for this individual. How long would it take for your pocket to be empty, and his or her pockets to be full?

Now imagine that each time that you focus on positive thoughts about yourself and your own ability to manifest positive experiences, you can put a dollar bill into a high-return bank account. Imagine that this bank account doubles in value each day. Wouldn't this be a better way to make yourself feel good about yourself and your life? After all, by focusing on your positive traits and releasing jealousy and judgment of others, you end up living the abundant life that you are so jealous of!

You see, living well is **truly** the best revenge—and to do that, you must think well about yourself, your life, and even those that you dislike or resent.

Questions and exercises:

1. Who in your life has hurt you so badly that you desire revenge on them? Have you heard of their success and it feels like salt in a wound to you? Do you find yourself visualizing ways to take revenge on those that have hurt you in the past? If so, what would you like to do, and why?

2. Is there anyone in your life that you are jealous of? Do you know someone that is unethical, mean, or just not a good person, but who seems to "have it all"? How often do you feel envious of this person? What do you say about them? Have you taken revenge on this person in any way? If so, what did you do, and did it make you feel any better, or do you feel worse?

Retuning statement: "I focus on my life for my good. I am grateful for my success and happiness."

3. As an exercise, I would like you to print two pictures of a piggy bank. On a page in your journal, paste the two pictures across from each other. On one bank, write your name. On the other, write the names of all of the people for whom you feel envy. For a week, each time that you think vengeful or jealous thoughts about someone that you envy, write a dollar sign on their bank. If you speak these thoughts to others in a negative way, write a dollar sign for that. However, when you think or speak in positive ways about yourself, or stop yourself from thinking jealous thoughts, give yourself two dollar signs. At the end of the week, evaluate. How much energy did you give others? How much did you give yourself?

If you find yourself having difficulty with jealousy, please use the retuning statement*: "I am in charge of my own life. I feel fully powerful. I release others to live the life that they need to, and I live my own life."

* In the next section, you will learn how to forgive those that have hurt you in order to free yourself of any vengeful feelings.

"Negative" Emotion Number 4: Fear

There is no doubt in my mind that the emotion of fear—and the uncomfortable physical sensations associated with it—creates negative and limiting belief-holograms quicker than any other feeling.

You will easily understand this if you have had the misfortune of being in a car accident or other situation where your life was in danger. After the fact, did any of the sensations that you associated with the original event trigger feelings identical to those that you felt during the actual event?

It is likely that they did. It is a phenomenon often called a "flashback," and the reason for it is simple—the energy of the original event was so powerful that the frequency of fear combined with all the sounds, tastes, sights, and tactile impressions of that moment and instantly became a very strong memory-hologram, imprinting the experience and the frequency of any associated beliefs in your mind. Any encounter with anything that was an aspect of the original event instantly tunes your brain and body into the frequency of that reality, causing you to feel the same in the new moment as you did at the time of the actual occurrence. Suddenly, you go from being a confident, assertive person to being a completely panicked, scared mess, reacting in ways that may confuse you. Your present self may logically know that you are not truly in danger, but your subconscious self is writhing with fear and panic created by the past.

This is indicative of how powerful of an emotion that fear really is. Worse, the desire to avoid the fear may cause you to not only avoid similar situations (limiting your life), but it may also cause you to give your personal creative power over to other

288

"authorities" in the effort to have a solution to the fear that you feel. The knowledge that a fearful person will believe almost anyone who seems to provide a salve for the pain that they feel is a fact used every day by the media, politicians, religious leaders, and even people in your everyday relationships. By pushing the fear trigger, these "authorities" can convince you to do what they say— even if it goes against your own sense of logic or ethics—just because you so desperately want to alleviate the discomfort that comes from the fear response. In the end, the fear wins, because you have given your personal creative power over to others' beliefs and desires, and that never tunes you into the life of your dreams.

To begin the process of dealing with fear in a more positive way, it is important to learn to distinguish between the two basic types of fear: "survival" and "learned." "**Survival fear**" is the emotional response that you feel when you are truly in danger. It is programmed into your system from before you were born, and has a great deal to do with the basic instincts that ensure your survival. However, "**learned fear**" is the emotional response that you feel because you have been taught that a situation is frightening, either by your own past experiences, or through repetitive messages given to you by authority figures in your life. For instance, when you were young, you were likely taught to never talk to strangers because strangers do bad things to little kids. After learning this, you may have felt afraid if any stranger approached you, whether or not that person meant you harm; you simply labeled any unknown person as a "stranger," and the stranger frequency was scary, causing a fear response in you. Because of this early programming, you may still feel a little fear upon having a stranger approach you, even as an adult.

Once you have been **taught** that a situation is scary, you approach all such experiences as frightening, **whether or not the situation is actually threatening.** When you believe that you should be afraid of a situation, you effectively turn off your basic survival instincts, and you are unable to rely on your intuition to assess the true threat level of any situation. At this point, you simply react from a programmed response—one which may or may not be appropriate to the situation.

Worse yet, learned fear always limits your life—**always.** It does not matter if your fear was developed from a past frightening experience or the fears of everyone around you, **all learned fear limits you**. After all, if you have been taught by your dad that you must protect every cent you have less someone steal from you, then you will never be able to trust others and develop the business that you desire. If you believe the news when it says that the world is getting worse every day, then you will be unlikely to take risks in your life that might lead you to the job of your dreams. If you have been hurt by a girlfriend in the past which has lead you to believe that relationships are scary and painful, then you will limit your ability to find your soul mate.

One of the easiest ways to develop a learned fear is embarrassment. If you have ever been embarrassed or humiliated in a situation—maybe done something accidental that made you the focus of negative attention, or were made fun of for anything— then there is no question that you have a learned fear about ever putting yourself in that situation again. For instance, you may have a fear of speaking in public. When you think about it, you remember that you had to give a speech in the 5th grade, and other kids laughed at you. Or, perhaps you have a fear about having clothes show off certain parts of your body. Upon consideration, you realize that this fear might have been caused by other kids making fun of these parts when you were in school, although there was nothing actually wrong with them at all. In any case, you may avoid doing things that you think will cause embarrassment again, but the reality is that you may be limiting your life from doing things that you will enjoy or even be good at. Release this fear and embrace the limitless, powerful you that exists in your soul!

To understand how you are limiting your life because of fear, think of something that you are afraid of. What do you avoid because of this fear? What concessions do you make in your life in order to not put yourself in a situation where you might feel this fear again? I imagine that it is shocking to you how many decisions that you make and experiences that you miss in order to accommodate this fear. If you are even limiting your life in only **one** way, it is too much—there is no reason for your life to be limited in **any** way.

As you start doing the questions for this section, realize how essential it is that you have outlets to express the fear that you feel. When you always hold in fear because you feel that you need to be the "perfect one" or the "strong one," you can develop serious anxiety and panic disorders as the fear builds in you with no release. The belief that you can't show fear for fear of looking weak will cause a panic reaction in you as you worry about losing control and breaking your perfect, strong façade. This pressure will build to an unbearable point, creating disease and disorder in you every time.

For all these reasons, give yourself a break!

Questions:

1. Have you had situations where you were afraid for your life? What did you learn in this experience? What physical reactions did you have at the time? Have you ever had flashback moments triggered by one or two aspects of the original event? Do you avoid certain experiences because of the fear of repeating the experience? What can you do today to take a small step toward healing this fear? How can you express this fear in a safe way in order to begin to release it? For example, you could journal, punch something, scream, cry, or choose to do something else liberating to express it.

2. How have others' fears created your own? What fears have been taught to you by the media, political figures, religious teachers, or other people in your life? How do these fears limit you? Can you find examples where some (or all) of these fears are unfounded?

3. Do you feel that you have good instincts? Have you had experiences where your survival fear kicked in? Can you tell a difference in this instinctual reaction as

opposed to the reaction caused by learned fears?

4. Have you ever had a truly embarrassing moment? Do you avoid similar circumstances now because of this? How might you express this embarrassment in healthy ways now? Can you turn this experience into something positive?

Retuning statement: "I am perfect in all ways. Others' opinions of me do not matter—I am confident in who I choose to be."

5. What are your greatest fears? Where did they come from?

Retuning statement: "I am confident. I am safe in all ways and at all times."

6. Do you hold in the feelings of fear because you are afraid of looking weak or imperfect? Do you fear losing control and embarrassing yourself or exposing an emotional side? Does this make you feel vulnerable? What effect does holding in your emotions have on you? To begin to express this repressed fear, journal about the times when you have felt fear, and how you would have liked to express it. Can you express some of that now? Choose to do this on your own, or with a trusted friend.

Retuning statement: "I allow myself to feel and express all emotions with ease. This is true strength."

"Negative" Emotion Number 5: Hate

Hate is not a stand-alone emotion.

Hate is always caused as a **reaction** to one of the above emotions, and is actually a way of distancing yourself from experiencing those emotions again by empowering yourself to hate a particular thing, person, or group of people. For instance, you may be so jealous of someone else's success that you "hate" them. Or, you may have been threatened by a group of people as a child, and the fear that you felt (and that they caused in you) has developed into a hatred for all people "like them." Of course, focusing hate at the problem experience seems to give you power over it, but that is an illusion.

Regardless of the cause for feeling hatred, the bottom line is that it is **always** a learned emotional response. In fact, the truth is that you do not know hatred as a baby—it literally does not exist. As you grow, you learn to hate because of your own experiences, what your "authority figures" teach you, and other influences—such as the portrayal of different groups of people in the media. In fact, hate often rises from Station 1 issues—fears over personal survival—and this ends up pitting one group of people against another for no real reason.

Any way that you look at it, hate is the most destructive emotion that you can feel. Since it is the polar opposite frequency of love, when you hold hate in your being, you negate all love that flows to you, and this creates a life that is not only harmful to you, but to the entire world. After all, since we are all one, when you hate another person you are really choosing to hate yourself, which doesn't make much sense, does it? Why hate any part of that which is the beauty of existence? There is never a good reason to hold hate toward another.

Choose to truly evaluate that which you "hate" in order to release negativity from your life for good!

Questions:

1. To evaluate the real cause for your feelings of hate toward another person or thing, please use this exercise: If you have ever been around a 5 year old child, you will know that he or she will ask "why" a million times

until you either get to the root of the answer, or give up in frustration. I would like for you to use the same idea to get to the root cause for your feelings of hatred. Write down someone or something that you think that you hate. Now, ask yourself, "Why do I hate this?" After you write down that answer, ask why **that** is. Continue to ask "why" until you get to the fundamental issue. As an example, let's say that you feel that you hate a certain group of people. After asking why this is, you realize that your parents always spoke badly of them. Why would your parents have spoken badly of them? They were of a generation that was afraid of change, and this group represented a threat to that. So, the real reason that you hate this group of people is because of your parents' fear. Is this a real reason to feel hate? Do you have any personal fear of this group? Once you understand the underlying reality of why you have learned to hate anyone or anything, deal with that issue—either releasing the underlying emotion, or doing research to come at the issue from a place of logic and reason, eradicating the hatred for good.

Retuning statement: "I feel love for all. We are all one."

"Bad" emotion number 6: Guilt

Guilt is a nasty little bugger isn't it? It can make you do things that you don't want to do; it can make you hate yourself for years over things that you think you shouldn't have done. It seems like you have no choice about feeling guilt, but here's the dirty little secret:

Guilt isn't a real emotion.

Yes, you feel it, and therefore it is real as that goes, but it is another **learned** emotion—it does not exist until you are taught what it is and when you should feel it. In fact, there is a great deal of solid evidence that shows that as a baby, you do not even know what guilt is, let alone know how to feel it. However, as you grow and are taught that you should feel bad for certain actions, thoughts, or feelings, you learn to respond to these things with a sense of guilt. Of course, this is in direct conflict with the common belief that guilt is part of your innate sense of right and wrong, or "conscience." Put simply: it isn't. Guilt is **taught** to you by the authorities in your life.

There is no question that a sense of learned guilt accompanying truly wrong or harmful actions is valid and even good, as it pushes people to take actions to make amends for these wrongs against others. A conscience mixed with the feeling of guilt causes many rapists and murderers to confess, which is certainly a positive result of guilt. However, depending on how you were programmed by authority figures in your life, you can also feel guilt even when the action that you took (or were going to take) is perfectly appropriate, and even harmless. Becoming aware of this fact when you sense guilt allows you to understand what an authority figure might gain by programming you to sense guilt in certain situations. Sometimes the motivation is just to keep you on the "straight and narrow," but just as often it is to keep you fulfilling **their** needs and desires. If this is the case, then you will notice that you feel guilt when certain "buttons" are pushed, and you will feel compelled to do what the other person wants, even when you truly want to be doing something else. For instance, your boss might push some "guilt buttons" when you resign, telling you that the business will fail without you. It's not true—the boss just doesn't want to have to do all the work that he had wrongly pushed off on you—but this will push a button that causes you to feel guilty about leaving, even when it is the appropriate decision for you. If you do not recognize your boss's manipulation, the sense of guilt that you feel might be so overwhelming that you stay at the job, which is not best for you. Guilt is a very strong trigger, indeed.

This learned guilt can develop into self-imposed guilt, taking away your ability to enjoy experiences where you think that you "should be" feeling guilt. I am speaking from experience here, because if someone could have a black belt in self-imposed guilt, it would be me. I never feel that I am doing enough for others, even when I am doing as much as I possibly could do. Because I am concerned about the environment, I often find myself unable to just sit and enjoy the nature that I love so much; instead obsessing about the fact that I have not done more to protect this lovely creation. I worry about buying items that are not organic, sweat-shop and cruelty-free, so I fixate over every purchase, often passing up beautiful clothes because I feel guilty that they might have been produced in ways that would have harmed a person or animal. If I stand up for myself and turn down an invitation simply because I am exhausted, I feel guilt that I might have hurt the person's feelings, even though I had no intention of doing so.

I tell you all of this not only because I want you to understand that even those of us that are in teaching or guidance positions struggle with the same limiting beliefs that you do, but also because I am guessing that you might be able to relate to these feelings and thoughts. Most of us that are focused on improving ourselves are also trying to improve the world and never feel that we are doing enough. The problem is that when you are always feeling guilt about what you **could** or **should** be doing, you can never enjoy the present moment for **what it is**. This is the power of guilt—it can take you away from loving and enjoying life, leaving you instead in a terrible place of dissatisfaction and worry.

Don't you think it is time to get rid of guilt for good, and get to the business of truly feeling and enjoying life? Let's get to it!

Questions:

1. What do you feel most guilty about? Are there experiences that you still feel guilt over? Are there certain people that can push those "buttons" most easily?
2. The next time that you feel guilty over something, ask yourself if you are truly harming anyone by making this

decision or taking this action. Is the action for your best? Is this feeling of guilt coming from old programming? Is it tapping into old fears about hurting others or disappointing those in your life? If the guilt is not caused because you are truly going to harm someone or something, then breathe in deeply and say to yourself, "I release anything that is not for my best. I am not responsible for others' lives. I am only responsible for my own."

3. Do you impose guilt on yourself for things that you think that you should be doing instead of enjoying the moment? When do you do this? Why do you think that this is? Can you identify the main issue that causes this? Do you have an over-inflated sense of personal responsibility for others lives?

Retuning statement: "I deserve to enjoy life. I choose to fully enjoy the present."

Clearing the slate: forgiveness

Would you like to know the most essential thing that you can do to assure that you live a healthy, fantastic life?

Forgive.

Forgive others for their wrongs against you. Forgive yourself for things that you have done. That's it. That is the big secret.

I know that it sounds simple, but unfortunately, forgiving is perhaps the biggest challenge that you will ever face. The good news is that you are already through the first step to forgiveness, which is to express any blocked emotions (you didn't know that was what you were up to, did you?). Blocked emotions create blockages in your system—by expressing your "bad" emotions, you allow yourself to move that energy and give yourself the dignity of feeling the sadness, fear, anger, jealousy, hate, or guilt that you feel toward the person or event that has harmed you.

Giving yourself permission to express your feelings frees you from having to carry that burden, and opens you to the next step to forgiveness—which is to truly let it go.

In this step, you will totally release any anger or hurt that you feel toward those that have injured you. Because you may have been holding onto painful experiences for most of your life, this can be difficult. However, you now have knowledge essential to making forgiveness as easy as possible. That knowledge? You chose the experiences of your life based on the frequency matching the expectations and beliefs that you held at the time. That may seem like a simple realization, but a good part of what makes forgiveness so hard is that you likely focus on the specific **person** or **situation** that harmed you; however, you can now understand that the person or situation actually does not matter at all—you would have chosen the frequency of that experience no matter who or what the exact situation was, due to the underlying beliefs that you held at the time. So, while you may be angry at a specific person who hurt you, you must choose to view them not as an individual, but as simply an **energetic frequency** that you tuned into due to some matching negative programming in your mind at that time. If it was not that person, you would have tuned into another person or experience matching that exact frequency.

I'd like to give you a good visual to help you understand this: imagine that you are in a boat floating down a lovely river. The river represents your life, and as you float along, you see different experiences of your life played out—some from childhood, some from young adulthood, and so on. Suddenly, you come to a place where the river divides into three streams, and you must decide which way to go. After worrying for some time about the right decision, you decide upon a stream. You move along and begin to meet some new people and have a bunch of different experiences with them. The final scene shows you being injured in one of these experiences with these people. You feel hurt and angry, and hate the people involved for being so unkind. Quickly, you begin to chastise yourself for being so stupid as to have decided to take this path instead of one of the other ones. Angrily, you look back to see if you can still make another decision. With shock, you realize that all three streams—all the paths that you had decided between—came to this same spot in the river. It did not matter which choice you made, you would have had the same experience regardless.

This is just how life is. As you go along in life, you are given many choices to make—like choosing between the three streams. While you might fret over the choices, they will all take you to the same energetic experiences based on the beliefs that you now hold. So, while you may chastise yourself for making "stupid" choices, the truth is that you would have tuned into an experience matching that one no matter what—you could not have tuned into anything different unless you changed some underlying beliefs. The people who hurt you are simply representative of the energy that you were flowing with at the time—and they could have (and would have) been replaced by others with matching energy.

The beauty of this knowledge is that it allows you to forgive yourself for things that you believe that you have done wrong, or mistakes that you have made. Sure, you may have made some "bad" decisions, but they were based on the frequency of your mind at the time. Now that you know better, you would choose better—you no longer match that experience energetically or otherwise.

The message? Stop beating yourself up! Stop beating other people up! Remember, the **past no longer exists** except in the ways that you re-create it in your current life. When you forgive yourself and others for past experiences, you release your mind to create beauty and love in your **present moment**—and that is what you are here to do.

Forgiving others also means releasing emotional scars that have become part of "who you are," and that can also present a challenge. After all, emotional scars can be used to control others by talking about the horrors that you have lived through, or can be used as a great excuse for why your life is the way that it is—and why you cannot do anything about it or be anything different than you are now. This allows you to put the responsibility for the difficulties in your life on someone or something else, and that can seem like a relief.

These scars can be such a part of your identity that you literally introduce yourself with these wounds. For instance, you may tell everyone that you are a survivor of abuse or that your father was an alcoholic. You may even frequently use the acronyms for these issues, as if they were degrees that you have earned—such as "I am a SSA" (Survivor of Sexual Abuse).

Yes, these things happened to you, but you do not have to choose to define yourself by them. The decision to take your personal power back—even from the most awful of circumstances or the scariest of diseases—is **always** yours. To make it easier to release this old pain, ask yourself how long you have been defining your life by these old wounds. 10 years? 20? Even 30? It is often startling to realize how long ago painful events occurred—and how long they have influenced your life. Isn't it time to let go of this pain and release yourself from its negative influence on your life?

Defining yourself with emotional scars robs you of your ability to create a powerful, flowing life. The only way to take back your power and free yourself from the destructive patterns caused by this injury is to forgive old wounds and heal them for good.

To help you with process of healing and forgiving any old pain, use the upcoming exercises. Believe me, after doing these simple exercises, you will feel both lighter and more open to life—and better yet, you will learn the truth that your life can be unbelievably wonderful when you forgive fully!

1. Cutting the cord

Imagine each of the people that have harmed you. Visualize that you have a cord (or cords, depending on the amount of hurt that you feel) connecting you to them. Watch as you try to turn and move toward a life experience that you desire, and really feel the cords preventing you from moving toward something better in your life. Allow yourself to feel how much harm not forgiving is doing to you. Do you want to continue being attached to this experience or person? When you truly feel in your spirit that you are ready, choose to cut the cord with each person, saying to each,

"I now release you, and I release myself. I forgive you, and we are both free." How do you feel after each cord is cut? Are some more difficult to cut than others? You may need to repeat this exercise a few times to totally clear out any cords that are holding you back.

2. Using the Art of Connecting to rewrite the past

Have you ever heard the term "make-believe"? If you were a fan of Mr. Rogers, you certainly have.

To "make-believe" usually means to pretend that you are something or someone that you are not, for fun or for play. However, for our purposes, it will be much more than that. In this exercise, you are going to **make** your subconscious **believe** that a painful past experience ended in a more positive way—and you will literally create a different frequency in your mind as a result. Of course, that is the key—because your mental frequency now contains the beliefs set during this past experience. However, by using make-believe and the Principle of Repetition, you can completely change that frequency, releasing the hurt and pain—and creating a better flow for your mind and life.

To do this, you can either use your imagination, or you can journal this exercise. To start, select one experience that is particularly painful or difficult for you. Imagine everything as it was at the time—try to re-create the experience in your mind or on paper in as much sensory detail as you can. As you see the situation go forward, imagine that the experience played out in a much better way. What do you **wish** would have happened? What would you have liked to say? What do you wish the other person (or people) had said? Imagine that it happened just the way that you would have liked. What emotions do you feel when this experience plays out in a more positive way? Allow those emotions to flow over you for several minutes to really connect with that frequency.

As you bring your awareness back to your present self, say or write several times, "I seal these positive emotions in my mind. I choose to believe this reality, and I release the past completely."

How do you feel after this exercise? Write down all your thoughts and feelings. Repeat this exercise as many times as you need for any and all experiences that you would like to rewrite.

3. The energy beat-down

Sometimes you would like to really harm those that have harmed you.

Of course, doing this in reality would be truly harmful to you on every possible level, but it is sometimes necessary to do this in your mind to be able to move into a place where you can effectively cut the cord and rewrite the past, allowing yourself to forgive.

Once again, you can either use your imagination or your journal to do this exercise. Imagine a person who hurt you. What would you like to do to this person? Kick them? Punch them? Harm them financially? What do you think that they deserve? Imagine that all of it happens to him or her.

Now, can you imagine sending this person unconditional love? As you send this person love, imagine that you get that love back ten-fold. After all, we are all one, so when you send love to anyone, you send love to yourself. It is my opinion that sending love to those that have hurt you must be worth more energetically—so, I figure that 10 times the love coming back to you seems fair!

Do you feel better after doing this? Do you feel freer? A caution on this one—do not do this exercise more than once every few weeks. You do not want to use the Principle of Repetition to tune **you** into harmful experiences and emotions!

4. Releasing scar-power

By doing the other exercises, you have already begun the process of healing old scars. However, if you are finding yourself holding on to some more than others, please use this exercise:

Pick one old wound that is a particularly deep and painful one. Close your eyes and envision what this emotional wound might look like if it was a physical wound on your body. Where on your body would it be? How deep would it be? Would it be a bruise, bump, or cut? How much pain would it cause?

When you are ready, imagine that a healing light starts flowing into and around this wound. Watch as it heals, revealing beautiful, glowing, healthy skin. Feel this healing energy flow throughout your body, from the bottom of your feet to the top of your head. As you allow these good feelings to flow all over you, repeat to yourself, "I am completely healed. I am free to create my life my way. The past no longer exists."

After opening your eyes, please journal about this experience. How do you feel different without this wound? Do you feel more confident about taking on your life with fervor and joy? Celebrate this new you by taking yourself out to a nice dinner, popping open some champagne, or whatever else makes you happy. Imagine that this day is the first day of the new you—because it is!

Connecting to the best emotions

Love.
Joy.
Faith.
Peace.
Compassion.
Just reading these words uplifts your spirit, doesn't it?

These are the great emotions of life—when you flow with these emotions in your daily life, you easily create a life of satisfaction and abundance. Better yet, when you open your heart to just one of these emotions, you gain access to all of them. By opening yourself to experience love, you feel joy, which helps you to feel faith, which allows you to feel peace, and this increases your compassion for yourself and all of life. You can start with any of these emotions and have the same progression.

Best of all, you can always choose to connect with these positive, life-giving emotions in any situation, just by changing your perspective. For instance, when you are fully aware that you are a spirit choosing to have a human experience, you can always feel joy at the fact that you are able to feel anything at all—the very experience of your humanity can bring you joy in even difficult and painful experiences. I know that sounds strange, but as you learn to connect with great awareness to your emotional self, you will fully understand this truth (I promise!).

Before you go forward with the exercises designed to help you connect with these positive emotions, I would like to talk about compassion for a moment. Compassion is perhaps the greatest emotion, as it is love taken to the point that you love and emotionally connect with all beings and truly understand their experience as yours. It is a beautiful emotion that has the power to change the world, because compassion always increases kind and generous action.

However, you can be **over-stimulated** by compassion, which can lead to energetic burn-out—especially if you happen to be a particularly empathetic person. While there is no doubt that the ability to truly feel others' pain can allow you to help others (and yourself) heal in a most profound way (all the very best healers are always empathetically connected to their patients to understand the profound issues that are causing their illness, and to allow them to heal with compassion and love) it can also connect you so strongly to others' pain that you begin to resonate with their negative beliefs, issues, and even disease. Your desire to help a person in need can then cripple you with the power of their pain, and you will end up riddled with the same issues—like a tuning fork, you become tuned to their negative frequency, and lose energy to the same issues.

It can also connect you so strongly to the individual that you end up giving up your own energy completely to try to help them. To protect yourself, understand that while you can feel and understand others' pain, it is still *their* pain, not yours. While you can help them as much as possible, they have lessons to learn for themselves that you cannot and should not carry for them. If this is an issue for you, combine your new awareness of compassion with detachment (Station 6) to develop an approach that allows you to stay clear of negative energy, while still emotionally connecting with others.

You can also be *under*-stimulated in compassion (or any of the positive emotions, for that matter). In this case, you are unable to feel anything for anyone, having no regard for others' issues and only concerned with your own life. This may have been caused by your environment when you grew up, or it can be caused by an experience so traumatic to you that your emotional circuits were blown out, causing you to be unable to feel anything at all. The good news is that the following exercises will heal you of this issue, allowing you to open yourself to feel things you have not felt in years—and believe me, that is a truly life-changing experience.

Finally, remember to turn compassion on yourself. You are human, and you deserve as much understanding and love as you would give to others. The more compassion that you show to yourself, the more energy you are able to give to everyone else in your life. And keep in mind—it is your right to feel life fully. It is your right to have the best emotions of life flowing through your daily existence, tuning you into more fantastic experiences. Open your heart and you will open yourself to the life of your dreams!

Using the Art of Connecting to flow with the "positive" emotions

Can you remember a time when you felt pure love and joy?

I would like for you to call up that experience in as much detail as possible—imagine everything that you can about it. Allow your body to flow with the emotions of the moment. When your body is tingling all over with these good emotions, repeat to yourself: "I choose joy and love as my reality every moment of every day."

While staying connected to these "good" emotions, imagine yourself exactly as you want to be, living the life of your dreams. Visualize this in as much detail as you can, taking in every sensory detail. As you "see" yourself in this reality, seal it in your mind by repeating to yourself: "I choose to create this reality now. I deserve this reality."

Allow a smile to come across your face, and when you are ready, bring yourself back to the present time.

How do you feel after this exercise? Pretty darn good, I bet! Repeat this exercise as much as you want—the more that you do it, the better your results will be!

Connecting to joy

If you have done the above exercise, you are now connected to joy, but I would like to give you another quick exercise that works wonders. Close your eyes and smile. Imagine that this smile has gone down into your feet, and feel as if your feet are smiling. Allow this smile to move up each body part, feeling that every cell in your body is turned into a little smiley-face. Repeat the word "joy" over and over to yourself as you do this. This is a great quick fix **anytime** that you are feeling down!

Connecting to love and compassion

Are you disconnected from the emotion of pure love? If so, you can easily reconnect to this beautiful emotion by surrounding yourself with pictures of those you love. Each morning, take five minutes to say to each picture, "I love you and am grateful for you in my life." Then, sit down and close your eyes, and imagine that you feel the love that you have just given out coming back to you from each person. As you feel this love multiplying, bring your awareness to your heart and imagine that it is glowing with a bright light—you can give the light a color (such as pink, green, or white), if you like. Focus your mind on your breath, and feel the light in your heart growing with each breath. As you breathe out, imagine that you send the love that you feel out to everyone in the world. As you breathe in, imagine that this love comes back into your heart, creating warmth and love. As you do this, say to yourself, "I am open to love. I love all beings."

How does this exercise make you feel? Do you sense the beauty of love and compassion? How can you put this feeling into action in your life today?

Questions:

1. How often do you feel each of the "positive" emotions in your daily life? If you feel restrained, why do you think that this is? Can you choose to view your life experiences from a more positive place, staying connected to joy, love, and faith even in difficult circumstances? Do you allow yourself to get excited about the good experiences of your life? Do you celebrate your victories? What can you do now to celebrate your life and accomplishments? How can you make this a habit?

Retuning statement: "Today, I choose love. Today, I choose joy. Today, I choose faith. Today, I choose compassion. Today, I choose peace."

Emotional body language

I said it before, and I will say it again:

When awareness is brought to an emotion, power is brought to your life.

One of the ways of becoming aware of your emotional reaction (and the emotions around you) is to notice the way that your body is reacting in any situation. Instead of reacting from a programmed habit, become conscious of the first signs of panic, fear, anger, sadness, and guilt. When you feel that first twinge of a negative emotional trigger, ask yourself what it is about the situation that is triggering this reaction in you. Where might this emotion really be coming from? What underlying belief might you be tuning into?

When you are conscious of your emotional triggers, you can always choose to make the best decisions in any situation, instead of letting your emotions get the best of you. From a conscious place, you can choose to express yourself in new ways that are in perfect alignment with who you are (and want to be), instead of tuning into who you have been **programmed** to be.

One of the easiest ways to develop awareness is to notice how you are using your arms and hands in different situations. The arms are an extension of the heart energy—and can be very representative of your true feelings about the person or situation that you are dealing with. When you are with someone you love, you touch them frequently, hug them, touch their arms, and hold hands. If you are feeling confident and comfortable in a situation, you will often talk with an expressive use of your hands—conducting the power of your message out the tips of your fingers.

This will be markedly different when you are with someone who threatens you or makes you feel uncomfortable. You will certainly refrain from touching them, often crossing your arms in front of you, as if to say, "I am not emotionally connecting with you!" Of course, if you really don't like someone, your arms can be used to harm them.

Your arms are representative of the choice between creating a moment that flows with love or with hate. Become aware of what your body is trying to tell you about the energy of the moments that you are in, and choose to retune any negative emotional triggers into a new, empowering pattern!

Station 4: Body language

I want you to look at each of the parts of the body in Station 4 symbolically—for what they might be able to tell you about any energy imbalance that may be going on here. For example, let's say that you are having an issue with your lungs. What is the function of the lungs? Well, they take in oxygen (something that we need in order to live), and they remove carbon dioxide from the body (a toxic waste product). What could this tell you about the beliefs that you hold that are causing your difficulty? Look at your life to see if you are having a hard time fully taking in life (breathing it all in, as it were), or if you feel that some emotional hurt has been so bad that it has taken your breath away. Do you have a tumor? Ask yourself if you are blocking emotions or nursing any old hurts against you.

Learn to use your inner wisdom to understand the diseases and pain that you may be experiencing in this Station. The more that you feel that you have the power to understand your own circumstances, the more that you can take control of your life—and truly change any difficult or negative experiences.

Action Plan for resetting Station 4

- ✓ Select 2-3 retuning statements to reset your preset.
- ✓ Go to page 409 and take the Reality Type Test, if you have not already done so.
- ✓ Select 4 Reality Type exercises, and do these for 40 days.
- ✓ Become conscious of your emotional response to situations.
- ✓ Find positive ways of expressing all emotions.
- ✓ Based on the best emotions, make all choices in alignment with the feelings that you associate with the life of your dreams.
- ✓ Learn from "negative" experiences.
- ✓ View all emotions as a choice—you are always in control of your emotions.
- ✓ Practice forgiveness.
- ✓ Connect daily to the "positive" emotions, and live "in the flow" with these.
- ✓ Become aware of the bodily reactions associated with emotional triggers.

STATION 5

The Strength of Positive Communication

Station Motto: Say what you mean, and mean what you say.

Location of Station: Throat

Problem Playlist: If you are preset with negative Station 5 beliefs, you will find that you have some of these behavior patterns and difficulties:

- Procrastination and difficulty getting started on improvement programs.
- Lacking the willpower to take the actions necessary to achieve your desires.
- Taking actions that are opposite to your goals.
- Saying one thing, but doing another.
- Knowing what you want to say, but not being able to say it.
- Feeling exhausted after being around certain people.
- Not being able to say "no."

- Either speaking too loud or too soft.
- Criticizing yourself in thought or in word.
- Gossiping, judging, and criticizing others.
- Having others criticize you, judge you, or be malicious toward you.
- Communication problems where you are not heard or taken seriously.
- Difficulty communicating your emotions or needs properly.
- Misunderstandings with others.
- Inability to create what you want in your life because of self-criticism and fear.
- Fear of expressing your real self and real truths.

Station 5 Body Issues: If you are tuning into negativity here, you will find that you have disease, pain, or extra weight in these areas:

- Throat
- Trachea
- Thyroid
- Mouth
- Jaw
- Teeth
- Esophagus
- Vocal cords
- Skin of the throat and jaw
- Vertebrae of the neck

Action-taking made easy

If you have ever heard the phrase "actions speak louder than words," then you will know the importance of doing what you say that you are going to do.

You can say that you want to lose weight, but if you keep

eating unhealthy foods and never exercise, your **action** is communicating that you do not really want to lose weight. You can decide that you want to write a book, but if you never sit down and write, you are not going to have much of a book. You can decide that you want to have a better relationship with your spouse, but if you keep choosing to go out with the guys until all hours of the night, you are **really** communicating that your friends are more important than your spouse.

Each of these examples shows the need for actions which back up your goals and dreams. Your mind will never be convinced that you truly want what you say that you want if you keep on taking actions contrary to your goals. Each action that you choose to take communicates your intentions to the world, and speaks volumes about whether you intend to go toward the life of your dreams, or to keep turning back to old habits and issues.

It is quite obvious that doing what you say that you are going to do has some serious advantages. So, why in the world do you choose to do anything else? Why isn't it easy to take the action necessary to bring your dreams into reality?

Put simply, it's hard for you to take actions in alignment with your desires because you have been taught that you don't really deserve to take the time to do the things that bring you to the life of your dreams. Others' needs must always come before your own, causing you to rush around fulfilling their needs, but never making time to do the things necessary to meet your personal goals. Additionally, you may be afraid of looking foolish, hurting someone, being made fun of, or putting in the effort and then failing. You might even be afraid of making others feel bad about themselves by improving **yourself**.

Everyone has been given these beliefs and fears somewhere along their personal journey—I think it is impossible to not be preset with a few of these worries. However, tuning into these beliefs will cause you to keep having experiences where, although you mentally **know** that one decision is better for you than another, you feel unable to take the right path. Perhaps you have decided that you are going to leave a job or relationship that you can clearly see is not for your best, but can't seem to find the words or take the actions necessary to actually leave. Or, you know that procrastinating on finishing a project or making an important call will be counter-productive to your goals, but you still put it off.

Mentally knowing (Station 6) what you want out of life is not enough. You must pair the mental acceptance of your new beliefs with actions that communicate these beliefs to your mind. For instance, you can decide to take on the new belief, "I deserve my best life," but if you do not make choices in alignment with that belief, you are not going to convince your mind that you actually want to tune into your best life. Instead, you will just keep tuning into the old patterns that you say or think that you don't want. To quote Henry David Thoreau, you must choose to "go confidently in the direction of your dreams" in word and in deed in order to truly reset your presets to tune into the life of your dreams.

It really is this simple: **You're never going to get what you want until you take the actions necessary to bring it into your life.**

Reread that last sentence, please—and let it sink in.

Here's where the nasty word "willpower" comes in (you knew it was going to eventually come to this). I say nasty, because just the utterance of this word can conjure up images of food deprivation, long workouts, battering-ram success habits, and adherence to strict time management principles. If you don't exhibit "willpower" and stay on the exact program, you immediately label yourself pathetically weak, a terrible failure, or a serious loser.

It is time to erase all that you know of willpower. Your ability to achieve the life of your dreams has little to do with a force of strength that keeps you on track, and much more to do with the fact that you now believe that you are worthy of making choices which take you to your goals.

In fact, what I am asking of you is to love yourself and your goals so much that you are able to take the healthiest, most life-affirming actions that you can because you **want** to, not because you have to. Instead of **forcing** yourself to stay with an action plan, you do what you need to do to realize your goals because your needs are truly important to **you.**

This is very different energy from common thought. In fact, what you think of as "willpower" is really "you-power," because it has to do with developing confidence in yourself so that every positive action becomes easier and easier. Feeling this confidence allows you to move yourself into the primary position of importance in your life, giving you the time and focus necessary to complete everything that you need to do to realize your dreams, instead of casting your dreams and needs aside to meet others' desires. Best of all, this "you-power" is not a mysterious force—it is within you right now, waiting for you to discover the joy and satisfaction you can have by simply taking actions that shout, "I deserve my dreams!" By tapping into "you-power," you **will** get your dreams, because you're actively expressing your trust in the process, and **also** making the effort to choose the right actions for you.

In order to uncover your own stash of "you-power," start looking at the kinds of beliefs that you now hold about how, why, and when you feel that you are allowed to take actions that are important to you, and, perhaps even more importantly, what amount of authority you feel that you have to do so. Perhaps you were programmed with limiting beliefs about your ability to do something just because it was good for you, or with a fear of hurting or letting down others by making choices for your own good. In the past, you may have been made fun of upon starting a self-improvement program, or been told that you do not have the right to experience certain things because of your gender, sexual orientation, race, religion, or any other random reason people come up with. Maybe you have chosen to do something truly important to you rather than giving in to others' needs, and were called selfish, self-centered, uncaring, or told that you were abandoning someone.

If you have had these kinds of experiences, starting to take empowering actions and holding to your plan can seem daunting. Old, programmed beliefs and the negative feelings associated with them can swirl in your head as you worry about whether you are really doing the right thing by taking the time to do the things necessary to bring your dreams into reality. I know it is hard, but

315

please put these worries aside. Choosing to put yourself first and sticking to your improvement plans is not selfish, it is **loving**— both to yourself, and the world at large. When you are at your best, you can help others so much more than when you are tired, depressed, and worn out. You can contribute more to the world by simply being true to yourself and using your personal power in positive ways. By reaching your goals, you will truly lead by example, enriching the world by encouraging others to live **their** dreams.

Even knowing this, you likely have quite a bit of conditioning to reset. There are going to be times when you slip up and find yourself making negative choices based on old habits, or giving in to people's requests that are not for your best. When this happens, don't berate yourself, criticize yourself, or decide that you are hopeless. Remember, everyone slips up. **I slip up.** Learn from the experience, let it go with peace, and become vigilant to not do it again.

Even more important, **congratulate** yourself each time that you make some progress. Any progress counts. It may be as simple as finally telling your boss that you will not take on extra work when you normally do, or just getting to the gym instead of going out with the girls after work. It doesn't matter the level of significance, each time that you take an action that is authentic to your intentions, it's a **victory**. You have reset your preset in that moment—and made a choice keeping you solidly on the path to your goals.

This is important, because each act of expression, no matter how small, communicates to the universe the frequency that you are seeking. This communication allows your personal TV to scan the hologram of life to tune you into the experiences matching this intention. Each little action is actually a **big** action, because any shift in frequency means that you cannot tune into the same kind of experience anymore. When you take actions that match the frequency of your desires, you **get** your desires (you simply can't tune into anything else!).

And remember, don't focus on past failure. That is exactly like heading out for a wonderful journey and then turning around and going home. It will get you nowhere, and will definitely tune you into past results. **Who cares** if you didn't succeed before? It doesn't matter why or what the circumstances were. You are different now. You have tools now. You can take the actions that allow you to flow right to all that you desire. Focus on the end result and celebrate your success every moment of every day. You have created this moment, and you are now truly creating your journey.

You-power: designing an action plan that you can stick to!

To develop real "you-power" and have a true path to total self-improvement, you need an action plan designed just for you. Best of all, once you do this, positive action becomes automatic because you authentically believe in the power of your dreams.

To develop this plan of action, take out your Flow Journal. On the top of each page, write an area of life that you would like to improve, or a goal you have. Areas of life might be "mental/emotional health," "physical health," and "financial health," while goals might be "write a book," "lose 20 pounds," or "win company trip." On each page, please draw two arrows, one pointing to the right, and one pointing to the left (see Figure 5.1, *page 318*). At the "pointy" end of one arrow, please write down a goal. For example, for the area of life "mental/emotional health," you might write "reduce stress." At the same place on the other arrow, write down the opposite of your goal, maybe "freak out" or "have a nervous breakdown." Now, make horizontal lines all the way up the arrows. On one side of the arrows, write down an action that you feel that you need to take in order to flow with this goal. For "lose 20 pounds," an action might be "work out once a day" or "eat whole foods." On the other side of this line, write the opposite action, for instance "sit on couch" and "binge on cake." For the goal "win company trip," you may put "get to work early" with "sleep in" on the other side. Do this same thing for each page, using one goal on each.

317

Figure 5.1

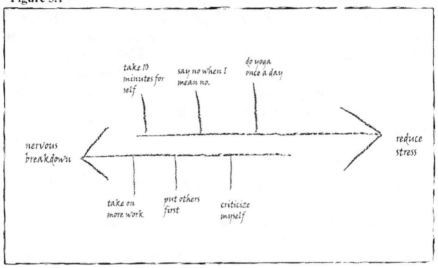

When this is complete, look at the list of actions leading to your goal. Above the positive actions, write down how you will **feel** by taking these actions and achieving this goal (see Figure 5.2, *opposite page*).

Now look at the other side of the page—the one listing actions taking you away from your goal. How will you feel if you take these actions, and end up far away from your goal (or worse, making the negative goal a reality)? Write these observations down on the appropriate side of the page. When you are done with all of your goals, look at your list of feelings. Which set of feelings seems more attractive? Which is going to provide you with better experiences?

By doing this little exercise, it will be very apparent that you will feel a good deal better by doing what you say that you are going to do. Even better, by matching your actions with your words, you will experience results that you never even dreamed of—**and** you will begin to respect yourself more than you ever have.

Figure 5.2

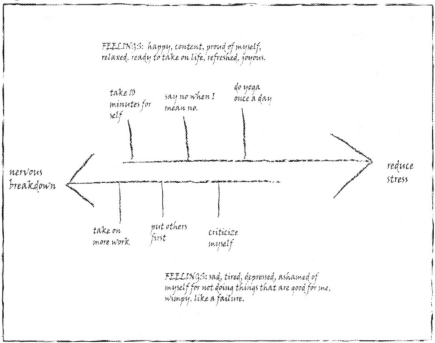

FEELINGS: happy, content, proud of myself, relaxed, ready to take on life, refreshed, joyous.

take 10 minutes for self

say no when I mean no.

do yoga once a day

nervous breakdown

reduce stress

take on more work

put others first

criticize myself

FEELINGS: sad, tired, depressed, ashamed of myself for not doing things that are good for me, wimpy, like a failure.

To develop "you-power" and be able to easily take the actions that you need to take to achieve your goals, keep focusing on the feelings associated with taking positive action. Write down the words associated with these good feelings on an index card or the back of a business card. Your list might be: "I feel proud, happy, confident, optimistic, and successful!" Keep your list of positive feelings in your car, purse or wallet, and at your work station. When you notice yourself feeling like procrastinating or avoiding positive action, simply ask yourself which choice would be of the same frequency as these good feelings, making this statement come true. Do you want to flow with these feelings or the opposite of them? It is much easier to take the actions that you need to take when you consider the alternative!

If you find that you are still having difficulty taking the positive actions that you have listed, read your list of good feelings over and over. Start your statement with "I feel," and allow yourself to really connect with these feelings. Once you are buzzing with these good feelings, it is much easier to decide to go ahead and take action—after all, you want to keep this good feeling going!

As a final bit of encouragement on this, just remember—the **instant** that you take an action that is in line with your new beliefs and goals, you change your energy frequency. When you change your energy frequency in positive ways, you tune into what you desire and (best of all!) begin to flow with your goals.

Questions:

1. Have you tried to reach your goals before and found yourself not doing what you knew that you needed to? Did you feel that you lacked willpower? Can you now see that you did not believe in yourself enough to succeed? What beliefs do you think you were operating on at that time?

Retuning statement: "I easily take actions for my best. I am important to me."

2. How do you feel about your ability (and right) to take the actions necessary to get your goals? Does this feel scary or unattainable? Do you feel that you have the right to take the time necessary for taking these actions? Have you been told that a person "like you" does not deserve certain desirable experiences? What actions would you take right now if you truly believed that you had the right to attain your dreams? What is keeping you from doing what you feel that you need to do? How can you support yourself so you can take these actions?

Retuning statement: "I have the right to live the life of my dreams.

I show love and respect for myself by taking positive actions."

3. What are the biggest obstacles to taking the actions necessary to get the life of your dreams? Are there people whose needs you put before your own? Can you begin to make choices that are for your best, prioritizing yourself as of primary importance?

Retuning statement: "I am important. I am worthy. I count."

4. Begin making a list of your accomplishments. Keep a steno pad with you (maybe with your "good feeling" words on the top) and write down each time that you make a decision that expresses these intentions. Every in-frequency action counts—so write down "took five minutes to meditate" and "decided to wear bright red dress" along with "made a huge sale." Every little action is a reset of your preset. Be proud of yourself!

Express yourself (you know that you want to)!

If you cannot speak up for yourself, you will not be able to take the actions necessary to get in the flow with the life of your dreams. For example, you have to be able to develop the confidence to ask for that sale or raise that you want. You must be able to say "no" when you mean no, or actually speak up and tell someone that they have hurt your feelings.

Your ability to speak, how and where you have the right to speak, and what is appropriate for you to say has been programmed into your mind by everything and everyone around you. If you are a woman, you may have been taught that girls don't yell, or asking for what you want makes you a "bitch." You may have been told that you do not have the same right as a man to voice your concerns, thoughts, and needs. If you are a man, you may have been taught that men don't express emotions, or that you must yell and curse to get your way. Maybe you have been taught to see every encounter as a win-lose proposition, or that you can't ever show fear, worry, or sadness.

Whatever negativity you have been taught, it is all rubbish. **Whoever** you are, you have the right to speak up and be heard. You have the right to express yourself in any way that you see fit. You do not have to be restricted by old beliefs, patterns, or fears anymore. You can choose to change your voice right now to one flowing with all that you desire.

Learning to speak in a way that is in alignment with your goals is very important, because each word that comes out of your mouth is literally an act of creation. In fact, while you may not realize this, your voice is completely unique to you—truly, it's a vocal fingerprint. When you speak, you are touching the universe with your unique perspective at your unique frequency, and creating a moment that no one ever has nor will again. You can either create the moment that flows with the highest attributes of love—love for self, love for life, love for others—or you can put yourself and others down. It's up to you.

This is not just figurative—it is true on the physical level as well. Your vocal cords vibrate just like musical strings. The frequency of the words that you speak causes the particles all around to vibrate in time with your words. Because of this, you can think of your vocal cords as the mini-remote control of your body—when you send out a vibration in words, you are instantly causing everything around you to tune into that frequency.

Since it is a fact that speaking your truth in action and in thought makes it real for you, begin to speak it now. When you have decided that you want a new belief to be true, speak as if it has already happened. This communicates the important energy of expectation to your mind and energy system—and (as you now know) you always get what you expect to get. If, for instance, you want a new car—tell everyone that you talk to that you are getting a new car. Maybe you want to lose ten pounds—tell everyone that you meet how successful you are on your new eating plan (even if you have not changed a thing yet!). Perhaps you want your business to be more successful—tell everyone how happy you are with the success of your new business plan. Again, this is not from a place of ego (of having to prove something in order to impress someone else), this is simply speaking the truth according to you. This is powerful—whatever you expect—in word and in deed— you will get.

Don't say things like, "I am **trying** to get a new job," or "We'll see **if** I can lose ten pounds." This communicates that you are not sure that you are going to get what you desire. Speaking these kinds of words will just lead you to more experiences where your goal is just out of your reach. By communicating in the present tense, you are using the power of expectation and optimism, and this will connect you to the frequency of your desires.

Learning to do this may feel very awkward at first. In fact, it can be downright scary. Just gently persevere. Some people may reject what you are saying. Some may make fun of you. A lot of people will notice the difference in you, and ask what you are doing to look so good. Just keep at it. Focus on affirming that you are getting positive results and being greeted with helpful, understanding people at every turn. Remember, you are reprogramming years of using your voice in a certain way—give yourself the time to adjust.

Soon, you will be shocking yourself at the confident way that you speak!

Questions:

1. What were you told about your voice? Were you made fun of? Were you taught to yell or to be quiet? Were you allowed to speak when you wanted to?
2. Do you find yourself in situations where you are arguing with or yelling at others? Are you the one being yelled at? How do you feel about these situations? Where might you have learned this behavior? The next time that you start to yell and argue with someone, take a breath. Ask yourself if this is a moment that you want to create. If

you cannot calm down the situation, walk away; it is better than using your voice to flow with the frequency of anger, fear, and hate.

Retuning statement: "I communicate with harmony and love, and get only harmony and love in return."

3. Look at your desires, dreams, and goals. Write each one down in an affirmative, present-tense statement. For example, if you desire a new job, write the statement, "I have a new, exciting job that exactly meets my needs." Start to work these new truths into your daily speech. Take out phrases like, "I am trying to," or "I think I will," and replace them with "I am," "I have," and "I enjoy." If you keep saying that you are trying to get your desires, you will just keep trying to get your desires. However, if you say that you have the things that you desire now, you connect to that reality.

4. Bring your focus to what you say about your goals. Do you use "if," "trying," "might," "maybe," or any other qualifier? Are you afraid of stating that you really deserve the things that you desire? In your conversations, start to notice how habitual it is for you to use qualifiers. Don't judge yourself—we all have patterns and habits— just start to exchange these statements for affirmative ones.

Retuning statement: "I deserve all that I desire, right now, right as I am. I am important to me."

Getting rid of people in your throat

When you are unable to find the words that you need to say or have a hitch in your throat, it is common to call this having a "frog in your throat." Kermit the Frog called this having a "people in your throat."

I have to say, I agree with the Frog.

Certain people seem to become "throat-dwellers"; they figuratively climb in and block your vocal chords, tighten your throat, and change the pitch of your voice. It is fairly easily to identify them—when you're talking to one, you will know clearly what you want to say and the decisions that you need to make, but somehow the words come out wrong (or don't come out at all). Maybe you have decided that "today's the day" to ask for a raise, but when you try to talk to your boss, you just can't actually do it. Perhaps you have attempted to say "no" to your church group when they want you to volunteer for "just one more thing," but you find yourself saying "yes," even when you had planned a day for yourself. You may have tried to end a relationship, but the person starts sobbing and you end up acquiescing. In all of these examples, you know that not saying what you need to say is causing you to make choices that are not in alignment with the life of your dreams, but you still keep doing it.

If you find yourself in these situations and walk away from the person feeling bad about yourself, weak, and defeated, then you have most definitely got a people in your throat.

Don't despair—you **can** learn to people-proof your throat (and the rest of you as well), but it is going to take some work. You lose your voice with particular people because you have been trained how to express yourself in certain situations. You may have been taught that you were not supposed to stand up to men, or that you could not question your parents. You may be very afraid of conflict, or fear losing someone's love if you say what you need to. Maybe you just don't want to hurt someone's feelings. These feelings and reactions have been programmed by authority figures, past experiences, and personal fears, causing you to react out of habit.

Habits are just that—habits. You can't change them instantly, but you **can** change them—it just takes practice. After all, you did not develop these negative beliefs overnight; rather, you learned these patterns of behaving from being in similar situations over and over. The good news is that practicing this skill can (and should) be done without the throat-dweller around, giving you time to start to develop the self-assurance necessary to voice your truth in even the most difficult of circumstances.

To begin speaking your truth, sit in front of a mirror. As you are looking at the mirror, imagine that you are speaking to a person who you have difficulty standing up to. Start to have a conversation with the mirror, just as if you were talking to this individual. Say what you want to say to them aloud, and then imagine their reaction to this. Practice responding with strength and love, even as you hold your ground. Realize that the throat-dweller can have any reaction that they need to have (trust me—it is likely they will try just about everything to manipulate you into doing what they want), but be prepared for this. Write out some reactions that you think that they might have, and then come up with some power statements for your response (these can be something like, "I am just not going to do that right now," or simply, "No."). Practice your power statements until you are truly comfortable.

Getting people out of my throat was a major issue for me, and let me tell you, it caused me to have some very negative experiences. I have had strange hair color simply because I did not want to hurt my hairdresser's feelings. When we had a contractor working on our house, he managed to convince me that he could only find certain colors of sinks, toilets, and stained glass (it was really just less work for him), so we ended up with things that I did not want. I have gone out with men because everyone else liked them (even though I really wasn't that impressed), purchased items that I did not really like because everyone else loved them, and lost money because I did not speak up when the down payment seemed excessive. And why did I do such things, even though I absolutely knew in my gut that they were wrong for me? Because I was afraid of not being liked, hurting someone's feelings, or having anyone think badly of me. Most of all, I was terrified of conflict of any kind, and figured by acquiescing I would avoid pain.

However, I did not avoid pain; I **invited** it. I developed swollen lymph nodes, TMJ, chronic sore throats, painful teeth, and cold sores. My body was screaming at me for not speaking up, and this resulted in all of these problems. It was no coincidence that I would have jaw pain right after talking to one of my throat-dwellers—by holding back the words that I wanted to say, I was allowing myself to tune into the truth that I was not very important. Because of this, I tuned into many more experiences where I felt very unimportant and unloved.

By practicing speaking my truth, I no longer tune into these experiences. You can absolutely find your voice as well, but it takes both patience with yourself and a willingness to deal with difficult people head on. It is important to realize that no matter how much practice you do (and how good you get at dealing with difficult people) you will still find yourself in situations where old patterns reemerge. For instance, you might be having a seemingly normal conversation when suddenly you are put on the defensive by a comment or question. You try to respond, but find that you feel terrified of speaking your truth, causing you to become hoarse, start to cough, and feel as if your throat is tightening.

In these situations, stop and take a deep breath. Give yourself a moment. Walk away if you have to. Let's say that your hairstylist says that you "absolutely have" to have the hair color of the season or the $100.00 bottle of mousse. Take a breath. Tell her that you don't think it's for you. If she continues to pressure you, ask for something to drink. Do something (anything!) to move the attention somewhere else for a moment so that you can gather yourself. If she still insists, just get up and leave. Yes, you will feel uncomfortable. Yes, you will be nervous. But you know what? You will not have orange hair or a bottle of mousse that you don't want (and isn't that a relief?).

This strategy can help in any situation. Maybe you have a friend that wants money, or Aunt Sally is grilling you about your life choices again. Take a breath. Say "no," or try to change the subject. If the person continues to put pressure on you, walk away. Go to the bathroom. Do whatever you can to get yourself away from the situation for a moment—long enough to regroup. Remember, their opinion has no authority in your life. They can hold their needs or desires, but you do not have to do what they ask of you. If you still feel pressured, respond with "I need a moment to think about how I feel about this before I make a decision," or,

"I'm really private about my life, and I'd prefer to not talk about this anymore." Always remember that it is your choice to be in the situation, and you have the right to choose to walk away.

As you make this transition, it is sometimes helpful to work with a counselor, psychologist, life coach, spiritual healer, or other person trained in positive communication. Before you settle on one, ask for references. Interview a few of them to see who you are really comfortable with. A professional can often help you to see your patterns, and may have helpful suggestions for ways to handle difficult situations. Certainly this goes doubly if you are being emotionally or physically abused. If this is an issue, there are many wonderful organizations that can help you get out of this situation. Please see the "Resources" page at the end of the book for a list of selected organizations.

Learning to speak your truth can be daunting, scary work—but remember, each time that you change your patterned behavior and speak up for yourself, you are sending out a signal to the universe that shouts, "I deserve the life that I desire!" And you'll get it too, because you will be convincing your mind in deed **and** in word!

Questions:

1. Do you notice you speak more "qualifier" statements (as in "I am trying to") with one person over another? Do you find yourself lying about what you really want? If so, realize that this person is someone who scares you, or who is not supportive of you or your dreams. Limit your exposure to this kind of person, and DO NOT tell them your dreams, desires, or wishes. They will not support you, and could try to tune you into their own fears in order to keep you in a place that they are comfortable with.

2. When you imagine yourself speaking your truth with someone who is difficult, what is your greatest worry about their reaction? Do you feel that you are not being

nice, will hurt them, or make them angry? What does this say about your importance? Do you feel that you are not important enough to stand up for? Where did you learn how to relate to the people that you have in your throat? Past experiences? Childhood conditioning? Can you think of situations that taught you how to relate to each person? Can you detach from each situation, and see the negative belief that you learned from this interaction? Write down these negative beliefs, and then write a new, powerful belief that you want to operate on with each person. Use these beliefs daily, especially repeating them mentally when interacting with each throat-dweller.

The dance of resonance: are you in a mosh pit or waltz?

Being around negative, demanding people can do more to you than just frustrate you; it can also bring your frequency down to theirs, causing you to feel drained, angry, and negative. As you can imagine, it is not too difficult to identify these people in your life, as you walk away from interaction with them more exhausted than when you arrived. You'll feel like you've been in a mosh pit for hours, and find yourself beaten and weary.

Actually, in many ways, you **have** been in a mosh pit. You have been beaten up by their negative frequency, and it is causing your particles to vibrate in beat with theirs. The result is some rather unpleasant dancing about of your energy.

To keep from being pulled into their negativity (and having it affect what you tune into!) become an observer of what is actually being said in every conversation. Begin to notice how each person is speaking and behaving. Are they gossiping, judging others, or putting themselves down? Are they saying things that are critical, hateful, and make fun of other people? Do they tell off-color jokes? Do they focus on illness and fear? Do they shout at others (waiters, cashiers, and co-workers, for example), or say belittling and hurtful things to put people down?

Now, turn the attention on yourself. Are you speaking this way as well? If so, do you find yourself only becoming negative with particular people, or are **you** starting this mosh pit, bringing negativity into all of your relationships?

When you are around people choosing to express themselves in this way or choosing to do so yourself, you are engaging in communication that is creating vibrations of hate and fear, hurting yourself and everyone else. Remember, by interacting with negative people, you are choosing to use your energy in the same way, and will find that you begin tuning into difficult experiences where hate and judgment is turned upon you as well. This sets up a vicious cycle where you criticize and judge others, which sends out that frequency, causing you to tune into experiences where others criticize you. You get angry about this and begin criticizing more, causing you to pull even more critical people into your life. This is clearly not the path to take to get you to your dreams.

The path that you **want** to take is to be around people who flow with the positive qualities of love, faith, joy, peace, and success, **and** to also become a beacon for these qualities yourself. By combining your own positive thoughts and feelings with theirs, you can create amazing change in yourself and the world as you will actively be creating moments that have this energy, not only for yourself, but for those with whom you are engaged in conversation. In fact, when you speak from the heart, you can even change the dynamic of a whole group of people. Martin Luther King is an amazing example of someone who not only chose to use his voice to flow with power and love, but who caused others to resonate with his vision. Each time that he spoke, his entire being was aligned for the purpose of equality, allowing the power of his conviction to come through in his voice. Do you think that he would have been as effective if he chose to incite violence and hate? It's not likely.

You may not be Martin Luther King, but even so, you **can** create positive change just by choosing to speak from a place of nonjudgment and love. By doing this, you will allow yourself and others to flow with life in a way that is more waltz than mosh pit.

No matter what, remember that you are actually creating the moment by being in conversation at that time. Who you are with and how you speak to them is **your choice**—you do not have to be in this situation if you choose not to be, no matter what anyone tries to tell you. Limit your contact with negative people, and do not say negative, critical things yourself. Don't judge or criticize other people, after all, they're part of the Source too. Don't gossip about others—it tunes you into experiences where the gossip turns on you.

Instead, seek out and surround yourself with positive people, and use your voice in positive ways. By doing this, you are communicating to yourself, your mind, and the entire world that you are taking full responsibility for creating your life in the best way possible.

Questions:

1. Think about recent conversations that you have had with people with whom you regularly interact. Are these people critical and judgmental? Are you critical and judgmental when you are with them?

Retuning statement: "Harmony and love are within me and within everyone that I come in contact with. I express only love."

2. Make a list of all of the people that you know. Next to each name, write down whether you feel drained or uplifted with each person. How much time do you spend with the draining people? The uplifting people? How can you begin to limit your interaction with the draining ones?

Retuning statement: "I deserve uplifting relationships, and I choose to be uplifting to others in my words and actions."

3. You were just asked to find ways to limit your interaction with draining people. How hard was this for you? What was your first reaction—fear, doubt, worry, or obligation? Did you begin to make excuses for why you could not limit your time with them? Why do you think that this is?

Retuning statement: "I am only obligated to my own happiness. I choose to do good and be good."

4. What are your most common criticisms and complaints about others? About life in general? Do you want these things to continue to be true? How difficult would it be for you to not complain about any of these things for one day? Pick a day this week to do just this, and write down your observations about the experience in your Flow Journal.

Retuning statement: "My voice only flows with love. I focus on the positive in each person and experience."

Do you talk to yourself?

Yep, you do, and yes, someone is listening.

So, **who's** listening to your self-talk? You, your mind, and the Source (kind of an important triad, don't you think?).

At every moment, your mind is whirring along, processing thoughts and judgments, and having quite an interesting conversation. Many of these thoughts are directed at yourself, and they may not be quite what you really want to tune into (perhaps an understatement, no?).

In fact, directing judgments and criticism at yourself is just as bad as speaking it about others, although you may not be aware of this. After all, there are many rules and sayings about how you speak to and about others, but there are no rules about how you speak about yourself. We are all taught the golden rule, "Do unto others as you would have done unto you," but we aren't taught, "Do unto **yourself** with kindness, love, and worthiness." What does this tell us? It clearly indicates that criticism of the self isn't that bad, or that we are not as deserving of being treated with respect as others.

This is just completely false. You are every bit as important as others. In fact, you're a lovely creation. You have talents and needs and unique abilities. You glow with inner light and wonder. You are no less important than those that you might criticize. However, you say things to yourself that you would never **dream** of saying to others. For instance, how often do you put yourself down because of your weight? Or, maybe you tell yourself that you are a failure, a loser, or a sorry excuse for a human being.

When you do this, you are not only hurting your own feelings, but you are also communicating powerfully to your mind that this is how you want your reality to be. Remember, your subconscious mind does not take a joke, and you are the foremost authority on your life. Because your mind believes you, it also believes that you are fat, unsuccessful, and a loser (or whatever else you say about yourself), and begins tuning you into experiences that prove you right.

The message? Stop it, and stop it immediately. Do not tell others that you are what you do not wish to be. Do not put down your accomplishments to yourself or to anyone else. While it may be seen as bragging to speak with pride about yourself, it isn't. Speak about your life with pride and joy; speak about your struggles with hope and optimism.

Practice looking in the mirror and saying positive things to yourself. Tell yourself that you are handsome, lovable, wonderful, talented, successful, prosperous, or whatever else feels right. Do it even if it doesn't feel right. Tell yourself that you deserve all that you desire. Do it until you mean it. This may be very difficult at first, because if you are really good at criticizing yourself, it will not feel true. It also may just feel silly. Just keep at it. Remember, you did not learn to criticize yourself overnight—you practiced at it, and in some cases, perfected it. This deserves just as much practice!

Become aware how much of reflex it is for you to criticize yourself. Really listen to yourself in conversations, and notice what you are saying about other people, and about yourself and your life. You can even bring a tape recorder to a meeting or family event, and stick it in your briefcase or lapel. By taping yourself, you can review the tape later on, and notice your patterned "playlist"—the things that you say all the time—as well as how others speak to you. By doing this, you can begin to catch yourself **before** you think or speak something nasty about yourself, and you can take that moment to change it into something positive instead.

If you catch yourself putting yourself or others down, don't judge that either. You are doing the best that you can. You're human. You're breaking a lot of old habits. Just acknowledge that you took a little detour off your path, and get back on course.

Just keep at it. You'll be tuning into your desires faster than you can imagine.

Questions:

1. What are your most common criticisms of yourself? Write them down, and become aware of how often you say these things. Try to stop yourself before thinking or saying negativity about yourself.

Retuning statement: "I deserve to speak about myself with love and pride. I love myself."

2. Imagine that as a child, you were taught to never say anything negative about yourself. I mean, **really** imagine it. How would your life be different? Can you imagine living your life as if you had never learned to be negative about yourself? Try to do this at least once this week.

Be a creator, not a berator

You sit down to write and you seize up. You cannot think of a thing to say that doesn't, well…**suck**, for lack of a better term. You try to paint, and the colors go crazy. You try to compose a song, and every chord is wrong. You start to design a business presentation, but just give up in frustration.

Suddenly, you begin yelling at yourself, saying that you aren't really talented or that you are a "has been" or "an idiot," and decide that you are foolish for even trying to do what you are doing.

The problem is clear: you are holding a belief that you're not good enough, coupled with a serious fear that you or your personal creation will meet with criticism.

Bad beliefs be gone! You now know that you are good enough in every single way. You are great just as you are right now—you are just choosing to adjust things a little to make this you the "you" that you want to be. No criticism, just adjustment.

You learned to criticize your creative expression a long time ago. In school, your writing, painting, singing, dancing, woodwork, and other forms of personal expression were judged, rated, scored and just generally taken apart at the seams. You were likely left with feelings of doubt about your capacity to express that which is in your head and body in a way that is acceptable and that will be appreciated by others. Due to this, many, many people are terrified of creating anything (and really, who **wouldn't** be after all that!).

In order to take the actions that you need to take and make the decisions that keep you on course, you must be able to express yourself creatively. What you create is as much an expression of your personal truths as your voice is. Creation is **innovation**—it is making something so uniquely you that you are breaking new ground (it's rather exciting, really!). However, if you have met with criticism and fear over your personal power to create, you will be fearful now that you will **ever** be able to actually do something that is great—or even good (that zaps the joy right out of it, doesn't it?).

Or, perhaps you have been taught that nothing is accepted if you are not perfect—there is no room for error or adjustment. Obviously, this kind of thinking will stifle your ability to create every time.

The truth is that the way that you choose to express yourself in **any** medium can be powerful, both to yourself and to those around you. For instance, when you write from the heart, you are able to communicate with a power that can move people. Think about all of the people that have written songs that make you cry, and poems that have inspired feelings of love. If you want to change the law, you can sign a petition (contributing your written intent to the energy of group belief), and when you want to speak out on injustice, you can write letters to your representatives and governments. Think about the power of the Declaration of Independence—a document that formed a country, and changed the course of history. A marketing piece inspires people to come to your business; a spreadsheet can keep a company on track and allow it to grow, thus creating jobs. A piece of sculpture or a painting can make people aware of injustice, or inspire others to be artistic themselves.

There is power in all forms of material expression, whether you want to paint, create magnificent furniture, film a movie or series, or any other way that you actively vocalize your personal expression to the world. You **can** move the world with the power and beauty of your creative expression.

This being the case, why not choose to create all that you do with the energetic attributes of love, hope, expectation, and prosperity? Throw out old beliefs that cause you to worry that what you create will not be good enough. Toss out the feeling that your grammar is not right, or your spelling is horrific (thank goodness for spell check!). Do what you choose to do for the sheer joy of creating. You are smart enough to express yourself in a way that is good for you **and** for the world. Release the need to criticize your creative process—when you see something that needs to be changed, do not say "oh my goodness, this is horrible!" Instead, say out loud, "I'd like to adjust that a little. Each time that I do so, it gets better!"

Create from your heart, and it will tune you into more success and joy than you ever thought possible. Love yourself in the process—what you do at each moment is both brilliant and uniquely you. No one else could have done it the way that you did, nor will again. You **can** release your personal berator, and become the creator that you want to be!

Questions:

1. Think back to your childhood. What did those around you tell you about your writing, painting, dancing, woodworking, or any other way that you expressed yourself? Write down as many comments as you can remember. Write down whole anecdotes if you can. Look at what you have written. Do you now criticize yourself using these same words? Can you see that you simply learned this behavior, and you do not have to choose to tune into these words any longer? Change each negative statement into a positive statement. For instance, if you were told, "You are stupid; you can't spell right," change this statement to, "I am intelligent, and create lovely words and phrases." Post this list near where you work. If you begin criticizing yourself, retune yourself by reading the positive statements aloud.

2. Do you still feel anger at people that criticized you from your youth? It is human to feel this way, however, holding on to this anger tunes you into more anger. To release this, try to see these people as only human—with issues, difficulties, bad childhoods, and parents that did not love them as they would have liked. They couldn't have done better, because they did not learn better in their own lives. It is heartbreaking that they felt that they needed to criticize you for their own sad reasons. Can you start to forgive now?

Retuning statement: "I create my own reality from a place of personal power and love of self. I forgive those who hurt me."

3. What would you really like to create? Why have you not done this? Have you been told that it is not appropriate for someone of your gender, race, sexual orientation, or any other stereotype? How do you feel about this limitation? Research others "like you" who have done what you dream of doing (beaten the odds, as it were). Post their stories all around your workspace.

Retuning statement: "I have a right to be who I choose to be, and create what I choose to create. I am powerful."

4. Have you been told that you cannot make a living doing your heart's desire? Do you think that this is true?

Retuning statement: "There is always a market for what I create. People are willing to pay well for my services."

Your money is talking behind your back

And right in front of your face.

As you now know, the money that you have right now is simply part of your energy, and is a physical reflection of your beliefs.

What you may **not** have thought about is that the way you that use your money is actually speaking volumes about you, your confidence in your beliefs, and how you want your energy manifested into the world.

Each purchase that you make has its own energy—and is an experience that you have selected from the hologram of life. If you are buying things made by women in sweatshops, or conning people into selling things for less than their value, you are tuning into negativity. If you are working on a belief to be respectful of life, you need to think about the food that you buy and the clothes that you wear. Is buying chicken that has been held in tiny cages and coats that have real fur in alignment with respecting life? If you are working on bringing more love into your life, but purchase music and movies that are violent and hateful, you are asking to tune into the opposite of what you want.

Each of your purchases is a very tangible expression of what you believe, as well as what you desire. Make sure that each purchase is an expression in alignment with what you want to bring into your life.

Questions:

1. Do you think about your purchases? Do you know where your clothes, furniture, and food come from? If you would like to know more, log on to: **www.responsibleshopper.com**.

2. What kind of music or movies do you choose to listen to, watch, or purchase? Are they positive and uplifting, or hateful and degrading? There are many ways to purchase entertainment matching your highest desires; one that I highly recommend is the Spiritual Cinema: **www.spiritualcinema.com**.

3. Do you give money to charity? Is there a charity that you have always wanted to give money to, but have not? Why not?

4. Have you ever given money to a political or religious organization? Is this organization in alignment with your current beliefs? If not, find another that works for you.

Body language, part 1: acting lessons (who doesn't want to be a star?)

Imagine Marilyn Monroe's sashay, or John Wayne's swagger. Think about watching a lovely dancer interpret emotional music, or seeing the toothless grin of a baby. Picture the rooster-like show-boating of a WWE wrestler, or the grimace of a football player in pain.

Without a word, each of these images conjures up a whole slew of expressions, from "I am a siren," to "I am powerful," and on to, "I am going to drop the hammer on you."

The message is clear: your body language is speaking volumes about you all the time, but it may not be the story that you are trying to tell. For instance, you may be trying to project trust and confidence during a sales presentation, but your fidgeting fingers and worried look are screaming, "I'm not sure that you really want what I'm selling!" You may be out on a date that you're really enjoying, but your sleepy eyes are telling her that she's boring you to tears. You might be working on the new belief, "I am joyous and optimistic," but your rounded back and eyes on the ground say, "sad and afraid."

These are just a few of the ways that you use your body every day to communicate to the world. Everything about you is an expression of you: the way that you walk, the way that your mouth forms words, the way that you dance, how you hold your arms, and more. In fact, it is said that body language accounts for 99% of what is actually understood. If that is the case, then you better know what you are saying when you are moving!

Do you think that you move in a way that exudes confidence? Do your movements scream, "I am running my life with authority!" or, "I am scared, afraid and depressed. Don't bother me"? To get a good grip on how you really move, practice talking and walking in front of a mirror. Stand as if you are giving a presentation or chatting at an office party. Notice if your back is straight or curved, where your arms are (are you fidgeting?), and how your hips move when you walk. If you have someone that you really trust to be both honest and kind, ask them to watch you and give you any impressions.

Now practice walking with authority and confidence. What changes from your habitual movements? Speak as if you are excited and optimistic. Do you notice a difference? Take notes of your observations, and start to be aware as you fall back into old habits. Make sure that your movements are expressing what you really want to tune into!

When you feel ready for it, choose one day a week to act like someone completely different from yourself. If you feel unattractive, become the God or Goddess. If you feel shy and demure, become outgoing and assertive. If you feel like a failure, act like the most successful person in the world. If you are fearful, become an adventurer. Whatever you choose, dress the part. Walk the walk and talk the talk. Think about every single aspect of this person's day. What would they eat? How would they speak? What decisions would they make? Who would they surround themselves with? What would their body language be? Carry yourself in all regards exactly as this person would. Have fun with it. At the end of the day, write out how you felt being this new person. Can you see that you can choose to change your personal expression in all regards to be exactly the person that you want to be? If this is a person you want to be, then **be** it. Be it permanently. Make this a life-long exercise, until it becomes a reality.

By acting as if you are what you dream to be, you reset your Stations to make that a reality.

Body language, part 2

Not only do you talk with your body, your body also talks to you.

Pains, colds, aches, weariness, cysts, tumors, and the like are all your body's way of telling you that one of your Stations is tuning into negativity, and it needs reset.

Do you listen to your body's communications to you? When you ignore your body's signals that something is wrong, you are tuning into the frequency "I don't deserve my best life. I am not important." You will have more and more experiences that prove this truth.

Remember, your body is wise. Your subconscious mind wants you to not only survive, it wants you to thrive. When your body tells you that something is getting in the way of thriving, stop,

341

assess where you may have negative beliefs or made negative choices, and work to reset your problem Stations.

When you do this, your body and life will improve in ways that you can't even imagine.

Questions:

1. Do you listen to your body, or do you ignore signs of trouble (working out through pain, going to work sick, tight muscles, etc.)? If you ignore these signs, why? Do you not feel important enough to listen to yourself?

Retuning statement: "I respect myself and my body. My body is important to me, and I am important enough to take care of."

2. How do you treat your body? Do you treat yourself to massages, baths, moisturizers, good food, or anything else that you find comforting to your physical self? If not, why not? Do you feel that you do not deserve it, or that people who are spiritual do not worry about the needs of the body?

Retuning statement: "I deserve to treat my body with love. I deserve treats."

3. Bring your awareness to the way that you use your body to express yourself. Are you tight, inflexible? Do you flow easily, opening yourself to life?

Retuning statement: "I am flexible. My body moves easily, and I am open to life."

4. Are your body movements the same as someone you know, such as a parent? If so, know that you are tuning into similar beliefs to theirs. Is this something that you

want?

5. Ask someone that you trust to tell you what your body language conveys. Listen with love (not anger) and write down their observations. You might be surprised at what you are saying without speaking.

Station 5: Body language, part 3

Look at each of the parts of the body in Station 5 symbolically—for what each is telling you about any energy imbalance going on here. For example, maybe you are having constant sore throats. What is the function of your throat? It houses your vocal chords, allowing you to speak. What could this be saying about the beliefs that you hold that are causing your difficulty? Take a look at your life to see if you are refusing to speak your truth in a situation, or if you are unable to stand up for yourself. You may have someone in your life that you find impossible to talk to reasonably. You may have a people in your throat.

By doing this, you will learn to use your inner wisdom to understand the diseases and pain that you may be experiencing in this Station. The more that you feel that you have the power to understand your circumstances, the more that you can take control of your life and change any difficult or negative experiences.

Action plan for resetting Station 5:

✓ Select 2-3 new beliefs to reset your preset.
✓ Go to page 409 and take the Reality Type Test, if you have not already done so.
✓ Select 4 Reality Type exercises, and do these for 40 days.
✓ Have faith that you have mapped a clear path to your goals.
✓ Evaluate every choice for whether it keeps you on this path, or detours you.

- ✓ Have confidence in your ability to make correct decisions.
- ✓ Keep your list of actions close by. Refer to it often, and make sure that you are doing each of these each day.
- ✓ Speak your truth with confidence. Love your voice.
- ✓ Practice saying what you need to say to difficult people. Practice over and over in a mirror until it is second-nature.
- ✓ Congratulate yourself for small achievements.
- ✓ Avoid or limit exposure to negative, critical people.
- ✓ Speak with love, faith, and confidence.
- ✓ Do not judge yourself. Do not judge others.
- ✓ Make purchasing decisions that match the frequency of your beliefs.
- ✓ Move with confidence.

STATION 6

The Power of Mental Creativity and Intuition

Station Motto: I have the power to make decisions and choose my experiences.

Location of Station: Middle of the forehead

Problem Playlist: If you are preset with negative Station 6 beliefs, you will find that you have some of these behavior patterns and difficulties:

- Difficulty making decisions—constantly looking for the better or more perfect choice.
- Fear of making wrong decisions or taking the wrong path.
- An inability or unwillingness to self-evaluate, or look at your motivations for acting as you do.
- Becoming a control freak, micro-managing every aspect of life.
- Looking to others to solve your problems.
- Blaming others for your difficulties.

- Not taking responsibility for your mistakes.
- An inability to leave situations that are no longer right for you.
- Being afraid of taking chances, or jumping at calculated risks.
- Being stuck in a rut—being unwilling to think in new ways or to have new experiences.
- Feeling an extreme fear of and complete resistance to change.

Station 6 Body Issues: If you are tuning into negativity here, you will find that you have disease, pain, or extra weight in these areas:

- Brain
- Eyes
- Ears
- Nose
- Head
- Skin of the nose, cheeks, forehead, and ears

Are you willing to use your power?

You now know that you have more power to change your life than you ever thought possible. While this is exciting, if you have been programmed with negative Station 6 thinking, this will frighten you as much as excite you. The good news is that some of the reprogramming work in this Station has already been done by the new empowering thought process in the Flow Principles. The Flow Principles have taught you the new truth that you contain the complete hologram of life within you, and it is your beliefs—the things that you take on as truths—which select the experiences in your life from all the possible experiences of life. You truly contain the Source within you—and because of this, you must consciously use your mental powers to resonate with the highest energy possible, and choose the best experiences for your life.

Obviously, this is a **big** responsibility! Even more important (and daunting), it is your **choice** how you use this power. Like the video game example I used earlier in the book, you can choose to struggle through all the different levels of life, fighting the bad guys and having difficult experiences, or you can decide to use your conscious and subconscious mind as a secret passageway—and walk right to the winner's circle, where all your dreams await you. It's your free will to decide what you want.

If you use this power wisely, you become a super-hero of sorts. I am sure that you had a favorite super-hero as a child—maybe Superman or Wonder Woman. Eyes glued to the TV, you watched with amazement as these seemingly normal humans transformed from average people into powerful, commanding personas. Inspired by this, you dressed yourself in your super-hero "Under-roos" and cape and dreamed of becoming a hero yourself.

As difficult as it is to believe, you actually have this seemingly super-human power, Under-roos or not. Right now, you have the power to change your thinking and transform completely at a moment's notice, and become all that you ever dreamed to be.

Put on your cape and gold bracelets and become your own hero! Imagine that you have all the power that you need to move mountains and make all your dreams come true right now. What would your special powers be? A love magnet? Financial wizardry? Love for humanity? Studly-ness that makes every woman swoon? Like any super-hero, imagine that you have these powers within you right now, just waiting to be used. Have complete confidence that you can move the world when you need to, easily removing any obstacles in your way. After all, Superman never walked up to a car and worried about whether or not he would be able to move it. He had **absolute confidence** that he could call up the power to do what he needed and wanted to do at that moment, and move it he did.

Walk up to every moment in your life with this kind of confidence. When you are worried or scared, imagine yourself changed into your mental super-hero cape and big kid Under-roos. Call upon your super-powers, and become certain that you can do what needs to be done. Believe in your powers, and you will truly change your world.

Of course, like any hero, it is your choice as to whether you use your powers for good or evil. When you use your power positively, you increase the energy and experience of every part of life. When you use your power negatively, you bring the collective energy down.

Are **you** going to be Superman or Lex Luther? It is up to you—but remember, when you hurt another, you hurt yourself.

The only one responsible for you is <u>you</u>

I know, I know—it is easier to blame someone else for your difficulties, your weight, your loss of money, your failed marriage, and anything else that is rotten and annoying in life, but you can't anymore. Being in the flow means being fully aware that you are creating the experiences of your life, and willing to do the introspection it takes to look within to see where your thoughts and beliefs are tuning into the wrong stuff.

You may feel frightened by this realization, especially if you have a pattern of being afraid of taking full responsibility for yourself, or if you have had a victim mentality for a long time. If you have found that being a victim of life has given you some advantages, it will be even more difficult for you to positively use your personal power. For instance, if you have always been seen as "the one with the chronic illness," you may have found that people cater to your every need and give you lots of attention, just for being sick or in pain. You may also play the victim to get others to fix your life for you, or use their sympathy to get what you want. At just the right moment (and with the right people) you can say things like: "Things just never seem to go right for me," "I always pick the bad relationships," "I just can't find a way to be less stressed out," and "I know that my boss is terrible, but what am I to do?" Suddenly, the person sweeps in and helps you to get what you wanted all along. Playing the damsel in distress (and yes, you can do this as a man, with or without pantaloons) can seem like a good way to go, because you get your needs taken care of with little effort from you.

However, no matter how long you have used the victim mentality to your advantage, believing that you are a victim will only tune you more victim experiences. Yes, at first glance, it may **seem** easier than taking full responsibility for yourself, but you will never truly get the life of your dreams in this way. Because you refuse to take responsibility for your own ability to create your own life, you will keep tuning into experiences where you must look outside yourself for the fulfillment of your needs and wants.

On the other end of the spectrum, you can choose to use your mental powers to become a dictator, constantly dreaming up ways to manipulate others into doing your bidding through guilt, fear, or intimidation. You can specialize in knowing how to push someone's buttons to get them to give you what you desire. If someone refuses to do something that you want, you may blow up, berate them, or turn the silent treatment on them. You may use your mental powers to con people, stealing to get what you want. In all of these cases, you may get what you **think** that you want, but again, it is not the highest use of your mental and creative powers.

The **best** way to use your creative powers is to come from a place of self-sufficiency. By believing in your own ability to tune into the life of your dreams without needing to control other people, you are truly flowing. Best of all, you will feel better about yourself than you have in years, because you will feel the pride of using your talents to make your life truly yours!

Let it really sink in: **you are the only one responsible for your happiness**. No one else can provide that for you—only **you** can choose to select experiences that make you happy and fulfilled.

If, upon reading this section, you notice that you have been tending to behave as either a "victim" or a "dictator," first of all, forgive yourself. You are **not** a bad person—you just learned this behavior by watching others, or being denied what you needed when you were growing up. While manipulation seemed like the best way to get what you wanted out of life, you now **know** that you possess the ability to get all that you desire by using your mental creativity in positive ways. Although it may be scary, difficult, or painful to do so, you must objectively look at the ways that you are using your mental power negatively. By doing this, you can finally release these patterns and become fully responsible for yourself, and be **truly** powerful.

Questions:

1. Say to yourself, "I am fully responsible for my life, and all the experiences in it." How does that feel to you? Is it scary? Do you sense any bodily reactions? Do you feel empowered by this statement? Write down all of your observations.
2. Look at the experiences of your life. Where have you not taken responsibility for yourself or your actions? Can you see a pattern of these kinds of experiences? When did they start? Did you learn this behavior from others?

Retuning statement: "I am powerful. I am able to be responsible for my own life."

3. Do you have chronic illness or pain? Do you get anything positive from continuing to have this problem? Do others cater to you? Do you get attention or concern from others because of it? What might happen if you did not have this illness or pain anymore? Does the idea of not having these advantages scare you?

Retuning statement: "I create positive experiences for myself. I take care of myself."

4. Do you feel that you are a victim in any way? Do you

have negative experiences in your past that you bring up again and again to get attention or to control other's actions? For instance, perhaps you bring up your abusive childhood to get attention, or to avoid doing something that you do not want to do. What would happen if you no longer saw yourself as a victim? What might you lose from this? What might you gain?

Retuning statement: "I control my own destiny."

Stuck on you, whether you know it or not

What's stuck on you? Toilet paper on your shoe? A Band-Aid? Some spinach in your teeth?

Maybe, but what I am actually talking about are your beliefs. Whether you know it or not, you may be stuck in a way of thinking that you are afraid to let go of, even though it does not work for you anymore. It might be the belief system of your family; it may be the thoughts and actions of your friends. It may just be thoughts so familiar to you that they're like a favorite pair of jeans—old, comfortable, and part of your personality.

Whatever your comfort zone, when you are either stuck in a certain way of thinking or absolutely positive that your belief system is the "right one," you are unable to learn something new that may benefit you. This attachment blocks your efforts to bring the life of your dreams to you, because you can't choose anything different from the frequency that you are clinging to. You may be afraid of being proven wrong, made to look foolish, or (worse yet) having to change your thinking, which causes your life to become a predictable pattern of experiences that are quite similar, and although somewhat unpleasant, comfortable in their own way.

The best way to combat this burning desire to be right (and trust me, when it burns it's an **inferno**) is to remember that every belief is completely relative to the person who holds it. The meaning of this is, of course, that every belief is as true as the ones

351

that you hold now, no matter how contrary they may be to your own. There is no right and wrong, there is just the choice of which truth **you** desire for your life.

It is because of this that you should not become overly attached to any religion, belief system, or school of thought. **Every** religion can be the right religion for you when it meets your needs at the time, and the same goes for every thought process, system, or belief that you may now hold. As your beliefs change, so may the religion or school of thought that you feel an allegiance to, and you can release this old system with peace and love. Best of all, you can move on from your current way of thinking without any judgment, criticism, or fear—you are simply changing your beliefs for what is appropriate for you based on your current understanding and learning.

I want you to understand that this even goes for this book. To be sure, I feel that I have brought together some wonderful information that I hope helps many people. I have tried to write from the heart and to be truthful from my perspective, but I also plan on continuing to learn and add new information to all of this as I live my life. I am not overly attached to any one truth—I will give the truths to the best of my ability at the time that I write, and I will add to them as I learn more. I encourage you to do the same.

Remember, no truth is the ultimate truth for all people all the time.

It is because of this that you must seek your own truth in a way that is totally detached from its social or cultural form. Remember, all theories are equal—you have the ability to choose the ones that fit the way that you want to live, and program your mind with just those thoughts. In order to effectively do this, you must take absolute responsibility for what you believe, which means making the effort to research and read everything that you can, and being open to new and contrary information. While it may seem easier to just take another person's word for it, you can no longer allow yourself to be spoon-fed others' views on the world. In every circumstance, you must make the effort to go out and find out what is truth to **you**. This takes more work than just accepting a set of beliefs at face value, but the reward is an authentic, joyful life, where you always know that you truly control your destiny, and tune into the best life for **yourself.**

Trust me; this is a prize worth working for!

Best of all, having this attitude will release you from the need to prove yourself to anyone, and will greatly reduce the amount of conflict in your life. You probably know many people who have made up their minds about something, and, no matter how logical the argument, refuse to see the issue from another point of view. Maybe you know someone who believes that their religion is the only "right religion," or that their understanding of a situation is the only correct viewpoint. It happens with every subject out there: science, politics, family matters, gender issues, and more. By bringing up an opposing viewpoint to such an individual, you may challenge their belief system to the point that you find yourself in an argument. At this point, both of you will become stuck in your position, arguing and screaming about the truth of your perspective.

People, **stop the madness**! Don't become a critical, inflexible person unless you want those kinds of experiences drawn into your life. Be open. Never, **ever** be afraid of hearing another point-of-view. In fact, look for every opportunity to learn something different than you are used to. After all, it can't hurt—you can always veto any set of beliefs that you don't agree with or don't want, and no one can force you to believe or think anything that you don't choose to believe. So **what** if someone proves that something you believe is false? Would you rather to go on believing something that is not really best for you?

The way that I see it, you've got nothing to lose except the possibility of having a better life. If you encounter a belief that is rubbish, just decide it's rubbish, give it the mental razz berries, and don't take it on or change your thinking because of it. However, you might just learn to see life from a different perspective—one that **does** change your thinking in such a profound way that you start to see your life improving drastically. You never know, so it is best to be open and just listen; after all, you just might have a breakthrough that really benefits you.

One point on this: because each person must find out the truth on their own, you **do** need to be aware that a shift in beliefs can be uncomfortable for a while. It may seem like you are all alone, and the people that you used to have much in common with now seem foreign to you. Don't worry—this passes. You will choose new companions when you are truly ready for them—and they, too, will be more open-minded and loving than those that are leaving your life.

Don't ever cling to old beliefs because they are "comfortable." **You** decide what you want to believe, and what is truly for your best. Unstick any old beliefs that are not you, pick the toilet paper off your shoe, and let the **real you** create the life of your dreams!

Questions:

1. Write down a few of your core beliefs. Which ones would be frightening to change? Are their perspectives that you cling to? How would your life have to change if some of these beliefs were proven wrong?

Retuning statement: "I am open-minded and willing to learn. I am willing to change for my good."

2. Are there people in your life that are very closed-minded? Do you find your viewpoint opposing theirs? Do you end up in arguments with them a great deal of the time? Which of their views are particularly challenging to you?

Retuning statement: "I am open to others' viewpoints. I am allowed to hold my own viewpoints as well. I am right for my life, and they are right for theirs."

3. Is it difficult for you to see another's viewpoint as true from their perspective, especially if it contradicts your own? Do you have co-workers that drive you crazy, because they won't do things your way? Do you find

yourself in situations where you are told that there is only one way of believing or of doing things?

Retuning statement: "Every person holds their own truth. I respect others, and they respect me."

When "things" become barriers to your best life...

As I am sure you know, you don't just become stuck on the beliefs that you hold; you can also have quite a grip on things, people, and experiences as well.

For instance, your current job may drag the life out of you, but you see it as the **only** job—so you do just about anything to hold on to it. Perhaps the house that you now have is so important to you that you refuse to take a risk—and do something that you really enjoy doing—simply because you are afraid of not making the kind of money that keeps that **exact** house. Maybe you refuse to give anything away, hoarding things that you don't even use, because you are afraid that you will have nothing to replace them with. Or, you stay in a relationship that is not completely fulfilling because it is what you know—it's "comfortable"—so you don't take the risk and leave, keeping you from the possibility of finding someone truly fulfilling.

Have you ever thought about how much power you are losing to these attachments? What dreams might you be blocking by refusing to let go of these things?

Release the death grip! You can't bring anything new into your life if you won't release what is wrong, worn-out, or unnecessary.

Don't worry, I am not telling you that you need to physically quit your job or give away all of your clothes to be able to tune into new experiences; rather, it just requires seeing everything in your life from a different point of view, called "detachment." Detachment sounds a little scary, but it really isn't. When you become truly aware that everything that is in your life right now is simply a product of the beliefs that you now hold, you can easily see that the job, relationship, car, money, or idea that you have now is just the one that resonates with the song that your beliefs are currently playing. Your beliefs brought you to this place with these things right now, but there is any number of similar items, people, or jobs that could replace the ones that you **currently** have and fulfill both your immediate and long-term needs. You do not ever need to give your power and authority to the particular things that you have in your life at this moment; they are just representative of a set of waves that could have come into your life in many ways and could be replaced with **any** of a myriad of same-frequency items or jobs. If something no longer fits you, just choose to release it—your brain will tune you into something else that will meet your needs (and, by connecting to your highest energy, it will be **better** than what you have now!)

Please note: this does not mean that you do not care about the things that are in your life now. You should care a great deal—you just should not be so attached to them that you are afraid of changing anything at all, in order to make sure that what you have in your life now **stays** in your life.

Now, let's deal with the fear part of this. What if you lose something that you are attached to without (seemingly) any personal effort? For instance, perhaps you get the pink slip at work, or your spouse walks in and says that he or she wants a divorce. What then? For so many of us, the response would be despair, disbelief, and grief. It is also likely that you will feel like a complete failure; perhaps taking it as a blow against your sense of self. That's understandable, and needs to be expressed in whatever way that feels right to you (just don't call yourself a loser, no matter how tempted you might be!). However, it is also **liberating**, and a powerful indication that you are starting to tune into new experiences. The changes have been caused because your beliefs have shifted—the beliefs that you held when you got the job or married your spouse are now different; you no longer need to tune into that experience, because you have reset your Station to tune into something better.

Celebrate the loss! It speaks volumes about your ability to positively increase your energy frequency to a higher, more abundant frequency. You can let this experience go in peace, and know that energy waves are now being organized that will allow you to have countless other experiences that will fulfill your new outlook on life. Like waves hitting the beach and going back out, when experiences leave your life, there is always another wave carrying one in. New experiences are ready to flow right to you and take you to a new level of fulfillment.

Again, you just need to realize that it is the **energy** of the situation that matters, not the specific situation or person that you are dealing with. You can simply look at the things in your life for what they are—a collection of energy resonating with your beliefs right now. Take this truth into your spirit, and let anything that is holding you back go.

Letting detachment work for you (without panic)!

I recently watched a show where a man was choosing items to send to auction. The antiques dealer appraised an old, unfinished chair at $4000, and asked if he could auction this chair. The man had saved the chair from a dump 30 years prior, and he had never actually worked on the chair at **any** point during that time. You could not sit on the chair, as it had no seat. However, the man adamantly said that he could not give up this chair, even at the excessive profit. The reason? This old, beat up chair had been in his garage for so long that the man felt that it was part of him; selling it would be like selling part of himself.

He came to his senses the next day and decided to fix up the chair and auction it. However, on the day of the auction, his adult daughter began to cry over the chair, saying that it held too many memories (mind you, it had been in the garage for her **entire life**).

The result? The man did not auction the chair.

I tell this little story because, like the man and his daughter, **you** may be starting to feel pretty stressed out and sad about releasing beliefs and experiences that you have come to know as "you" for most of your life. Logically, you may know that the old beliefs are limiting, and that some experiences have outgrown their usefulness years ago, but your fear of giving up part of who you are is becoming pretty darn scary. Although you know that you have will have an enormously better life if you let them go, you may still be emotionally reluctant to do so—a fact that just might be causing you stress.

Take a moment. Breathe. Repeat *"relax"* over and over until you feel the tension go. When you are ready, read on.

You are not going to give up part of yourself by giving away things that don't really fit you anymore. It is your emotions (Station 4) that are getting in the way of your objectivity, causing you to feel sadness and fear over releasing things that you really no longer want. Do not fret—your identity is intact regardless of what you let go of; you are **not** going to lose a sense of who you are.

You are not your job, your relationships, your religion, your gender, your weight, your money, your house, or anything else. You are not chairs without seats, no matter how long you have had them. You are beyond that. You are you, regardless of anything that you have in your life right now, or what you decide to get rid of.

Better yet, releasing that which you no longer want or need does not have to be a process wrought with worry or difficulty. You can change effortlessly, easily releasing the old and embracing the new. To do this, use your conscious mind. View everything as merely an energy signature, releasing your attachment to the people and things in your life now. If you are attached to things because of feelings of obligation or sentimentality, remember that when you get rid of something limiting or negative, you are consciously exchanging your current energy for something **better**.

Just know that all things end when you are ready for them to end (when your energy shifts), and they begin when you are fully ready to accept the new. You can't force this process; you can only work on releasing any negative beliefs, and know that you will absolutely get what you want when your mind is ready for it.

Remember, life is waiting for you to ask for better. You can only do that by detaching from the things in your life that you no longer need. When you start to feel fear over letting go of something in your life, think about the fact that attachment to **anything** limits your ability to make free choices in your life. If you attach yourself to the energy of disease, you cannot choose the experiences of health. If you attach yourself to the energy of a lost relationship, you cannot choose experiences that would bring you new, happy relationships. If you attach yourself to only one way of thinking, you cannot choose experiences that are different than that way of thinking—even if they are something that you would really enjoy.

You absolutely have the ability to have everything that you want, but you need to release the things that you no longer need! So **detach already!**

Questions:

1. Think about all of the material goods and titles that you have in your life right now. What are you attached to and afraid of losing? What if you did not have these things? Would your life be different? Would **you** be different? Would you like to improve some of these things? Is there something better that you long for? You must let go of the old in order to bring in the new—can you imagine letting go of the things that you no longer want?

Retuning statement: "I am more than what I have in my life. I am open to the flow of life."

2. Are you afraid of change? What do you think will happen if your life changes?

Retuning statement: "I am open to change. All change is for my best."

Mental power, mental intuition

When you are truly in touch with your thoughts and believe in your mental capacity, you will get flashes of intuition—a thought, an image, or a word—something that gives you a bit of important information about your progress and possible directions or decisions to be made. While many will try to tell you that intuition is a mysterious force, it really isn't. In fact, intuitive guidance is no more than your mind showing you some of the possible solutions to your problem given your current set of beliefs. When looking at it this way, you can easily see that intuition is not reserved for the psychic or clairvoyant among us—and that your intuition is hard at work right now.

Intuition is your energetic plug into the Source—the order of wave frequencies that organizes the way that everything comes into and out of everyone's life. Remember, every particle always knows what every other particle in the universe is doing, and every single one of us is connected to it all, every moment of every day.

The more aware you are of this connection to the Source, the more aware you are of intuitive guidance—and what your thoughts are trying to tell you. Flashes of intuition will indicate when a certain person is not the right one for you, or when a job is not as great as it appears to be. It will warn you of experiences and people that are not in alignment with the life that you desire. It will also let you know when someone or something is coming along that is completely perfect for you.

Perhaps you have woken up one morning and thought, "I shouldn't go to work today." You decide not to go, and realize that there was a horrific accident on the freeway at the exact time that you would have been going through. Even closer to home, your intuitive guidance alerts you to out-of-phase energy in your body. After all, don't you often know that something is wrong with you long before you decide to go to the doctor to check it out? That's your mind trying to get your attention and let you know that something is awry. Remember, your mind wants you to be the healthiest, happiest person around, and when you are choosing experiences and beliefs that are going against that goal, you develop illness.

Best of all, your intuition is also available to give you the solutions that you need to any problem, the ideas that you need for any project, and the visualization that you need for any creative endeavor. Rather than worrying over how in the world you are going to come up with the ideas that you need for your business or projects, or fretting over how it could ever be possible for you to make the money that you need to be able to launch a new endeavor, just let your intuition figure it out for you. There is no end of ideas and solutions available to you—let them come to you. To connect to your creative and intuitive power, sit silently and ask to be provided with all that you need on your particular issue. You can also do this as you go to sleep at night, asking the question over and over until you drift off. By doing this consistently, you will be amazed at the amount of ideas that come to you.

And who knows? By morning, you just might be the next Einstein.

When you truly align your energy with the positive frequencies of this Station, you can tap into this greater wisdom without effort. Remember, your subconscious mind always wants the best for you—and will tap into the waves of thought that you need in order to produce the best life possible with the beliefs that you now hold.

What's the overall message of this section? Always be respectful of random thoughts and visions—your mind is trying to tell you something about the presets that you are tuning into. Listen, and tap into the power of flowing mental creativity with ease!

Questions:

1. Can you think of instances when you had thoughts, dreams, or visions about someone or something that

warned you about dealing with that person or kept you out of danger? How did you feel when you heeded that warning? Have you had times when you ignored these thoughts? Did you find yourself in difficulty?

Retuning statement: "I trust my intuition. I am always connected to the Source and my highest good."

2. Write down a list of your current concerns—maybe your job, your relationships, or worries about money. Next to each, just start to write whatever comes to you—don't try to block anything; no one but you will ever see this. Look at what you have written. What is your intuitive sense trying to tell you? Are you able to see these situations more objectively by writing this down?
3. A great way to tap into your mental intuition and problem-solving capacity is to ask for answers as you are falling asleep. Pick a problem or concern, and simply repeat, "The solution to this issue will present itself in the morning," as you drift off. In the morning, write down your first thoughts, as well as any dreams that you have had. You will find that your subconscious is happy to provide you with direction on how to thrive.
4. Were you told that you were not smart? Do you feel that you do not have enough brainpower to figure out solutions to your issues? Do you believe that you cannot come up with the ideas that you need in order to make your dreams come true?

Retuning statement: "My brain is connected to every solution and idea that I need or want. I trust my intellectual abilities."

Using the force—and not forcing the flow

Do you spend a lot of time helping people who will not help

themselves?

How frustrating is this? How drained do you feel by this effort?

If this is a pattern that you see in your life, you are likely a "helper" personality—one who wants to improve the lives of others. You may also have a big heart—and feel that those that you are trying to help truly can't help themselves. Believe me, I couldn't understand more because this is exactly who I am, and I have had a terrible pattern forgetting my own needs and running myself ragged in order to try to help everyone that I possibly can.

What I have had to realize is that every person has the same connection to the Source that I do. They also have the same ability to use their mental creativity and intuition to solve their problems. They have the same ability to do the work that it takes in order to free themselves of their own patterns.

Finally, I had to realize that I am actually hurting other people by fixing their problems for them—and if you are doing this, you are, too.

I know that this runs contrary to what you may believe, but it's true. At one point in my life, I was so worn out trying to help others do things that they were fully capable of doing that I worked with a life coach to figure out how to help them without losing myself. To my shock, she told me that I was a "spiritual irritant."

I reacted with shock, "A spiritual irritant? Me? But I'm **helping** them!"

The truth is that she was right.

Every person must use their own co-creative power to fix their own problems and create a better life. By fixing other people's problems for them, you are robbing them of self-sufficiency and the ability to learn the lessons that they need in order to create a life that is powerful and fulfilling. You are a "spiritual irritant" because you are not allowing them to learn to listen to their own intuition, have the satisfaction of learning a new skill or healing a disease, or become truly independent. You are keeping them from truly taking responsibility for themselves and their lives, or ever using their own mental powers for their own good. No matter how much you want to fix other's problems for them or how painful it is to watch someone else suffer, at the end of the day, each person has to fix themselves—**they** must do the work to heal from an illness, fix their business, kick their drinking problem, leave an abusive relationship, stand up to their boss, or solve any other problem.

To understand this better, think of the movie *Star Wars*. Could Yoda have fought the battles for Luke? Of course he could. So why didn't he? Because it was much better for Luke in the long run to actually learn to "use the force" and truly accept his personal power, than to feel that he was powerless, always needing Yoda around for protection. By learning the tough lessons, Luke was fully empowered to do the things that he needed to do to protect **himself**.

Moreover, Yoda's decision to not fix all the problems for Luke and allow him to learn to use his own power was a **loving** decision. He was not abandoning him; he was not being cruel. Rather, he would have been hurting Luke (becoming a spiritual irritant) if he had not allowed Luke to become fully empowered.

I know that this is easier said than done. You may have a loved one who seems to keep having problems in his or her life—and who keeps asking you to fix those problems for him or her. Perhaps someone that you care about has a drinking problem, or continuously asks for money to get by. Someone else may keep asking you to cover their work, because they suffer from terrible headaches or have a bad home situation. The problems that people encounter are many, and, when you love someone, it is **awful** to watch them go through difficulty. However, you cannot give all your time, power and energy to helping someone that is capable of helping themselves, but simply chooses not to. It is not doing this person any good. Moreover, it is not selfish or horrible of you to either refuse to fix someone's problems for them or to remove yourself from a bad situation—rather, it is **loving**, as you are allowing them to truly learn the lessons that they need in order to use their personal power in a truly positive way.

No one changes until they are ready to—not you, not your friends, not **anyone**.

I am not for one moment suggesting that you should not try to help people—when people ask for your help, you should

absolutely offer it with love. However, if you find that you are getting pulled into their disasters, working harder than they are to get them out of a bad situation, or consistently fixing their problems for them, you must realize that you are in a place where you are losing power to the attachment. At this point, you may need to walk away. You've given them the tools necessary to live better, but they have to want to use them—and you cannot force that.

Always give people that are in trouble a lifeline, give them information, and give them your love and understanding. It is their choice on what to do next—and their decision on the course of their lives. It is terribly difficult, but you must wait and watch, and just hope that they are ready to change. You'll know if they are—they will start to truly take responsibility for changing their own patterns and mindsets.

Just remember, you cannot help those that will not help themselves. Luke always had the choice to ignore Yoda and go through life without the knowledge or power that allowed him to become all that he was meant to be. Every person has this same choice—to use mental power to learn to improve, or to block the flow of life and resonate with difficulty and disease.

Just offer your help, be loving, and wait to see if others are ready for the lifeline. If they are, throw it out there with joy.

Questions:

1. Do you have people that you are constantly saving from disaster? What would happen if you just allowed them to help themselves? Can you imagine how they would be if they became self-sufficient? What do you get by always being the one to save them? Satisfaction? Personal sainthood? A sense of love? As difficult as it might be, really look at this issue and be honest with yourself about your motivations.

Retuning statements: "I allow others to grow in any way that they need to. I love and approve of myself as much as I love and approve of others."

> 2. Do you give a great deal of time or energy to helping people that do not help themselves? How does this affect your life? Does it drain you? Do you give so much time to them that you do not do what you need for your own life? Why do you do these things, even when it is not for your best? Is it out of obligation? Past training? A desire to prove your worth? A fear of losing this person?

Retuning statement: "I am only responsible for my own happiness. Each person is responsible for him- or her-self, and can change when they are ready to do so."

Putting it together: decision-making made easy

Are you a "ditherer"?

If you have Station 6 issues, you probably are. When faced with a decision, you go back and forth, worrying about making the right or perfect choice. You make a decision then change it. You rush around asking everyone **their** opinions, changing your mind each time that someone presents a different argument. Then, the "what if" thinking starts to creep in there: What if I screw up? What if I move and someone in my family needs me? What if I say "no" and no one will love me anymore? What if...

Let's face it, when you've got Station 6 difficulties, decision-making can be a complete nightmare.

It needn't be this way. Making decisions can and should be easy for you, and I am going to show you how to do this in just three easy steps (seriously). Okay, here goes:

Step 1: Detach.

When faced with a major decision, detach from the fears, crazy aspirations, wants and needs of **anyone** but you.

I know that you are mumbling incoherently about guilt complexes and family responsibilities right now, but hang in there. You **can** detach—no matter how much your programming tells you that it is impossible.

Have you ever noticed that you can easily see what a character in a movie should do next? For instance, a tear-stained woman opens the door to her ex-lover (the abusive, drunk, cheating one) who begs her to take him back. Don't you scream at the screen, "Oh, **please**...kick him to the curb!"? Or, you watch with amazement as a man worries over whether or not he should follow his heart and take the job of his dreams, although it will temporarily mean less income. His wife tells him that he should stay put, but you want to shake him and say, "**Absolutely** follow your dreams!"

Not only can you see the right answer quickly, you can also see the motivations of the people involved in the situation. So, while the woman might worry about whether she should take her ex-boyfriend back, agonizing about his feelings and needs, you as the observer can see that the boyfriend is really a mean and manipulative man who is only going to continue to cause her heartbreak. In the man's case, you might clearly see that his agonizing is caused by his fear of change—and that his wife is only thinking of herself and her own comfort with her current lifestyle when she counsels him against taking the new job.

It certainly seems obvious! So why are these same kinds of decisions so difficult in your own life? Like it or not, you are actually **in** the movie of your life and personally involved with all the players and issues. Because of this, you are attached to the situation, motivations, and emotions, blurring the lines of right and wrong and causing you to miss the fact that **your** ex-boyfriend is trouble, or that **you** are afraid of change.

In order to make decisions that are in alignment with the life of your dreams, you must become the observer of your own movie, detaching from everyone and everything else and looking at it all objectively. To start the process, the next time that you are faced with a difficult decision, imagine that you are in the movie theatre watching an actor or actress play the role of you. Watch as your character has flashbacks on all the various scenes and events that lead up to this moment. Now (and this can be the hard part) start to just observe the way that the other players involved are acting, what they are saying, and what their motivations might be. Watch as you talk about your hopes and dreams to the other characters, and start to see where you may have inaccurate perceptions about the role of other people in your decision-making process. Do the people in your life have an unbiased input on your decisions, or are they counseling you to go one way or the other to fulfill their own needs? Can you see what they may get out of encouraging you to go a certain direction, or are they truly altruistic? What might their motivations be?

In other words, see the people and experiences for what they actually **are**, not what you want them to be, or what others may have told you that they are.

Now ask yourself, if this really were a movie, what would **you** be yelling at the actor playing you? What would be the completely, **ridiculously** obvious decision?

It should seem a good deal clearer now. Yes, these people may be important to you, but you are ultimately responsible for the quality of your life and your happiness—and no one else's. Write down your observations, and move on to step two.

Step 2: When faced with a decision, choose the matching-frequency option.

For a moment, I want you to imagine that you have gone to a travel agent to map out your travel plans to the life of your dreams. You've decided to drive, so she draws out a map for you, showing you every turn that you need to take and each interstate to get on to get you right to your intended destination.

You walk away, map in hand, and feel completely confident that you will get the life of your dreams, so long as you stay on the charted course. No choice would present a challenge or worry to you, because you could just refer to your personal map and go the direction that it indicated.

Wouldn't it be wonderful to know how to turn at every crossroads of life, and how to negotiate over every bump? Even better, wouldn't it be great to know that you were absolutely, positively going to get everything that you desire just by following the right path? It would certainly make decision-making easy.

The good news is that you absolutely **can** know that you are going to get to your intended goals as surely as if someone had actually mapped it all out for you. When you make decisions and take actions in alignment with the frequency of your desires, you are communicating to the Source that you want to tune into that frequency. Exactly like following a map, each matching-frequency decision that you make takes you a step closer to tuning into your true desires. You are simply working with the laws of the Source; you **must** get the experiences that you desire, because you can't tune into experiences that do not match the frequency that you are sending out. It is that simple.

Instead of spending an enormous amount of energy on worrying or stressing out about making the "right choice" or "perfect decision," choose instead to check in with your internal travel planner. When presented with a decision—no matter how small—check in with yourself. Which choice will keep you on course to arrive at the life of your dreams? Which will cause you to turn down the path of old habits or self-destructive behavior? The answer will be obvious.

Let me give you an example of how this works. Let's say that you are working on choosing the perfect job; one that would fulfill you in every way. Suddenly, you are presented with an opportunity to move to the place of your dreams, with a job that you will absolutely love. Your gut instinct tells you that this is everything that you have ever wanted, but you feel torn by your loyalty to your family, and are also somewhat apprehensive about moving to a place where you don't know anyone. What's the best decision?

Look at it in terms of frequencies. You could make a decision to stay put, because you are worried about how your family will react. What is the frequency of this? Fear. Obligation. Guilt. How about not moving because of not knowing anyone where you are going? Frequency: Fear. How about moving to this dream location? Hope. Trust. Optimism. Faith. Self-esteem.

Which matches the frequency of wanting the most fulfilling job for you?

Suddenly, a difficult decision is not such a hard decision after all.

Always pick the choice that is the same frequency as what you desire, and you can be assured that you will tune into the life of your dreams. You can't get anything else!

Step 3. Do not micro-manage the process: let the outcome come to you (<u>however</u> it decides to come).

By learning The Flow system, you now know that you have the ultimate ability to control your thoughts and beliefs and change the outcome of your life. As you likely do with any new idea, you can take this on as a project, and begin feverishly working on changing your beliefs, visualizing your success, and taking steps towards completing important goals. Of course, you have an exact picture of how things are going to be. For example, you read this book, and you decide to work on the beliefs, "I am successful in all areas of my life. I deserve to have a loving relationship." In truth, you already have the person that you want to have a relationship with all picked out—and you expect that you will soon be dating this person. Suddenly this person moves away, and you feel abandoned by the system—after all, you did what you were supposed to do, but didn't get the result that you expected.

You must understand that you cannot be this attached to a specific outcome. When you change your beliefs, your mind will tap into the best experience that resonates with that new frequency. So, that particular guy or girl is sent away (because he or she is actually extremely controlling, and no good for you), but the very next week, a perfectly wonderful person moves in right next to you. **This** person is a perfect match for your new beliefs—and the two of you have a happy, wonderful relationship with each other.

When you change your beliefs, you can expect to get exactly what you want. You must trust this process—even if it does not seem to be coming out exactly as you envisioned—**it will come out exactly as it should.**

Make your decisions, reprogram your beliefs, and keep your body and mind tuned into the **feelings** of the outcome that you desire. Develop an attitude of expectancy that you are tuning into your desired outcome.

Now it is time for a big **DO NOT**: Do not micro-manage every detail of everything along the way.

Micro-managing your life (or the lives of others) is tuning into fear. You fear the loss of control over your life if you let things just come to you. You fear that no one will continue to need you if you don't rush around like a chicken with its head cut off fixing things and doing, doing, doing. What will happen if you don't schedule every minute of your meetings and trips? Will the world fall apart if you don't have your ear on the pulse of everything? This feeling of erratic energy and outcome anxiety will tune you into experiences that have the same crazy, worrisome energy—and that is definitely not going to be the best decision for you.

Stop doing, and **be**. Be the person that you want to be in your heart, mind, and soul. Be the outcome that you desire in every decision that you make. Exude the feeling of optimism, and watch your desires begin to come into being. Work on developing right action (Station 5), balanced with right thought—and you will free yourself from the cycle of distress that you are likely experiencing now.

Best of all, details will begin to manage themselves without you doing **anything**. Now, isn't that wonderful?

Make your decisions, make sure that they are in alignment with your desired outcome, and release them to the Source. Allow your mind to tune you into the frequency of all that you want, and never, ever worry that it is not working. The process **will** work for you if you take your hands off the steering wheel and just let go.

Questions:

1. What would happen if you did not deal with all the details that you do now? How do you feel about just letting go and letting the minor details work themselves out? What are you afraid of if you did not try to control the process with your "doing"? Write this all out. Can you identify where you got these fears? Did your parents act the same way, or were you always the "responsible one," fixing everything for everyone?

Retuning statements: "I am only responsible for my own happiness. I see all that I want easily coming into my life. I am grateful for the abundant process of life."

2. Do you always feel alone? Do you feel that you have to "do it yourself or it doesn't get done"? Are you the one that does everything—organizes all the parties, fixes all the business issues, and takes charge of every meeting or group? Can you trust others to help you?

Retuning statement: "I attract helpful people into my life. Everywhere that I go there are people willing to help me make my dreams a reality."

Using detachment to heal

By looking at any experience in your life objectively, you can develop beliefs that allow you to detach from the experience and see it instead as a metaphor for some negative beliefs that you hold. For instance, you might be overtaken with fear when you are told that you have a life-threatening disease, but it **is** possible to detach from the fear and develop the ability to see the negative beliefs matching this experience. In this way, you can see the big red arrow that your body is pointing to show you that negative frequencies are present, and you can work to fix them. In doing so, you can return to optimum health.

If you have an illness now, you can use this knowledge right now in order to begin the healing process. You **can** detach from the illness and see the larger picture, and the message that your body is sending you. Remember, don't focus on the illness itself— that attaches you to the frequency of the illness, and gives the disease a position of authority in your life. For instance, if you find out that you have cancer, don't focus on the cancer. Totally detach from the cancer itself—think nothing about it. Feel as if you are simply watching this experience in a movie. Look at every experience that led up to this disease as a different scene in the movie of your life. Carefully analyze each scene for clues to the beliefs that might have tuned you into this illness.

Remember, you would not feel the same attachment to fear if you were just watching this in a movie, and you do not have to attach to that fear now. Instead, you can choose to use your mental power to focus on the positive frequency of expecting the best in all things. You can believe that you have the power to choose the experiences of your life in a positive way.

Detach from the illness, and attach to the experience of health.

Station 6: Body language

Because it is your free will to go with the flow or not, you can consciously choose to block the information and experiences flowing into your life from your subconscious mind, perhaps because of a serious fear of change. The result of this decision is not only an unsatisfying life, but also pain in your eyes, ears, nose, and head. If you stick with these fearful thoughts or deny your connection to the Source over a long period of time, real disease can develop.

A good example of how this happens is with headaches. Headaches are often the result of the conscious mind trying to reject what the subconscious is bringing to pass. For instance, you may feel intuitive guidance from deep within, but are either consciously trying to reject it, or don't feel that you have the power or right to bring your dreams into reality. To give you a good visual of what's going on here, you can think of this like a bottle of fine wine. Imagine that you try to pour the wine, but something clogs the bottle, preventing you from getting any of the wine out. This is exactly what you do when you consciously block the flow of experiences or inspiration from the Source—your co-creative power is trying to bring something good to pass, but you are putting a cork in it, which creates a headache.

As you start to deal with the disease that you are tuning into now, please keep telling yourself that there is no reason to put a cork in anything—you are worthy of all that you truly desire. Accept that you deserve the best in life, and the best in life will flow right to you.

Please look at any of the Station 6 issues that you may be facing with an eye to your intuition and ability to trust life. What I want here is for you to learn to use your inner wisdom to understand the diseases and pain that you may be experiencing in this Station. The more that you feel that you have the power to understand your own circumstances, the more that you can take control of your life and easily change any negative or limiting experiences.

Action plan for resetting Station 6:

- ✓ Find a willingness to change. If this is difficult for you, use the new truth, "I am ready and willing to change. Change is only for my best."
- ✓ Select 2-3 retuning statements to reset your preset.
- ✓ Go to page 409 and take the Reality Type Test, if you have not already done so.

- ✓ Select 4 Reality Type exercises, and do these for 40 days.
- ✓ Have faith that you can make decisions with confidence.
- ✓ Each time that you are faced with a decision, follow the 3 steps: detach, pick the matching-frequency decision, and allow the outcome to come to you (do not micromanage).
- ✓ Connect each day with your intuition. Become aware (and grateful) each time that you have ideas and solutions come to you with seemingly no effort.
- ✓ Look at any health issue from a detached perspective. See if you can identify what the disease might be saying to you symbolically.
- ✓ Take responsibility for fixing your own life and choosing your own happiness. Detach from anything that is not in alignment with this goal.

STATION 7

The Energy of a Higher Purpose

Station Motto: I am one with the Source. I am an expression of Source-power.

Location of Station: Top of head.

Problem Playlist: If you are preset with negative Station 7 beliefs, you will find that you have some of these behavior patterns and difficulties:

- Feeling disconnected from everyone around you
- Not taking joy in things that you used to take great pleasure in.
- A sense of being lost in life.
- Feeling unimportant, or feeling that you do not make a contribution to life.
- Not having a reason to get up in the morning.
- Feeling no drive to do your work.

- Not feeling taken care of.
- Feeling burned out—in work or in life.
- Having a nagging sense of dissatisfaction with everything and everyone around you.
- Having no idea what you want to do with your life.

Station 7 Body Issues: If you are tuning into negativity here, you will find that you have disease, pain, or extra weight in these areas:

- Muscular system
- Nervous system
- Skin of the entire body
- Scalp and hair
- Top of the head

A little enlightenment, please...

It is hard enough to trust a Source outside yourself to provide a good life for you, but when it comes to trusting your own ability to co-create a fulfilling life **with** that Source, it may seem like too much. Can you really trust life to provide you with all that you desire? Can you actually trust yourself to stay connected to your Source-power, even in the face of difficulty?

You absolutely can. When you flow with positive expectations in Station 7, you feel intensely connected to all of life. Every action and individual that comes into your life is proof of your expectations bringing into being all that you desire. Every flower that you smell, every fruit that you eat, and every person that you meet is seen as an aspect of the Source showing itself to you at that moment.

Better yet, with this true awareness of your Source-power comes complete trust in the creative force that flows through all of us. This force will provide all that you desire, if you just let it. By trusting your perfect connection and partnership with the Source you can create a fulfilled life and feel at all times connected to the universe in a powerful and very real way. You can create "supernatural" experiences, and you can make miracles happen at every moment—actually, you are already doing this by co-creating each moment!

This is enlightenment. By connecting to the reality that you are one with the Source and using your intention to create moments that flow with the highest frequencies, you literally lighten your load of negative expectations by turning them to pure energy and letting them go—**enlightening you**! Connecting to this enlightened state allows you to fine tune your Source-power so that you can be more of who you intend to be, with more creative force than you ever thought possible.

Trust your own connection to the Source

Who is the Source?

Inside your very soul, you **know** the answer to this question. You know the ways that the Source manifests in your life, and you know your own connection to its power. This sense of the Source is palpable—no one needs to tell you that the Source is real, or that you have a very personal relationship with this force.

Other people (Good Witches and Wizards and other "authorities") have tried to disconnect you from your own knowledge on the Source, and have made every effort to make you afraid of your own power and even the power of the Source. Because of this, instead of trusting your instincts on what and who the Source is, you have given over your power to them, choosing to believe their version of what a higher authority is and what you must do to earn the Source's love and good graces.

Once you have been convinced that your own inner knowledge of the Source is not to be trusted, you will easily believe **their** version of what it takes to have a personal relationship with this higher authority. Somehow, having others tell you what to think and how to pray seems easier than having to make your own judgments on the truth. Because of this, you may have found yourself giving all your power to the rules and regulations of a particular church—after all, you are told that if you follow the rules and words written in the chosen religious text, then you have a true understanding of the Source. The same is true of many esoteric, healing, or spiritual systems available—they may have convinced you that the **only** way to enlightenment, wellness, or connection to your creative power is to follow their plan exactly. Either way, the message is the same—if you deviate at all, the system either won't work for you, or you will have angered the Source. Believing this, you give more authority to the rules than to your own inner connection to the Source, and **that** creates problems in your life.

The reality is that no text, no book, and no set of rules will ever give you the personal relationship with the Source that you seek—or that you already have within your mind, body and spirit. You are one with all that the Source is, and you are your own authority on the aspects of the Source that you choose to experience. To know the Source on a personal level, you must **trust yourself to understand**. You must trust your instincts, and you must become aware of the hand of the Source holding yours as life is created in alignment with your expectations.

To do this, release the fear that you won't be right, or that you are not good enough to truly know or comprehend the Source. It is this fear that makes it seem easier to just take another's word on what and who the Source is, and how you work with it to get what you want out of life. After all, a true personal relationship with the Source takes a good deal more effort—**and** an authentic willingness to be open to all information about the Source, rather than just one or two "authorized" perspectives. The reward of this effort is that you will truly accept your own Source-power, and you will take back total authority over your life in a way that flows with the most positive attributes of life.

When talking about this I am often asked, "But how do you know if it is okay to trust your experience of the Source as real? How can you possibly know if you are good or bad, if you don't have some guidelines?"

It is actually fairly simple. You are programmed with an inner understanding of the Source, and of the best energies in life. To feel your own sense of the Source, ask yourself these questions: Who do **you** think the Source is? Do you have an instinct of what is good or bad? For instance, is killing good? Is love bad? The physical sense that you will have in response to these questions tells you that you absolutely have a trustworthy inner sense of not only the Source—but of what is good or bad as you judge it so. Further, when you truly connect with the reality that you are one with both the Source and all life on Earth, you will never choose to create in a way that is inconsistent with the very best frequencies. After all, anything that you do to another, you are literally doing to yourself **and** to the Source. Since this is the case, why would you ever choose to take actions that knowingly hurt another being, the Source, **and** yourself? You know the answer to that!

To fully accept your own authority on what the Source is for you, you must be willing to look at every belief that you now hold about a higher authority, and those that you encounter in your daily life. Instead of only knowing one religious text, read everything that you can about the various religions of the world, and their respective views on God. Read philosophers who wax poetic on the nature of the Divine and the divinity of nature. Read quantum physics books. Read different viewpoints on the beginnings of the universe, or the nature of the universe itself. Question everything. Do not **ever** accept something as true simply because someone says that it is. Seek your own holy grail on the wisdom of God. Seek this wisdom for wisdom's sake alone. Seek with a totally open heart—without a need for judgment or a fear of what you will find. If you find something that is different than your current notion of the Source, don't be afraid of letting go of your old beliefs for one that works better for you. Accept only the things that you feel are true for you. Throw everything else out.

I am passionate about this, because I think that if more people were less afraid of going against their family's or church's or friend's notions of the Source, and were willing to actually take the time to explore what the world has to say about the nature of the Source, there would absolutely be less hate, less fear, and certainly less war. We are not so different. Our beliefs are not so different. There should be no need for criticism—no desire to prove that one religion or way of thought is better than the other. They are all equal. Learn from them. Take what you want, believe what you want, and release the rest.

In this exploration, you will find that some writings seem more inspired than others. Within the truly inspired texts, you will find one true definition of the Source: that is, the Source is **unconditional love**. Because of this, in order to align yourself with the Source, choose to love unconditionally in all situations all the time. The truth is that the Source makes that choice at every moment—there is no love only **if** you are not a sinner, or only **if** you follow whatever rules have been set forth exactly. There is no love only **if** you give a certain amount of money to the church, or you make it to a religious service a certain number of times. There is no only **if** at all—the love of the Source **always** flows through you. You are **always** worthy of this love, however you choose to use your energy. You have earned the love of the Source by simply existing—you were created from this love and are never disconnected from it. There is no judgment, there is no fear—there is only faith in the power of love. That's it—the Source is love, and, as reflections of the Divine, each living being is charged with the task of aligning ourselves with the power of pure, unconditional love for ourselves and all of life.

Your relationship with the Source could not be more personal. Begin your journey **today** to align yourself with this power within, and to this beautiful connection to the Source itself.

Questions:

1. What have you been taught about the Source? Do you believe that the Source is judgmental? Vengeful? Unconditionally loving? Is it difficult for you to believe that you are one with the Source, and you are co-creating the aspects of the Source that are shown in

life? Is so, why is this difficult? In what ways would your life be different if you truly believed that you are co-creating life as part of the Source?

Retuning statement: "I am a co-creator."

2. Have you been taught that the Source is male or female? How does this teaching impact your ability to have a personal relationship with the Source?

Retuning statement: "The Source encompasses all of life. I am one with the oneness."

3. What have you been taught about having a personal relationship with the Source? Does this explanation match the relationship with the Source described in this book? Do you trust yourself to know who and what the Source is? If not, why not? Remember, you can choose to believe anything that you want to about the Source, and you can choose any school of thought or religion out there. Just know that whatever you believe the Source to be, it is.

Retuning statement: "I believe in my personal connection with the Source. I trust myself to understand."

4. How have the religious texts that you are familiar with been interpreted to you? If you read the text with this new viewpoint on the Source, how would it be different from what you have been taught?
5. This week, pick up spiritual or religious readings that you would normally avoid. Read these with an open mind. What do you find true? What do you dismiss as untrue for you? Are there similarities between your current way of thinking and this new way? Did you learn anything from this experiment?

Free will, flow-style

You have likely been taught that the Source has given you "free will" in your life. In the context in which this is taught, the idea is that free will is really just a ticking time bomb—you are more likely than not going to use this power to do something horrible to offend the Source, at which point, you must plead with the Source for forgiveness. Since the Source knows that He or She created you in a flawed state, so long as you are truly sorry, you are forgiven. Newly cleansed, you then go on about your day, just waiting for the moment when your free will causes problems again, and the cycle starts over.

This always seemed rather odd to me. After all, if the Source is the all-powerful being that most of us believe in, then why in the world would He or She create us so flawed that we would just constantly mess up?

It turns out that the holographic understanding of the Source provides enlightenment on the true nature of free will. Since you are one with the Source, and you have the ability to create anything that you choose, then free will is truly just that—you have the free will to use that creative power any way that suits you. The Source does not stand in your way—indeed, it cannot. The Source does not judge your creation, and there is no one looking for your forgiveness. You co-create the world in the way that you choose to—you have full authority to create negative or positive experiences, and the Source brings what you wish into being. That is true free will, and **that** is truly freeing.

This is not to say that free will is not a bit of a ticking time bomb, however. For one, you must actually live what you create, so it is important that you create in alignment with the best aspects of life and the highest creative ability. Further, this definition of free will puts a lot more responsibility on your shoulders (or, perhaps more correctly, in your mind), because you are **solely responsible** for your creation—you are never a victim of life or of the Source. If you choose to create chaos and negativity, you know that you are reaping what you sow—you cannot point to a higher authority and release your responsibility when chaos and negativity comes into your own life. Nor can you go to the Source and act like a bad teenager who knows that his parents will bail him out of jail, as long as he is truly sorry for his actions. Instead, when you take on the full responsibility of your free will to create each moment of life, you know that you are responsible for the product of your creative thoughts, words, and actions—and you must clean up your **own** messes.

So, while this co-creative understanding of free will seems freeing (and it is), it also means that you must take on a great deal more responsibility for your personal impact on the world. The truth is that you are having an impact on the creation of the entire world and on the collective experience of life, and that is a lot of responsibility to shoulder. In some ways, it seems easier to just blame a Source outside your control for the world being the way that it is, for so many people going hungry, for wars in far off-countries, and for your own life being so unfulfilling and messed up. However, to live in the flow, you need to take your creative Source-power very seriously, becoming consciously aware of not only your personal part in creating life, but also the way that your thoughts and actions affect everyone and everything else in the world.

When you choose to be aware of this, you can never see an injustice and shrug your shoulders and say, "What can I do?", because you will know the answer: You can choose actions that assist the situation. You can choose to create every single moment from a powerful place that flows with love, hope, joy, and prosperity. You can believe that your life is so abundant that you can easily and effortlessly give to others—whether it is in the form of time, money, or goods.

Further, when something "bad" happens in your life, you can never again turn anger at the Source, wondering why such a thing happened. You no longer have the convenience of saying that you're a victim of life, or that you have no power to change your life. Nor can you say that you are at the whim of a vengeful Creator—one that you must have angered in some way. Rather, when you fully accept your Source-power, you will always come back to your own mind to search for the problem beliefs and expectations that might have caused this difficulty or disease. From that place, you will be able to use your personal creative responsibility to change your life **that very moment.**

You may feel that you are not responsible enough to use your power to create your life—that the Source would be much better off having all that power, and you will just go along with whatever the Source decides for you. I hate to tell you, but the Source has already given you that power—you earned it at birth, and you have been using it all along. If the Source trusts you enough to allow you to use your co-creative power to create the world, shouldn't you trust yourself?

It seems to me that it is time that you did. Trust yourself to use your free will in a positive way, and begin to use it now to consciously create the life that you desire to live.

Questions:

1. Do you trust yourself to use your Source-power in a positive way? If not, why not? Where were you taught that you were not to be trusted? Write down any experiences, teachings, or beliefs that come to mind. If you continue to believe these teachings, what kind of life do you think that you will have? What kind of life has it already created for you? Is this the life that you desire?

Retuning statement: "I accept my co-creative responsibility with awareness and confidence. I choose to create in the most positive ways today and every day."

Have a little faith...

The blind kind, please.

While blind faith has often been used as a justification for you to ignore your own gut instincts and just take another's viewpoint "on faith," this is truly not what it means. The truth is that blind faith is the power that causes co-creation to work, because it means that you have complete confidence that what you desire to bring into being **will** come into being, regardless of the fact that you cannot see it now, nor see all the steps necessary to bring it to you. No doubts, no "what ifs," no worrying about all the little details—just blind faith and total focus that the outcome that you desire will flow to you.

You must have blind faith that you have the ability to co-create in your life, and that you are choosing the thoughts, words, and actions that are in alignment with all that you desire. You must have blind faith that everything that you desire is already connected to you and will come into being, and that even if it is not in the way that you intended, it will be in perfect alignment with what you truly desire.

Further, you must have blind faith that there is a perfect order in the universe, and that you are working with this order to bring about the world that you truly desire. This is difficult for us as humans because we have an inner desire to know **why** everything happens; to be aware of the cause and effect relationship of each and every occurrence. However, the process itself is beyond our conscious comprehension—it is outside of our human capacity to see and know every little wave that brings life into existence in a certain way at a certain time. For instance, when you send out an expectation that you are going to be successful, this expectation works with the Source, rippling out over the oneness of life to bring you the experience of success. You cannot fully know the whole process, or know every result of your decision to think or act in alignment with any frequency. Nor can you know how many events it will take to bring your desires into being, or in exactly which way that they will manifest, but you **can** know with complete confidence that you will get exactly what you desire, when you have faith in your ability to co-create your life.

This kind of blind faith is very difficult, especially when it appears that your life is becoming more chaotic, or that "bad" things are happening that are not in alignment with your desires. It is at exactly this point that it is most important to keep the faith—you must pull within yourself and know that all the changes that you are seeing are for a positive and perfect purpose. A client of mine is a perfect example of how "bad" experiences are actually for your best. He decided to start his own consulting business, and his original focus was to work with small businesses to help them succeed. To bring wealth and success to his business, he began to work on the 4 for 40 system, using exercises and belief statements to create this reality. Of course, he thought that his intention for success and wealth would create a prosperous small business consulting business, but his Source-power matched him with something very different. In fact, in the first 8 weeks of his business, he could not secure one contract with a small business, but other opportunities in various global consulting roles fell into his lap. If he had focused on the "bad" experiences in small business consulting, he would have felt like a failure, but instead, he had blind faith that success and wealth were coming to him, and he allowed this to flow in whatever way matched this expectation. The amazing thing is that by having blind faith in his desired reality, he made connections that he did not even know existed before this—and could never have made those connections consciously. He may have consciously thought that small business consulting was the way to success and wealth (not to mention happiness), but the Source answered his call in a way that was better aligned for his best life. He is still amazed about the synchronicity in his life, and the ways that his Source-power continues to bring him more than he ever imagined.

This is why the "devil's in the details"—when you disconnect from your Source-power and begin to focus on all the difficulties in achieving your desired result, or you worry about making all the necessary connections yourself, you are focusing on the "devil," and creating a reality wrought with difficulty and missed connections. When you focus with blind faith on the desired result and expect that all the connections that you need will flow to you in the right way at the right time, you are in alignment with not only your desired goal, but also with the best energy of the Source. Better yet, the results that you get are often better than you could have imagined, and easier than if you had tried to do it all yourself.

By putting blind faith in this partnership, you will find yourself easily doing the "impossible" with little effort.

This is the power of blind faith. Become aware that all events are coming into your life for a reason, whether you know that reason or not. Look for moments of synchronicity as proof that your reprogramming efforts are working—notice the books that you are drawn to, the songs that you hear on the radio, the people that you meet, and even the conversations that you overhear. By being aware, you will find that these little moments will show up just when you were looking for a piece of information, a new contact, or a new idea for your business. You will be amazed at how little events are actual big indications that you are co-creating your life with the Source, so be grateful for all experiences, and create every moment with the intention of love, faith, hope and trust. If chaos happens, be grateful that life is changing and moving to bring you all that you desire (because it is!). Laugh at chaos, if you like. By doing this, you can know—with absolute certainty—that life is just as it should be.

Questions:

1. Today, begin to write down everything that happens that seems to have some connection to what you are bringing into being. Maybe you open a book to just the right place to find the answer that you were seeking. Perhaps you meet someone who has the connections that you need. Maybe the song that you hear on the radio inspires you to take action on your life plans. Do you see a pattern? Choose to become aware of all experiences as proof of your co-creative power.

Retuning statement: "I am grateful for...," inserting what you desire in the space. Add to this, "I trust that all is well. Everything is for my best."

Don't want, just BE

A friend of mine will list on her fingers the things that she wants out of life. "I want jewelry. I want a new house. I want a baby. I want a designer purse. I want to be able to go to the spa anytime that I want." She says this over and over again, telling everyone that she meets that this is what she wants.

Clearly, she is articulating what she wants from life, but does she have any of these things yet?

No, she is still just wanting.

Some people would use this as proof that the Principle of Repetition does not work (or indeed, that you have no co-creative power), but I would point to it as proof that it works better than you ever imagined.

As I have talked about many times, words have creative power—each word has its own frequency. When you continuously say, "I want," you are communicating your creative expectation that you will have the experience of wanting. Because of this, you will never get what you want, but you **will** keep on wanting it.

However, when you use the true power of expectation to communicate about your desires in a way that conveys your trust that you have it in your life now, then that experience **must** flow into being. Remember, the Source is infinitely abundant, and you are co-creating with the Source to bring into being all that you desire. The Source can only respond with matching-frequency experiences. When, instead of saying, "I want," you use phrases like "I have," "I see," or "I am," then you are asking that your experience of the Source come into being in the way that you expect—and that it is in reality now.

Instead of wanting, try **being**. **Be** the success that you want to be. **Be** the wealth that you desire to have. **Be** the good person, **be** the toned body, **be** the solution that you seek.

I know you may be asking, "But how can I be what I so clearly am not right now?" You may not be or have something that you desire now, but you absolutely can pre-construct that reality in a way that makes it real for you right this moment. Remember, even when you do not see an experience that you desire, it is already in existence—you just need to reprogram your expectations to have it flow into your life. When you use the Art of Connecting to pre-construct your reality, the illusion is as real as "reality." Through repetition, you tune yourself into that very reality in, well, reality.

Beyond the Art of Connecting, you can cultivate the practice of being grateful for the experience before you actually experience the experience. (I know that is a lot—hang in there.) When you are grateful for all that you have in your life even before you physically have it in your life, you convey the frequency of absolute confidence that you will have that reality. This confidence (or blind faith) in your co-creative ability changes your you-hologram in such a way that you are assured to have those experiences in your life—or at least, matching-frequency experiences.

Catch yourself the next time that you begin to say you "want" something. Instead, change that statement right then and there to "I have," and be grateful that you have the Source-power to create all that you desire.

Questions:

1. How often do you say "I want"? Do you have what you want yet?

If this is an issue for you, please use "I have," "I am," "I will," and "I do" with each of your desires. You may also use "I am grateful for," if you wish.

2. Imagine that you truly believed that you had what you desired in your life now. How does that feel? How does it sound, smell, or taste? Use the Art of Connecting to pre-construct that reality now (for a review of the Art of Connecting, see Principle 3).

What is your purpose?

Have you ever wondered, "Why am I here?" or "What is my purpose in life?"

Since you are here in Station 7, I am going to guess that the answer to that would be "yes." You may have also worried that you did not have a purpose at all, or that you have one but will never find it.

If this is a concern for you, fear no more. Not only do you have a purpose in life, but you are fulfilling part of it right now.

The first part of your purpose in life is to learn how to use your mind to physically create in the world from a place of conscious responsibility. By working through The Flow system and accepting your personal power to create the best that you possibly can, you are fulfilling this purpose at the highest possible level. Go ahead, congratulate yourself—you've earned it!

While this first part of your purpose is a more universal purpose (all human beings have this initial calling), the second part is particular to you, and is your own higher calling to be and create in a way that is reflective of who you are as part of the oneness of the Source. It **is** spiritual work, because it is literally that which your spirit wants your physical self to do and be in this life. You may not realize that your spirit is calling to you, but it is—and when you answer that calling, you live your life in alignment with your higher purpose.

Most of us have encountered a person who seems called to do exactly what they are doing. These people are usually identifiable because of their natural charisma, their joy at being alive, and their passion for their work and for life in general. And, while we might not term it so, there is a definite sense of spirit in their demeanor—whether or not their job is what you or I might deem a spiritual job. In fact, it does not matter at all what job they are doing; it is much more important how they are creating in that environment, and their personal expression of that work.

In the presence of such a person, you might feel that you somehow came into the world without a higher purpose, or that your own calling could not possibly be as noble as all of that. You may feel that if your calling is not in a field that other people find significant or important, then you will be seen as a failure. Or, you may be afraid that you have messed up too many times to have any chance of really living such a passionate, beautiful life.

Don't believe it. You have a purpose in this life, it is unique to you, and it is significant in its own right. To discover what this purpose is (believe me, your spirit already knows), you must allow yourself to do some introspection on what truly makes you happiest in life. Listen to your own spirit—it will tell you what you are to do, if you just let it. You may suddenly feel a flash of inspiration as you are walking through a grocery store or driving to work in the morning—the calling that you feel may be as specific as suddenly wanting to be an artist, or it can be as general as the sense that you want to create something to make people happy or to inspire them.

Take out your Flow Journal and write down all the things that you wanted to be when you grew up. Is there anything in common with all of these different jobs? For instance, as a young child, I wanted to be the President of the United States, a research scientist, an oncologist (until I hit chemistry, that is), a dancer and choreographer, a writer, and a speaker. While these professions may seem on the surface to be very different, the underlying reason why I wanted to do each of them is that I wanted to change the world. If I asked myself why I wanted to change the world, I would say that I wanted to make a difference in people's lives—to help people. And that is my life purpose: "to help people." (Please notice—this is different than finding the actual job that you should be doing—you will be working on that in Station 2. Here, you are finding an **inner purpose** for doing what you are doing with your life).

What is the underlying reason that you wanted to be each of the professions on your list? If you are having a difficult time with that, try writing down everything that you love doing, or the moments that you have done something that you were really proud of. Why did you love those experiences so much? What might the underlying purpose be? See if you cannot put this into a simple statement, such as: "to provide solutions to others," or "to teach others." Read the statement aloud, starting with, "My life purpose is," then add your statement. If this is your life purpose, you will feel it deep within you—and you may very well have a physical reaction to it. I know that when I read mine aloud, the truth of the statement literally made my eyes fill with tears. That was when I knew I had hit the core of who I was to be in life.

In fact, to my utter surprise, I found that I had always been living this purpose, although I was not consciously aware of it. At the time, I was working as a benefits consultant—work that definitely helped people by providing health and disability benefits, but that I might not have readily identified as spiritual work. That reality changed when one of my clients introduced me to an entire table of people as "the girl who changed her life." At that moment, I realized that when you are truly living your life in alignment with your higher calling, all work **is** spiritual work.

More often than not, you may have found yourself very worried about choosing the "right job" or taking the "best opportunity," but the truth is that when you understand your life purpose, you can live that calling in almost any profession, although the right one will fit you like a glove—it will just flow. In my case, the realization that my purpose is "to help people" set me out on an interesting journey through life. Building on this awareness, I allowed myself to be open to other ways to help people. I studied and trained to be a Reiki Master—and I helped people heal. Because of my love of dance, I trained to become a Nia teacher, and I started to work with my students on releasing tension and loving their bodies. Finally, I felt the inspiration to write this book, and that seems to be the most perfect expression of my life purpose.

The deep calling to "help people" can be fulfilled by a host of choices and life paths—none of them wrong. For example, you might feel that your true calling is to help others through teaching. Wonderful. Now, think about how many different ways that you can fulfill this higher calling: You can teach in grade school, high school, or college. You can become a trainer for a company. You can write a book. You can teach windsurfing. You can become a mother or father, and pass along your wisdom to your children. Any of these would work, but one or two might seem to fit you best right now.

These are just some examples, and there are certainly many, many more. The idea here is to understand that it is not so important **what** you are doing—it is far more important **why** you are doing it. The job itself is literally irrelevant; when you have a clear idea of your higher calling, you can live that purpose in whatever employment that you find yourself. A perfect example of this is a man name Tony, who is the janitor of my old high school. His physical job may be to clean the bathrooms and sweep the floors, but his spiritual job is clearly much more than that. Anytime that you encounter Tony he has a big smile on his face, a kind word, and usually an enormous hug with his big strong arms. He seems to know when a student is having a bad day, and he is always there with a joke or a pat on the shoulder. His higher calling is certainly to brighten the lives of others, and he happens to be fulfilling that purpose by working as a janitor. The job itself is not important, but his **expression** of the job certainly is—he is one of the most lovely people that I have ever met, and he has made an unbelievable impact on the world simply by living his personal purpose in that particular place and job. Can you imagine how many lives he has touched by working in that profession and having contact with that many kids? I am truly grateful that this happened to be the way that he is fulfilling his life purpose, because he certainly made a difference in my life and continues to make a difference in people's lives to this day.

Once you understand that the profession itself is not as important as your life purpose, you can easily understand that every moment that you create—in or out of "work"—should be dedicated to living this purpose. In this way, **your work is your life**—whatever you do, say, or create in any situation or interaction **is** on purpose for your highest calling, and therefore, **is** spiritual work. You then become a perfect expression of Source-power and your own spirit every moment of every day, and there is nothing more beautiful than that.

Questions:

1. Write down your life purpose statement. What jobs can you think of that might fulfill that purpose? Which of these seems like the best fit for you right now?
2. List some ways that you might be able to live your life purpose in your daily interactions with others. Make sure that you include yourself on your list! How will you feel if you take these kinds of actions?

Poverty is not the only spiritual choice

What? You can live a spiritual life **and** have material success?

If that is what you desire, you absolutely can.

This may come as a shock, since it is ingrained in our culture that those living a spiritual life should be living in poverty, forgoing any worldly success. But what if you don't want to give up everything to follow your calling?

You do not have to. Your personal manifestation of your life purpose is completely up to you. **One** choice is to express your calling by living in poverty, like so many mystics and saints. St. Francis of Assisi came from a very wealthy family, but answered his calling by giving up all of his riches and living on the streets, becoming a vehicle for healing people and animals. Mother Theresa followed her calling by living and working on the streets of Calcutta, tending to the less fortunate. These were the manifestations of unconditional love and creative power that they each chose to create; it was how they decided to express their life purpose and personal alignment with unconditional love.

This can be your calling—your life path—and, if you feel that is what you are to do, by all means, you should do it. However, I would like to stress that following your calling and fulfilling your life purpose does not mean that you **must** live in poverty, sleeping on dirty streets, or anything else. There are many ways for you to manifest a life in alignment with your life purpose, all of them noble. Instead of choosing to be poor, you can choose to be wealthy and use that wealth in a positive way. After all, there is no question that a person who gives up everything to answer the calling of his or her spirit is always to be admired and applauded, but it is no less powerful to follow a calling that does not require you to give up all wealth and comfort in this world. Such wealth, when gained and used in a way consistent with your life purpose, can do a great good for yourself and for all of life on earth. While giving time to a charity is very valuable, so is giving money or goods that can help it stay in business and continue to do its good work for years to come.

No matter how you choose to express your higher calling, it is always an action that is in alignment with trust and courage, and a physical manifestation of your personal partnership with the Source. Any decision made out of the pure love of self (fulfilling your needs) and the love of others (using your power to create for the good of life) is always a decision flowing with the best creative energy of the Source. Choose to heed your higher calling and offer your personal creative expression to the world, in whatever form or fashion that takes.

You will be better for it, and so will the world.

Questions:

1. How do you want to manifest your calling? What are your feelings about living a spiritual life and having money? Can you imagine having wealth **and** feeling that you are living a life of the highest frequencies?

Retuning statement: "I choose to be abundant in every way. I earn and use money in alignment with my life purpose."

A spiritual crisis is sometimes just a breakthrough in disguise

Finding your higher purpose tunes you into a much higher frequency of living. While this is absolutely for your best, the adjustment to this higher level means that your current beliefs, identity, groups, work, and relationships no longer fit the person that you now know yourself to be. Everything that you know as your life and your comfort zone becomes challenged, resulting in discomfort, depression, and maybe even a true spiritual crisis, otherwise known as a "dark night of the soul."

While this process can feel uncomfortable, it is oftentimes a strong indication that you are transitioning to become truly powerful and in tune with most positive aspects of the Source. I speak from experience here, as I went through processing beliefs from this Station a couple of years before I wrote this book. Let me tell you, it is not necessarily a pleasant experience. I didn't feel like getting up in the morning. I knew that my own mission in life was "to help others," and I felt a deep calling to do so, but I did not know how best to express myself in the world. I felt so antagonized by everything that I had once seen as comfortable that I wanted to just cloister myself away from everyone and everything. Nothing seemed to fit me anymore—the experiences that I used to enjoy were now completely unfulfilling.

As you begin your journey to your true purpose, you may find yourself going through similar experiences and emotions. Caught up in this transition, you may begin wondering if you will ever find your way. You may feel abandoned by life, as everything that you trust and know seems to shake up or disappear all together. You may feel shocked that you are not able to accept the same behavior from others that you once considered normal.

Perhaps most difficult, you may feel conflicted about moving forward on purpose. Part of you may feel elated, because your spirit is **ready** to move forward—after all, your spirit has known your true purpose all along. However, your mind may rebel, perhaps due to a long-standing resistance to change. Worrying thoughts may creep up, such as, "What will I have to leave behind? What if I am crazy? What if I do this and totally mess up my life?" Worse yet, these feelings may be amplified by other people in your life, especially those who have some interest in keeping you as you are today. Of course, this outside reinforcement of your innate fear will only amplify it.

When this happens (or if it is happening now), take a deep breath. Remember that you are never lost, and you are never abandoned by the Source—you are one with the potential of the entire universe. Read your life purpose statement aloud, and connect with the emotions that you feel when you know who you are and why you are here. While connected to these positive emotions, ask yourself whether you want to connect to fear—and cling to a life that no longer suits you—or move forward with faith, and connect to a truly fulfilling life that allows you to make a real contribution to the world.

The choice becomes very clear.

Trust your calling and your connection to the Source and move forward, courageously choosing to make choices and create a life that is in alignment with your higher purpose. Take time each day to connect with the oneness of the universe through prayer, meditation, or simply sitting in nature. Feel the truth that you always fit into the oneness of the universe. Allow yourself to reconnect with your inner sense of purpose, be grateful for your creative power, and trust that you will have all that you need provided for you.

And so you shall. When you have the faith in yourself to follow your higher calling, you resonate with the power of love of self and of others. The most spiritual thing that you can do is to use your unique energy and talents in a way that betters the collective frequency of the universe. Not only will you be emotionally fulfilled (no matter what **anyone** thinks of your decisions), you will make a difference in the lives of all you meet.

Questions:

1. Do you feel full-body tired or depressed? Do you feel disconnected from the Source and from everything around you? Can you see where a shift in your beliefs may have caused this change in your life? Do the people and things of your old life (pre-Flow) fit who you truly are? If not, know that while these experiences no longer fit you, you will bring others into your life that match your new way of being exactly.

Retuning statement: "I am always connected to everyone and everything. I trust that I am moving forward into a better life for myself."

2. Do others in your life resonate with fear about the life that you need to lead to be on purpose? Do you feel shaky or depressed when being around these people?

If this is an issue for you, limit your exposure to these people. When you are around them, focus on your breath. While breathing in and out slowly, mentally repeat, "I trust myself. I have faith in my purpose in this world."

Give peace a chance

I am often approached with the questions: "How can I change the world? How can I help to bring about peace?" They are age-old questions, to be sure, but there is a real solution in sight.

In a world that seems filled with conflict, it is easy for each of us to feel that there is little that we can do to bring peace and love to the world. However, as discussed earlier in the book, each action that you take that is in alignment with the very best frequencies of life—love, peace, hope, joy, and faith (to name a few)—is causing a ripple effect that is changing the overall frequency of the collective consciousness. That, in turn, asks for new experiences to be called up from the Source.

That said, in the words of Ghandi, "You must **be** the change that you wish to see in the world." Following this logic, to change the world, you must:

1. Find peace in your life now.

To offer peace to the world, you must offer peace to yourself first. Choose to stop beating yourself up for "mistakes" that you have made. Accept who and what you are now, and love yourself unconditionally. Love every moment of your life as the new miraculous creation that it is.

This acceptance does not mean that you do not wish to change aspects of your life; it just means that you have chosen to love this moment now, and all that you have created in this moment. You must be at peace with all the decisions that have lead you here, and who you have chosen to be. Choose non-judgment in your life in this present moment, and be at peace with yourself as you move forward, altering anything that you wish to. **Peace in your life now always equals peace in your future life.**

And, every moment of peace that you choose to create in your life **also** increases the frequency of the world—which always creates a more peaceful world.

2. Make decisions that flow with peace and love.

Every day, in little and big ways, you are making creative decisions that either flow with peace and love, or flow with conflict. You are choosing how you respond to others; you are choosing how to speak to yourself. Instead of responding to anyone from a place of anger, step away for a moment, take a deep breath, and realign yourself with the frequency of peace and love. When you speak, do so with love in your heart, and a true belief that any differences between you can be healed, even if it means just walking away from each other.

When you make a decision about your own life, make it from a place of peace and love, not fear and hate. Choose to move forward in life with authentic faith in the good of life and with peaceful intentions for yourself and all of life.

Actions that flow with peace and love bring the world up.

3. Be compassionate.

As is discussed in Station 4, compassion is the true understanding of another person's issues and plight. By reacting with compassion to all of life, you stop judging anyone or anything because you truly understand their perspective and what they might be going through, and you see yourself as one with everything. You understand that all of life is a reflection the Source.

4. Get involved.

Find a cause that you really care about, and give a couple of hours of your time to it—or send off a percentage of your income, if that is how you'd like to do it. Take two hours a week to write letters and make phone calls to your political representatives about issues that interest you.

Think big. Believe in your heart that you are making a big difference, and know that you truly are. Be satisfied in knowing that you have done good for the world, and choose to do a little bit more of it every day.

To create peace in yourself and the world, please use the retuning statement: "Today and everyday, I choose peace. I am peaceful to myself and all of life. I choose words of peace. I choose thoughts of peace. I choose actions of peace."

Station 7: Body language

Like the oneness of the universe, the body issues in Station 7 deal with the oneness of your entire body, causing disease to show itself in two distinct manners. If you are overly connected to your spiritual self, you may stop caring about the condition of your body; the result of which is that your body becomes emaciated, worn out, and generally unkempt. A remedy for this is to remember that your body serves a very important purpose for your spiritual development—without it, you would not be able to experience the physical results of your thoughts, words, and actions.

On the opposite end, you may be a person who is completely disconnected from your own spirit or Source-power. Without a strong connection to the Source, the electrical connections of your body can break down, resulting in nervous and muscular system disorders. This makes a great deal of sense when you consider the way that you are able to co-create life with the Source, and the way that life is brought into existence. Just as your nervous system takes in and communicates wave information to your brain, your thoughts and expectations communicate with the Source in waves, and those waves are translated and made manifest in experiences in your life. When you do not trust your connection with the Source, you interrupt the communication, and your body tunes into the frequency of interrupted electrical communication as well. To create an open and flowing connection with the Source, use the Art of Connecting to connect with the oneness of the universe, and imagine that your thoughts and words are rippling out, bringing you perfect health.

Finally, if you feel like life is launching an all-out attack on you, then you may be experiencing full body skin disorders. The skin represents your ability to protect yourself, so, if this is the case for you, ask yourself a few questions: Why don't you trust your connection to the Source to provide protection for you? What would happen if you truly believed in your oneness with the Source?

If you are dealing with physical issues in this Station, I want you to look at the disease and affected system symbolically. Look to see what the issue is able to tell you about the underlying expectations and beliefs causing the problem. For example, let's say that you are diagnosed with Parkinson's disease. What is the effect of this disease? It affects your nervous system, causing your nerve synapses to break down, affecting your nerves' ability to communicate with your brain. Can you look at this symbolically? Your nerves are the conduit of waves all over your body—taking your thoughts and beliefs and making them physically real, as well as sending the frequencies of different experiences to your brain, and letting you know what you are sensing. Symbolically, the nervous system can be seen as the communication that you have with the Source-hologram. Do you feel a breakdown of your ability to feel the Source's love and communicate that to your life? Do you trust your ability to communicate your desires to the Source? What is standing in the way of a flowing communication with life?

What I want here is for you to learn to use your inner wisdom to understand the diseases and pain that you may be experiencing in this Station. The more that you feel that you have the power to understand and take responsibility for your own circumstances, the more that you can take control of your life—and truly change any limiting or difficult experiences.

Action plan for resetting Station 7:

- ✓ Select 2-3 retuning statements to reset your preset.
- ✓ Go to page 409 and take the Reality Type Test, if you have not already done so.
- ✓ Select 4 Reality Type exercises, and do these for 40 days.
- ✓ Have blind faith that you are on purpose in your life.
- ✓ Evaluate every choice for whether it is in alignment with fear or faith.

✓ Remember that the devil's in the details. Don't focus on worry over how something is going to come into being. Choose to set your expectations and focus on your Source-power to have these goals flow to you.

✓ Pay attention to little synchronicities that happen.

✓ Do not use "I want." Instead, be who and what you desire.

✓ Choose peace in your interactions with others.

✓ Choose to be peaceful in your self-talk.

✓ Avoid or limit exposure to negative, critical people.

✓ Focus on the truth that everything is one.

PART 4

4 for 40

4 FOR 40

40 Days to Total Life Transformation!

Are you ready to have the life of your dreams flow right to you?

To create the best program for your success, you are about to design your own "4 for 40." First, you will take the "Reality Type Test." This will identify your "Reality Type," which simply identifies the way that you process new information and create reality with your senses. Remember, the sensory information that you take into your mind creates the memory-holograms and beliefs that then tune you into the various experiences and illnesses that you manifest. To reset your problem presets the quickest, you want to use your **strongest** senses—the ones that allow you to have the strongest connection with reality. Your Reality Type will tell you which senses work the best for you.

Next, you will create your 4 for 40—you will choose 4 exercises that work with your Reality Type, and you will do these simple exercises for 40 days. Research has shown that by doing a specific activity for 40 days, you will literally change your brainwaves (which is exactly what you are going for!). In "The Flow" terms, that means in 40 days, you will have retuned your mind into a completely new frequency—creating new presets and habits that tune you into more positive experiences, behavior patterns, and health.

Very soon, you will be flowing with the life of your dreams!

THE REALITY TYPE TEST

Make a check after each statement that is true for you. When you are done with each section, total the checks in the column and put the total in the appropriate box in the last row.

Sight:

After seeing something new, I can remember exactly   ____
   what it looked like.

I took many notes in school.   ____

If I was stuck on a test, I could close my eyes and   ____
   picture the page of book the answer was on.

I can remember what someone was wearing the last   ____
   time that I saw them.

When I think about a past conversation, I can visualize   ____
   exactly where it happened.

When I walk into an empty room, I can visualize what   ____
   the room would look like decorated.

In school, I liked the subjects of art, photography, and technical drawing. _____

I love to read; I read everything that I can get my hands on. _____

When someone gives me directions, I like to have a map and landmarks. _____

I like color, and have a good sense of what colors go together. _____

I love colored pens and find myself doodling with them. _____

I write everything down. _____

I can easily visualize buildings, former homes, and rooms. _____

I prefer to use visuals to explain concepts (for example, creating a drawing or putting together a PowerPoint presentation.) _____

I can put things together using a diagram. _____

Total: _____

Sound:

I love to tell stories and jokes, and enjoy speaking in public. _____

I remember things better if I talk them out. _____

In school, I loved classes that had a lot of discussion. _____

English, languages, and choir were favorite subjects of mine. _____

I love listening to music as much as I can. _____

I enjoy singing or playing an instrument. _____

I can easily remember a tune that I have only heard a few times. _____

I love to listen. My friends say that I am a great listener. _____

Songs and jingles frequently pop into my head. _____

I have often been able to help others talk out issues and come to a compromise. _____

I don't like silence. _____

I find it easier to study or concentrate with some kind
    of sound on in the background. ____
I like to think aloud. ____
When I remember important events in my life, I can
    remember the music that was playing at the time. ____
Songs evoke strong emotions in me. I associate
    feelings with music. ____

Total: ____

Smell:

I can easily remember the smell of my father's cologne
    or my mother's perfume. ____
I associate a smell with being home. ____
I love to smell flowers. ____
I enjoy putting on clothing that smells good to me. ____
I put on different perfume or cologne depending on my
    mood or what I am going to be doing that day. ____
When I think about a memory, I can remember the
    scent of the moment. ____
I associate different feelings with different scents. ____
I love to cook, because I love the smell of good food. ____

When I someone walks by wearing the same cologne
    or perfume as a parent or a former lover, I
    immediately think of that person. ____
There are smells that absolutely make me sick. ____
It is important to me that my home smells nice. ____
I often smell my food before I eat it. ____
I think that there is a scent of love and a smell of
    money. ____
I love scented soaps and candles. ____
Certain scents immediately take me back to my
    childhood. ____

Total: ____

Taste:

I have certain tastes that I love (and/or crave). _____
I love to try samples at the grocery store. _____
When I go to a restaurant, I enjoy trying new things. _____
When I taste certain foods, I am reminded of events in my life. _____
I love to cook. _____
I am able to put foods together in non-traditional ways, but that taste great. _____
I have taken, or always wanted to take, a cooking class. _____
To me, certain tastes are connected with different emotions. _____
I can remember the taste of foods from my childhood. _____
I enjoy trying to figure out the ingredients in various dishes at a restaurant. _____
If I had to live without certain foods, my enjoyment of life would decrease significantly. _____
I believe that love has a taste. _____
When I am working, I must have something to munch on. _____
To me, taste is one of the great gifts of life. _____
I get excited about the taste of a succulent orange or a great steak. _____

Total: _____

Touch:

When trying to figure out how something works, I would prefer to physically handle it. _____
I love the feel of different fabrics. _____
I often stroke my hand, leg, or face as I am thinking. _____
I enjoy working with my hands. _____
I have taken, or would like to take, a sculpture, glass-working, pottery, or wood-working class. _____
I enjoy the feeling of soft cotton or clean sheets. _____

I like to wear different textures and fabrics. I like the way that they feel. ____

When trying to understand a new concept, I like to have something tangible to hold on to (example: a brochure, pen, book, or worksheet.) ____

I enjoy massages. ____

When someone touches me, I feel comforted. ____

I have been described as a "touchy-feely" kind of person. ____

I like to hold something in my hand as I meditate or think. ____

I enjoy gardening, working in the shed, or tinkering with a car. ____

I can remember the feeling of fabric, flowers, or tablecloths that were involved in past events of my life. ____

When I shop, I find myself touching things as I look at them. ____

Total: ____

Movement:*

I love to dance. ____

I use my hands and arms a great deal when I speak. ____

I find myself tapping out a beat when I am thinking or reading. ____

I watch people's body language for clues as to how they are feeling. ____

I often pace as I am thinking. ____

I like to be active—I don't like to sit still. ____

I love sports and dance, and can easily pick up on new skills. ____

I go on a walk when I want to think about a decision that I need to make. ____

I find myself fascinated with the body movements of other people (for instance, while watching a TV ____ show or presentation).

I have always liked using my body in new ways. _____

I like to doodle when on the phone or listening to a _____
    lecture.

I am drawn to physical activities. _____

When I hear music, I naturally want to move to it. _____

I can easily recall the movements involved in a sport _____
    that I played or a dance that I learned as a teen or
    young adult.

I coach sports, cheer, or dance, or I have thought about _____
    it.

Total: _____

* I have added "Movement" as a Reality Type, because research has shown that many people learn best when moving. In addition, movement has also been shown to create new neural pathways in the brain (which is what we are going for!).

Part 2

Place the total for each "Reality Type" in the appropriate box.

Sight	
Sound	
Smell	
Taste	
Touch	
Movement	

The top two numbers compose your personal Reality Type—your individual way of sensing and perceiving all information. To select your exercises, simply go to the matching sections in the upcoming pages, and choose 4 exercises total from your top two senses.

For example, let's say that you are a Smell-Sight Realty Type. After reviewing the exercises in the Smell and Sight sections, you decide that you would like to use these exercises with your retuning statements:

1. Light a scented candle
2. Look at a picture that reminds you of your goal
3. Choose a new perfume that matches the feeling that you want to embody, and
4. Write out your new "retuning statements" several times a day.

Of course, you **absolutely** can combine exercises any way that you desire, or even create your own. Just be creative, and trust your intuition on what will work best for you. Whatever you do, or however you do it, just do 4 Reality Type exercises every day for 40 days, and you will tune into a **total life transformation**!

SIGHT

W rite out the retuning statements that you have chosen to work on. Answer the questions. Select your exercises, and use these with the retuning statements.

1. What color would you associate with each retuning statement?
2. Does a picture come to mind when you think about what each retuning statement means to you? How about the way that each emotionally feels? Write your observations down.
3. Would you associate a style of dress with each retuning statement?
4. When you think about what each retuning statement means for your life, is there a physical location that comes to mind—perhaps the woods, a park, a building, or a home, for instance?
5. Is there a physical object that comes to mind in relation to each—perhaps a car, a piece of jewelry, a candle, or a bed, for instance?

Exercises:

1. Find ways to incorporate the colors that you identified above into your daily life. For instance, you can put these colors all over your house, in your car, in your office, or wherever else you frequent. Be creative. Buy new sheets for your bed. Get throw pillows in each color, and place them on the couches. Find colored paper and cut it up into little squares. Write your new retuning statements on the squares, and stick them everywhere and anywhere that you will see them. Make sure that you have one in your pocket, wallet, or purse. Each time that you see one of these little squares, repeat the retuning statement(s) aloud to yourself several times.

2. Try to work the colors into your wardrobe. For instance, you can buy a suit in one of the colors, or maybe just a pin or scarf. When you put this on, repeat the belief aloud to yourself several times.

3. Get a bunch of old magazines. Cut out any pictures that remind you of the feelings that these retuning statements evoke in you. Using a poster board, make a collage of all of these pictures—and also put a few of these pictures in your wallet, pocket, or purse. Refer to them often, saying the new belief each time that you look at them.

4. Get some blank paper and a bunch of colorful pens, markers, or crayons. Draw out images that represent these retuning statements to you. Repeat the retuning statements to yourself as you draw.

5. Go to a new age store, and buy crystals that remind you of your retuning statements. Place these crystals all over your house and work area. Look at the crystal as you say the statements to yourself.

6. Purchase candles that are the colors that you have identified above. Light one of the candles, and as it burns, repeat the statement(s) over and over several times. This is excellent to do right before you go to bed;

however, **do not do this** if you are feeling sleepy—you don't want to fall asleep with a lit candle!

7. If there is a physical location that you associate with these statement(s), drive there if possible. If that is not possible, visualize this place in your mind as you repeat the statement(s) to yourself.

8. Gather up any physical objects that you associate with these retuning statement(s). If possible, hold one of the actual objects and look at it as you repeat the statement(s) to yourself. If it is not possible to hold the physical object, just visualize the object in your mind.

9. Find pictures of yourself that were taken at a time when you felt more confident and powerful. Connect with the positive feeling of that time as you look at the picture. Tell yourself, "I love and approve of myself."

10. Find and cut up all pictures that you absolutely hate of yourself. If possible, burn them; if not, cut them up into little pieces. As you do so, repeat the statement, "I am in control of my destiny."

11. Look at yourself in the mirror, either in your bathroom or in a compact. Repeat your retuning statements aloud as many times as possible while looking yourself in the eye. (This is a good one to do while brushing your teeth and washing your face).

12. Buy soap, bubble bath, or mineral soaks in the colors that you have identified above. Each time that you use them, repeat the retuning statement(s) to yourself.

13. Paint your nails in one of these colors.

14. Sit with a partner, and look into each other's eyes. Take turns saying each of your retuning statements aloud. Complete the exercise by telling each other, "I love you unconditionally," as you connect with the physical feeling of love.

15. Write your retuning statements out as many times as possible. Choose to do this instead of doodling while you are on the phone or sitting at a lecture.

16. Create your own exercise, using these as inspiration.

SOUND

W rite out the retuning statements that you have chosen to work on. Answer the questions. Select your exercises, and use these with your retuning statements.

1. What song might you associate with each retuning statement? For example, the retuning statement, "My life is filled with love and joy," might make you think of the song: "I'm Walkin' On Sunshine."
2. What sound might you associate with each statement? How about a sound that projects how each one emotionally feels?
3. When you think about what each retuning statement means for your life, does the sound of any physical location come to mind? For example: the sound of the woods, a park, a building, or a home.
4. Look at the following words: love, happiness, peace, health, prosperity, wellbeing, contentment, joy, success, abundance, loving oneself, safety, and speaking one's truth. What sounds do you associate with each of these words or concepts? Is there a song that you would associate with each? Write these down, not only for use

in the following exercises, but for future reference. When you want to work on resetting a preset with one of these concepts, you already have a ready-made list!

Exercises:

1. Burn a CD or make a mix-tape of the songs or sounds that you associate with each retuning statement. You can also make a theme CD or mix-tape for different emotions. For instance, you could have a "happy tape," "a prosperity tape," "a healthy tape," and so on. Play these songs all day, everywhere it is possible to do so— in your car, as you are falling asleep at night, at work, as you are taking a walk—anywhere and everywhere. Connect emotionally to the feeling of the music, and say your new retuning statement(s) aloud over and over.

2. Make a song out of these retuning statements(s). You can make an original tune, or just put the words of the statement and what you desire to the tune of an old song—perhaps one that you would associate with this particular statement or goal. Sing this aloud several times a day. Sing it while you are cooking. Sing it in the shower. Sing it in the car. If you are at work and cannot sing it aloud, hum the tune as you think of the words, or just "hear" it in your mind. However you do it, just do it as much as you possibly can.

3. Record your own voice reading your retuning statement(s) over and over. Listen to this recording often, especially as you drift off to sleep at night.

4. Go to a toy or gadget store and purchase a toy that will record what you say (there are stuffed animals and other toys that can do this). Keep the toy somewhere convenient to you, allowing you to push the button and hear your retuning statement(s) frequently.

5. Look in a mirror. As you do, repeat the retuning statement aloud several times. Look in your eyes and really connect to the emotions associated with the statement(s). Do this as often as possible.
6. If there is a physical location that you associate with these statement(s), drive there. If that is not possible, imagine hearing the sounds of this location in your mind as you repeat the statements aloud.
7. If you have a fireplace, light a crackling fire. As you sit and gaze at the fire, hear the sounds of the logs burning, turning matter into energy. Imagine that the logs represent the negative beliefs that you wish to release. As you watch it burn and hear its sounds, say aloud, "I release all negativity from my life. I love and approve of myself."
8. Find pictures of yourself that were taken at a time when you felt more confident and powerful. Connect with the positive feelings associated with that time as you look at the picture. Say aloud, "I love and approve of myself."
9. Find and cut up all pictures of yourself that you absolutely hate. If possible, burn them; if not, cut them into little pieces. Say aloud, "I am in control of my destiny."
10. Clap aloud as you repeat your retuning statement(s). Feel the joy of knowing that you are tuning into your goals each time that you do this.
11. Make sure that everything that you say in your daily life is in alignment with your goals and dreams.
12. Sit with a partner and look into each other's eyes. Take turns saying your retuning statements aloud. End the exercise by telling each other, "I love you unconditionally."
13. Create your own exercise, using these as inspiration.

SMELL

Write out the retuning statements that you have chosen to work on. Answer the questions. Select your exercises, and use these with your retuning statements.

1. What scent would you associate with each retuning statement? For example, the retuning statement, "I am filled with love," might cause you to think of the scent of roses or chocolate cake.
2. When you think about what each retuning statement means for your life, is there a scent of a physical location that comes to mind—for instance, the scent of the woods, a park, a building, or a home?
3. Look at the following list of words: love, happiness, peace, health, prosperity, wellbeing, contentment, joy, success, abundance, loving oneself, and speaking one's truth. What scents do you associate with each of these words or concepts? Write these down, not only to for use with the following exercises, but also for future reference. When you want to work on a retuning statement that involves one of these concepts, you have a ready-made list!

Exercises:

1. Go to the store and smell everything that you can; for instance, fruit, veggies, bakery items, and anything else that you want. Keep a little notebook with you as you do this, and write down the feelings that you associate with each smell. Can you summarize each feeling with a retuning statement? Do any of these scents match the retuning statement(s) that you are working on? If so, purchase some of this product to use with those retuning statements.

2. Go to a natural foods store or a new age shop and smell their aromatherapy oils. Use your notebook to write down any feelings that you have about each. How does the smell make you feel? Buy any oils that you would associate with the feeling of your retuning statement(s).

3. Take the oil of your choice and make a room spray out of it. Get an old spray bottle and wash it out thoroughly. Fill the bottle with water, and add 10-20 drops of the oil. Use this spray everywhere that you can: on your pillows, in your car, on your couch, and in the bathroom. Each time you spray the scent, repeat your retuning statement(s) aloud as you inhale the scent.

4. Make a spray bottle for different emotions or desires. For instance, you could have a "happy spray," "prosperity spray," "healthy spray," and so on. Spray these scents when you want to connect to this feeling or concept. Repeat your retuning statement(s) aloud as you do this. End the exercise by saying, "I am choosing to invite this into my life and my surroundings. I am in control of my life."

5. Make yourself a hot bath. Just before you get in, mix a few drops of the oil of your choice with a little witch hazel astringent (available at any drug store, usually in the first aid aisle). Pour this into your bath, saying, "I am pouring (insert belief or feeling) into my life. I take

it into in every fiber of my being." Climb in the bath. Soak a washcloth in the tub, and put it over your face. As you breathe in the scent, repeat your retuning statement(s) to yourself.

6. Fill a sink basin with hot water. Put a few drops of the oil of your choice into the water, and then soak a washcloth in this. As you wipe your face with this oil, repeat your retuning statement(s), along with, "I am washing away negativity."

7. Is there a perfume or cologne that you associate with a happier, more confident time in your life? Perhaps there is one you would associate with "the life of your dreams." Buy a bottle (or at the very least, get a sample of it). Each time that you wear this scent, allow yourself to connect with the positive feelings that it embodies. Spray this scent on small pieces of paper, and smell it during the day, repeating your retuning statement(s) to yourself as you do.

8. Buy soaps and shower gels that remind you of the retuning statement(s) that you are working on. Use these in the shower and bath while repeating these statement(s) to yourself.

9. If there is a physical location that you associate with this retuning statement(s), drive there. If that is not possible, imagine smelling the scent of this location as you repeat the statement(s).

10. If you have a fireplace, light a crackling fire. As you sit and gaze at the fire, hear the sounds of the logs burning, turning matter into energy. Imagine that the logs represent the negative beliefs you want to release. As you watch it burn, breathe in the scent of the fire, saying aloud, "I release all negativity from my life. I love and approve of myself."

11. Sit with a partner and look into each other's eyes. Spray the room with a "feeling" spray, or light an oil burner with this scent. Take turns saying your retuning statements aloud. End the exercise by telling each other,

"I love you unconditionally."

12. Create your own exercise, using these as inspiration.

TASTE

W rite out the retuning statements that you have chosen to work on. Answer the questions. Select your exercises, and use these with your retuning statements.

1. What taste would you associate with each retuning statement?
2. Does a food come to mind when you think about what each retuning statement means to you? How about the way that each emotionally feels?
3. Would you associate a restaurant that "feels" like each retuning statement?
4. What tastes do you associate with each of these words: love, happiness, peace, health, prosperity, wellbeing, contentment, joy, success, abundance, loving oneself, and speaking one's truth. Add any of your own. Write your observations down, not only for use in the following exercises, but also for future reference. When you want to work on a retuning statement that involves one of these concepts, you have a ready-made list!

Exercises:

1. Go to the grocery store and buy a bunch of different foods—especially concentrating on foods that you love. Get hard candies in an array of different flavors. As you try each, write down what comes to mind with each taste. What kind of belief or feeling would you associate with each? Write these down. If you find some that you would associate with the retuning statement(s) that you are working on, circle those. Each time that you take a bite of one of these tastes, repeat your retuning statement(s) to yourself.

2. If you can, find a hard candy that goes along with the tastes that you identify as being associated with your retuning statement(s). Put these candies all over your house, your car, your office, or wherever else you frequent. During the day, suck on one of the candies, and repeat the statement(s) to yourself. Really connect with the feeling of this. How does this taste make you feel?

3. If there is a special meal that you would associate with the retuning statement(s), commit to cooking this meal once a week. Make this night a special night. Set the table with nice linens. Put the good china out and drink from the crystal. Light candles. Splurge on yourself, and enjoy the entire experience. Dedicate the meal to the fulfillment of this retuning statement or goal.

4. If there is a restaurant that you associate with your statement(s), dine there, if possible. If not, call the restaurant and ask if they might give you the recipe for your favorite meal. At worst, make a meal as close to the taste of the restaurant food as possible, and repeat the retuning statement(s) as you cook and eat.

5. To reinforce the idea that you are open to the changes flowing into your life, try one new food a week. For example, if you always order the same thing every time

you go out to eat, try something that you have never tried before, or maybe normally would not try. Each bite you take say to yourself, "I am changing. I am becoming the person of my dreams. I greet my new life with a feeling of excitement and adventure."

6. Each time that you make coffee or tea, make it a ritual. Notice everything about the process as you do it. Bless the drink with love. Smell the drink, and say to yourself, "I am fully taking in life." As you sip on this drink, feel the warmth going down your throat, and say your retuning statement(s) to yourself, adding "and I am taking this into my body, mind and spirit."

7. Create your own exercise, using these as inspiration.

TOUCH

W rite out the retuning statements that you have chosen to work on. Answer the questions. Select your exercises, and use these with the retuning statements.

1. What part of the body would you associate with each retuning statement?
2. When you think about what each retuning statement means for your life, is there a particular fabric or texture that comes to mind—perhaps silk, cotton, warm dirt, or grass, for instance?
3. Is there a sensation that you associate with these retuning statements—for instance, cold, hot, or wind against your skin?
4. Look at the following list of words: love, happiness, peace, health, prosperity, wellbeing, contentment, joy, success, abundance, loving oneself, and speaking one's truth. What fabric, textures, or sensations do you associate with each of these words or concepts? Write these down, not only for use in the upcoming exercises, but also for future reference. When you want to work

on a belief that involves one of these concepts, you have a ready-made list!

Exercises:

1. Go to the grocery store and touch everything that you can: fruit, veggies, bakery items, cans, jars, or anything else (be prepared to buy what you touch!). Keep a little notebook with you as you do this, and write down what feelings that you associate with each texture or sensation. Can you summarize each feeling with a retuning statement? Do any of the textures match the retuning statement(s) that you are working on? If so, use these items along with your retuning statement(s).

2. Go to a natural foods store or a new age shop and buy some crystals. Notice how different crystals feel to you. Choose some that seem to feel like your retuning statements. Keep these next to your bed, in your office, in the bathroom—anywhere that you will remember to pick them up frequently. Each time that you touch these crystals, repeat your retuning statement(s) to yourself.

3. Go to a fabric store and feel as many fabrics as you can. Keep a notebook handy, and write down your feelings about each. Purchase some fabric that you associate with your retuning statement(s). Cut it into little squares and keep a square in your pocket, on your desk, in your purse or wallet, or wherever is convenient for you. Feel this fabric often—rub it between your fingers while repeating your new statement(s) to yourself.

4. Take some of the fabric and sew it into throw pillows, or at the very least, a pillow cover for your bed pillow. As you lay your head on this fabric each night, repeat your retuning statement(s) over and over until you fall asleep.

5. Make yourself a hot bath. Add a cup of Epsom salts and

a cup of baking soda to your bathwater (this is an excellent combination both for detoxification and for softening the skin). Swirl the bathwater to make sure that it is all dissolved. Stay in the bath for at least 20 minutes. As you begin to sweat (believe me, you will), wipe the sweat away with a soft washcloth as you say, "I am wiping away all negativity from my life. I release all negative thoughts through my skin." At the end of your bath, feel the water going down the drain, and visualize that all negativity is going with it.

6. Fill a sink basin with hot water. Soak a particularly soft washcloth in this. As you wipe your face, notice the feeling of heat and soft on your skin, and say to yourself, "I am washing away negativity." Then, repeat your retuning statement(s) to yourself.

7. Is there a style of dress or an item of clothing that you associate with a happier, more confident time in your life? If you have it, wear it once a week. If it doesn't fit you or you no longer have it, go to the store and buy something that really makes you feel great, or that looks like "the life of your dreams." As you put on the clothing of your choice, connect with positive feelings while repeating your retuning statement(s).

8. Buy an assortment of scarves or ties. Assign a retuning statement to each. Select one to wear each day. As you do, touch this item—focusing on the feel of the fabric—and repeat your new statement(s) to yourself throughout the day.

9. Tap your finger on the part of your body where the problem Station is. For instance, if you are having issue in Station 4, tap on your sternum. As you do so, focus on the sensation of the tapping. Repeat your retuning statements as you tap, connecting with the positive feelings that you would associate with the life of your dreams.

10. Buy some really soft or luxurious sheets for your bed. As you fall asleep at night, imagine that you are in a

cocoon vibrating with the frequency of your retuning statement(s). Fall asleep connected to this feeling.

11. Find and cut up all pictures that you absolutely hate of yourself. Pick them up, rip them apart, and throw them in the trash. Feel the pictures release from your hands, and say aloud, "I am in control of my destiny."

12. Sit with a partner and look into each other's eyes. Hold hands, or place your hand over the other person's heart. Take turns saying your retuning statement(s) aloud. End the exercise by telling each other, "I love you unconditionally."

13. Create your own exercise, using these as inspiration.

MOVEMENT

W rite out the retuning statements that you have chosen to work on. Answer the questions. Select your exercises, and use these with your retuning statements.

1. What movement would you associate with each retuning statement? Is there some body language that you can think of that reminds you of each? What would that be? For example, the retuning statement, "I am filled with love," might make you want to cross your heart or hug yourself.
2. When you think about what each retuning statement would mean for your life, is there a physical movement that comes to mind? For example, the retuning statement, "I am successful," might be associated with a broad smile, a victorious punch in the air, or a high five.

Exercises:

1. Pick out some music that you love. Make mix tapes or CDs of the music that reminds you of the retuning

439

statement(s) that you are working on, or that just makes you feel good. Play these tapes everywhere that you can—in the car, at home, at work. Dance around to the music, repeating the retuning statement(s) to the beat of the music.

2. Make up a little dance that goes along with your retuning statements. This doesn't have to be anything fancy or elaborate—it could be as simple as swaying or stepping side to side. As you move, repeat your retuning statement(s). Allow yourself to really feel it in your muscles and bones. Do this as many times a day as possible.

3. Make a cheer out of your retuning statement(s). Again, nothing elaborate is necessary. For example, if your retuning statement is "I am prosperous," you could clap on "I," on "am," and punch in the air victoriously on "prosperous." Do this as many times a day as possible.

4. Kick your leg out, or punch the air. As you do this, say aloud, "No more negativity for me! I am strong!" In addition, you can shadow-box with yourself in the mirror, imagining that you are knocking the negativity out.

5. Take an aerobics, dance, yoga, nia or Tai Chi class. Dedicate that class to embodying your retuning statement(s). Repeat the statement(s) to yourself throughout the class.

6. Find out the sign language equivalent of different words, feelings, or the retuning statement(s) that you are working on. For example, you could find out how to sign love, happiness, joy, health, prosperity, abundance, success, or whatever else that you would like to have in your life. Sign this throughout the day as you repeat your retuning statement(s) aloud, connecting with the positive feelings of the life of your dreams as you do so.

7. Pace back and forth or take a walk as you repeat your retuning statement(s) to yourself.

8. Create your own exercise, using these as inspiration.

RESOURCES

The National Domestic Abuse Hotline:
1-800-799-SAFE (7233)

National Sexual Assault Hotline
1-800-656-HOPE

American Psychiatric Association
1000 Wilson Boulevard
Suite 1825
Arlington, VA 22209-3901
Phone: 703-907-7300
http://www.psych.com

BIBLIOGRAPHY
(And Recommended Reading!)

Branden, Nathaniel. *The Six Pillars of Self Esteem*. New York: Bantam, 1994

Chopra, Deepak. *How to Grow Younger and Live Longer: 10 Steps to Reverse Aging*. New York: Three Rivers Press, 2001.

Choquette, Sonia. *The Psychic Pathway: A Workbook for Reawakening the Voice of Your Soul*. New York, Three Rivers Press, 1994.

Crum, Thomas. *The Magic of Conflict: Turning a Life of Work into a Work of Art*. New York: Touchstone, 1987.

Dreamer, Oriah Mountain. *The Invitation*. Harper San Francisco, 1999.

Dyer, Wayne. *Your Sacred Self: Making the Decision to be Free*. New York: HarperCollins, 1995.

_____ *Manifest Your Destiny: The Nine Spiritual Principles for Getting Everything* You *Want*. New York: Harper Collins, 1997.

_____ *The Power of Intention: Learning to Co-Create Your World Your Way*. Carlsbad, CA: Hay House, 2004.

Forward, Susan. *Emotional Blackmail: When the People in Your Life Use Fear, Obligation, and Guilt to Manipulate You*. New York: HarperCollins, 1997

Greene, Brian. *The Fabric of the Cosmos: Space, Time, and the*

Texture of Reality. New York, Vintage Book, 2004.

Hay, Louise. *You Can Heal Your Life.* Carlsbad, CA: Hay House, 1984.

Herbert, Nick. *Quantum Reality: Beyond the New Physics.* New York: Anchor Books, 1985.

Jacobsen, Mary-Elaine. *The Gifted Adult: A Revolutionary Guide for Liberating Everyday Genius.* New York: Ballantine Books, 1999.

Keith, Kent M. *Anyway: The Paradoxical Commandments: Finding Personal Meaning in a Crazy World.* New York: Berkley, 2001.

Miller, John and Kenedi, Aaron (editors). *God's Breath: Sacred Scriptures of the World.* New York: Marlowe & Company, 2000.

Moring, Gary F. *The Complete Idiot's Guide to Theories of the Universe.* Indianapolis, IN: Alpha Books, 2002.

Myss, Caroline. *Anatomy of the Spirit: The Seven Stages of Power and Healing.* New York: Three Rivers Press, 1996.

Prophet, Elizabeth Clare and Mark L. *Creative Abundance: Keys to Spiritual and Material Prosperity.* Corwin Springs, MT: Summit University Press, 1998.

Siegel, Bernie S. *Love, Medicine, and Miracles.* New York: HarperCollins, 1991

Thoele, Sue Patton. *The Courage to Be Yourself: A Woman's Guide to Emotional Strength and Self-Esteem.* Berkley, CA: Conari Press, 2001.

Walsch, Neale Donald. *Conversations with God: an uncommon dialogue.* New York: Putnam, 1996.

Zukav, Gary. *The Seat of the Soul.* New York: Fireside, 1990.

ABOUT THE AUTHOR

Tara Meyer-Robson is an emerging new voice in the field of life transformation and personal growth. She is CEO and Creative Director of The Flow, a company dedicated to helping individuals, companies, and health care organizations achieve success and wellness with ease.

Tara brings her unique voice and sense of humor to this book, breaking down difficult concepts in ways that are easy to understand, completely engaging, and enjoyable to learn about. It is her authentic love of people and desire to help others achieve their best that drives her, and this authenticity comes across in everything she does.

In addition, she has consulted and conducted seminars and transformation workshops on a national basis for health care organizations, associations, hotels and spas, and companies ranging in size from Fortune 500 to small businesses.

BONUS

A little extra flow for you!

Keep the good flow going and get a bonus just for you! Visit **flowwithlife.com** to find out how you can get a free Flow Transformation Toolkit—just click on "get my bonus" at the bottom of the home page to get all the details!

While you are there, make sure to sign up for the newsletter and join the online Flow Community. As of this writing, we are in the process of developing community forums, discussion groups, and creating an online "4 for 40" tracker in order to create the perfect support environment for your total life transformation!

And, if you have found this book valuable, please let me know by posting a five-star review for it on **Amazon.com**.

Printed in the United States
126711LV00003B/34-45/A

9 781598 009835